Praise for

WELL

"Sarah's storytelling is so engaging that you won't want to put this book down, but it is her heart that will grab you. Her observations are honest and gritty at times, and you will wrestle with her through difficult tensions. But in her exploration of brokenness, you will also find grace and beauty. On a planet loaded with pain, death, and poverty, Sarah's words are a gentle reminder that each of us is called to participate in the healing of our world as we seek to follow Jesus."

—Santiago "Jimmy" Mellado, president and CEO,
Compassion International

"With a style and voice that is powerful, eloquent, and sincere, Sarah Thebarge takes us on a journey of faith through her own physical struggles as well as those experienced while working in a hospital in Togo, West Africa. Many books attempt to provide answers, but few do it in such a profound way—while walking us through the honest, deep questions that arise from the messiness of life and the mystery of God. WELL is an important book that will stand the test of time and it will profoundly shape and inform your understanding of Christian spirituality and the love of God."

—Ken Wytsma, founder of The Justice Conference and
author of Pursuing Justice and Create vs. Copy

"This is a beautiful and soul-piercing story of Jesus with skin on, walking the halls of an underfunded, understaffed, and overcrowded hospital in West Africa. Of selfless love poured out. Emptied. And then poured out some more. Told with such self-effacing honesty and emotional transparency, it wholly unmasked my own indifference. I closed the last page in tears, and said, 'Lord, I am so sorry. Please help me love like this.' I haven't been this moved by a story since Heavenly Man."

—Charles Martin, New York Times bestselling author of Unwritten,
Long Way Gone, and The Mountain Between Us

"WELL is a powerful book—the kind that knocks you out of the complacency that infects our lives and shows you the beautiful, brutal drama of life. I understand what compassion means in a way I never have before."

—"Mike the Science Guy" McHargue, author of Finding God in the Waves
and host of Ask Science Mike and The Liturgists Podcast

"Words like *love, compassion, courage,* and *faith* easily become clichés... feel-good sentiments that go on greeting cards. If you read Sarah Thebarge's new book, those words will become more meaningful for you than they've ever been... sturdy, substantial, incandescent. Sarah is a supremely gifted writer and she has a powerful story to tell that is worth your precious time."
—Brian D. McLaren, author of *The Great Spiritual Migration*

"With a faith shaped through service and sharpened by real experience, Sarah Thebarge responds from the depths of her heart with the question we should have been asking all along: not 'Why does God allow suffering?' but 'Why do we?' Sarah's piercing, loving insights in this book, told through the stories of her medical service in West Africa, will grow your faith, improve the questions you ask, and help you on your journey to find better answers. WELL will move you."
—Michael Wear, author of *Reclaiming Hope: Lessons Learned in the Obama White House About the Future of Faith in America*

"This book shook me to my core. It is harrowing and beautiful. It challenged my faith and strengthened it. Sarah asks the hardest questions over and over. She sifts our platitudes until all that's left is truth and love strong enough to hold us all."
—Sheila Walsh, author, cohost of *LIFE Today*

"In the course of our lives' adventures, some of us learn how to practice compassion, and some of us run away from it. Sarah Thebarge's work reminds me that compassion is not a character trait as much as it is a learned behavior. Pressing through the pain of life, as well as embracing its glory, has the power to teach us that all will be well. Sarah's most recent work demonstrates the truth that compassionate action is something that transforms lives. People who wonder about the cost of transformation owe it to themselves to share in Sarah's journey."
—Paul Fromberg, Rector of St. Gregory of Nyssa, San Francisco

"In a brilliant story perfectly capturing the heart of Divine Love, Sarah Thebarge gently proves we are never too far for rescue, never too broken for wholeness, and never too sick to be made well."
—Reba Riley, author of *Post-Traumatic Church Syndrome*

WELL

Also by Sarah Thebarge

The Invisible Girls: A Memoir
NIV Bible for Women (contributing author)
*Talking Taboo: American Christian Women Get Frank
About Faith* (contributing author)

WELL

Healing Our Beautiful, Broken World
from a Hospital in West Africa

SARAH THEBARGE

New York   Nashville

FaithWords
Hachette Book Group
1290 Avenue of the Americas, New York, NY 10104
faithwords.com
twitter.com/faithwords

First Edition: November 2017

FaithWords is a division of Hachette Book Group, Inc. The FaithWords name and logo are trademarks of Hachette Book Group, Inc.

The publisher is not responsible for websites (or their content) that are not owned by the publisher.

The Hachette Speakers Bureau provides a wide range of authors for speaking events. To find out more, go to www.hachettespeakersbureau.com or call (866) 376-6591.

Brief quote from "The Myth of Sisyphus" (p. 48) from *Parables and Portraits* by Stephen Mitchell. Copyright © 1990 by Stephen Mitchell. Reprinted by permission of HarperCollins Publishers.

Unless otherwise indicated, Scripture quotations are from the Holy Bible, New International Version®, NIV®. Copyright © 1973, 1978, 1984, 2011 by Biblica, Inc.™ Used by permission of Zondervan. All rights reserved worldwide. www.zondervan.com. The "NIV" and "New International Version" are trademarks registered in the United States Patent and Trademark Office by Biblica, Inc.™

Library of Congress Cataloging-in-Publication Data has been applied for.

ISBNs: 978-1-4555-5319-8 (hardcover), 978-1-4555-5318-1 (ebook)

Printed in the United States of America

LSC-C

10 9 8 7 6 5 4 3 2 1

For the people of Togo.

Thank you for trusting me with your pain.

All shall be well, and all shall be well and all manner of thing shall be well.

—JULIAN OF NORWICH

WELL

A T 10 A.M. at a hospital in rural Togo, West Africa, I stood at the bedside of a forty-year-old man who had come in the night before with altered mental status—he was confused, he couldn't walk in a straight line, and his family said the man's level of alertness had waxed and waned over the past few days.

The hospital didn't have a CT scanner or an MRI, so the doctor had to make her diagnosis based on a few blood tests and a physical exam.

Soon a diagnosis emerged. His HIV test was positive. He was running a fever. His neurological exam showed he had increased pressure inside his head, which indicated he likely had a brain infection because of his weakened immune system.

Within an hour of arriving at the hospital, his condition worsened. He needed a hole drilled in his skull to release the pressure or else, in a matter of minutes, his brain stem would herniate through the hole in the back of his skull, where the brain meets the spine, and he would die.

The doctor paged the surgeon, who ran to the hospital and rushed the man to the OR. As soon as the surgeon drilled a hole in the man's skull, copious amounts of clumped white fluid started pouring out. *Like cottage cheese*, the surgeon said later. In my ten years of working as a physician assistant, I had never heard of anything like that. Clumped white fluid that looked like cottage cheese pouring out of someone's brain.

The hospital didn't have a microbiology lab to identify the pathogen that was causing the brain infection, but the doctors concluded that the man likely not only was HIV-positive, but also had end-stage AIDS and, because his immune system was almost nonexistent, had contracted a rare fungal infection called cryptococcus.

The patient came out of surgery with white gauze wrapped around his head, like a soldier from the Revolutionary War. His bed was propped up at a forty-five-degree angle to keep the pressure off his brain. The doctor ordered every antibiotic she could think of, as well as two medications to decrease the pressure in his brain. But the hospital pharmacy didn't have the anti-fungal medications needed to treat cryptococcus.

The following morning, I reported to the hospital to work my twenty-eight-hour shift. I arrived at 7 a.m. and wouldn't be off until 11 a.m. the next day.

I stood at the man's bedside during rounds, where the doctor who'd worked the night before, as well as the surgeon who had performed the operation, summarized the patient's clinical course to me and the doctor I was working with that day.

The anesthesia had had plenty of time to wear off, but the man still hadn't woken up.

When we finished rounding on the other patients, I came back to the man's bedside and studied the monitor above his head.

His blood pressure was high and his pulse was low, indicating there was still too much pressure on his brain. But there was nothing else we could do.

The doctor I was working with took the man's two brothers to a quiet room around the corner and explained in French that the man was HIV-positive—which no one had known until then—and had a dangerous infection. She told the brothers that we'd tried everything we could, but the man hadn't woken up from surgery, and his condition was worsening.

"We're probably going to lose him," she said.

The older brother, six inches taller than the younger, brushed a tear away from his eye and nodded.

When they returned, the brothers stood at the foot of the bed and silently looked at the patient, whose head was still wrapped in white gauze, his bed still propped up at a forty-five-degree angle.

The hospital only had three patient rooms with doors, which were reserved for patients with contagious infections, like tuberculosis or meningitis. Because the man's infection wasn't airborne, he had been placed in a large alcove with two other beds. There was just a curtain across the entrance, and no partitions between the beds. On the patient's left was a ten-year-old boy with malaria. On the patient's right was a fifty-eight-year-old man with pneumonia.

I watched as the patient's oxygen level dropped to 70 percent, then

54 percent, then 35 percent. I watched the heart rate as it went from a regular 100 beats per minute to erratically swinging from bradycardia, 30 to 40 beats per minute, to tachycardia, in the 170s.

The ten-year-old boy looked on with fear in his eyes.

I retrieved a privacy screen—a large piece of cloth hung on a wheeled metal frame—from the hallway and placed it between the ten-year-old and the man who was dying.

I brought two chairs to the bedside so the brothers could at least sit down while they watched their sibling die.

We had done everything we could do for him, but he was dying, rapidly decompensating before my eyes.

I had other patients to see, medications to order, and lab results to review, and yet I continued to stand at his bedside. *If I can't prevent his death*, I thought, *the least I can do is witness it.*

Maybe I was standing there for them—providing physical presence and visible support for the man and his brothers. Or maybe I was doing it for me—because it made me feel like I wasn't completely powerless. I felt like I was doing something, even if it was just watching the monitor as his vital signs became more and more unstable.

After a few minutes of an erratic heart rate and an oxygen level so low the monitor couldn't register it anymore, the tracing of his heartbeat turned into a flat line on the monitor, and it started blinking 0. ASYSTOLE, the monitor blinked, and alarmed loudly.

I reached up and turned the monitor off.

The last word Jesus said on the cross before he died echoed in my head in the profound silence that followed my patient's death.

Tetelestai.

It is finished.

The monitor's screen went black.

It was over.

Just like that, as I stood there watching, the man's soul left his body. He was still sitting up in bed, his eyes closed, his head wrapped in gauze. He looked like he was sleeping, and his body was still warm. But he was dead. He was gone.

I wanted to journey with his soul to God. I wanted to hold his hand as he passed beyond the veil of the physical world and into the other side of eternity.

I wanted to accompany him because I wanted to ask God why. Why did some people in the world have so much, while others had so little? Why were some people in the world so comfortable, while others suffered so much? Why did we have lifesaving treatment for some patients but not for others?

The injustice and unfairness were maddening.

I felt helpless as I stood silently at the bedside, resting my hand on the younger brother's shoulder while he buried his face in his hands and wept.

Later that afternoon, the ten-year-old boy with malaria lapsed into a coma and died. His father collapsed into the chair I'd drawn up to the boy's bedside when it became clear that his son was leaving this earth, and there wasn't anything else we could do to keep him here.

After his son took his final breath, the father frantically searched the pockets of his shirt, pants, and jacket, looking for money to pay his son's medical bill so he could take his son's body home and bury him.

The fifty-eight-year-old with pneumonia was a wealthy man from Nigeria. He motioned to me, and I walked over to his bedside. He asked me to hand him his wallet, which I retrieved from the pair of pants that were hanging on a hook near his bed. He opened his wallet and pulled out enough money to cover the ten-year-old's medical bill.

"Take your son home," the Nigerian man said to the grieving father, who nodded his head in gratitude.

And then the father picked up the limp body of the son we couldn't save, and carried him out of the hospital.

I worked through the morning, then into the afternoon, then late into the night.

Patients kept coming.

And for the next three months, patients kept dying.

THE HOSPITAL OF Hope (or, in French, L'Hôpital de l'Espérance) is located in Mango, a rural village in northern Togo, West Africa. Togo lies between Ghana and the Ivory Coast to the west, and Benin and Nigeria to the east. Burkina Faso is directly north.

In 2013, the United Nations performed a survey of 170 nations. According to that survey, Togo was the least happy country in the world. Political corruption, conflicts between people and groups, a poor economy, a decrepit infrastructure, a high infant mortality rate, a low life expectancy, and a lack of educational and employment opportunities all contributed to the unhappiness of the Togolese people.

The Hospital of Hope opened in March 2015 to offer medical care to people who, before then, had to drive as long as two days to get to the closest medical facility. The most common medical problems included malaria, typhoid, malnutrition, poisonous snakebites, hemorrhagic viral fevers, and childbirth complications.

Some friends of mine were on the email list of the missionaries who had started the hospital, and my friends forwarded to me the first newsletter written after the hospital opened. The hospital director, Matt, wrote that they had enough staff to see a hundred patients in the outpatient clinic every day, but more than five hundred lined up at triage each morning, desperate to be seen.

The doctors who worked in the inpatient wards of the hospital were overworked and overwhelmed. There was already a long waiting list of patients who needed surgical procedures, because there weren't enough surgeons or support staff to perform the operations fast enough.

"If you know any doctors, nurses, PAs or NPs, please ask them to come," Matt wrote.

I reread the letter several times over the next few days, wondering whether I should pursue the opportunity.

When I started college, I had planned to become a clinician so I could practice medicine internationally. Then, inspired by journalists like Celia Dugger and Nicholas Kristof of the *New York Times*, and others who did exceptional reporting about health issues in developing countries, I added a journalism minor. In addition to practicing medicine, I wanted to write the stories of suffering people in the developing world, and I wanted to start a public conversation about how our global community could work together to solve these problems.

After college, I earned my physician assistant degree at the Yale School of Medicine and, a year after that, I began earning a master's degree at the Columbia University Graduate School of Journalism.

Getting into two Ivy League grad schools convinced me not only that I was on the right track, but also that medical journalism was a divine calling God had placed on my life. I couldn't wait to finish my program at Columbia and begin what I was sure would be a successful, rewarding, world-changing career.

But my plan came to a sudden end when, after my first semester in journalism school, I was diagnosed with breast cancer. I was twenty-seven years old.

I had a bilateral mastectomy. At my post-op appointment a few weeks later, the surgeon said, "We got it all," and assured me the cancer wouldn't come back.

But a year later, the cancer recurred. I had four more surgeries plus months of chemotherapy and radiation, followed by a nearly lethal battle with pneumonia that led to sepsis and landed me in the ICU with less than a fifty-fifty chance of making it out of the hospital alive.

After a month of five different IV antibiotics, the infection was finally under control. When the doctors were getting ready to discharge me from the hospital, I knew I couldn't stay in New Haven, which was now haunted with painful memories. I needed a clean slate, a fresh start, a new chapter.

Maybe now *it's time for me to head overseas*, I thought.

I applied with several short-term missions agencies. They all turned me down because of my recent cancer diagnosis.

I ended up moving to Portland, Oregon, because it was as far away from the East Coast as I could get without dropping off into the Pacific Ocean. I worked full-time in an ER and did some freelance journalism on the side.

Shortly after I arrived in Oregon, a seemingly chance encounter with a Somali refugee mom and her girls on the train one Portland afternoon led to a lasting friendship. Two years after our first encounter, I wrote *The Invisible Girls*, a memoir that wove my story of cancer and a sudden move to the West Coast together with their story of fleeing the violence of Somalia only to end up nearly freezing and starving to death once they got to the United States. I used the proceeds from the book to start a college fund for the five Somali sisters I wrote about. At its heart, *The Invisible Girls* is a story about finding redemption in the most unusual places at the most unexpected times.

As I traveled around the country telling the story to tens of thousands of people, I often said, "After my cancer diagnosis, I couldn't go to Africa, so God brought Africa to me." To put it bluntly, I thought that working with the Somali family in Portland was my consolation prize because first prize, traveling and writing internationally, was out of my reach.

In the spring of 2015, as I contemplated the letter from the Hospital of Hope's director, it occurred to me that practicing medicine in Togo could be the fulfillment of my lifelong dream. Finally, I would have the opportunity to do "the real thing," to help people on their native soil instead of helping refugees who had landed on mine.

I had the summer off before resuming my book tour. *So, I could go…* I thought.

And then I hesitated.

Because I had never been to Africa, I had never practiced medicine internationally, and I was still on anti-cancer medicines to prevent a breast cancer recurrence.

And—here was a significant detail—I didn't know where Togo was.

AFTER I THOUGHT it over for a few days, my anticipation overcame my hesitation, and I applied with the missions agency that ran the hospital. They quickly accepted my application. I raised support from family and friends to cover the cost of the trip, booked my plane ticket, and applied for a visa from the Togolese consulate.

Less than three months after I got Matt's letter, I was on a plane to Togo.

On July 7, 2015, I touched down at the country's only airport, located in Lomé, the capital city, on the southern coast. It was a nine-hour drive north from there to get to Mango.

When we first got off the plane, my fellow passengers and I had to wait in a health screening line where two Togolese workers in white hazmat suits used temporal thermometers—handheld wands waved across a person's forehead to detect their temperature—to screen each passenger. Anyone who had a fever got pulled out of the line and taken to an adjacent room, where they were more thoroughly screened for Ebola or any other potentially contagious and life-threatening infections.

Once I had been cleared by the health workers, I stood in the immigration line, where a man checked my visa and then stamped my passport without asking me any questions about where I was from or what I was doing in Togo.

Then I went to baggage claim. I spotted my large, blue wheeled duffel bag that held three months' worth of clothes, books, and toiletries. As I was pulling it off the conveyor belt, a broad, six-foot-two-inch Togolese man came up and tried to take it out of my hands.

"What are you doing!?" I asked.

"I'm helping you," he said in French, yanking the handle out of my hands.

"No thank you," I said firmly as I grabbed it back.

Next, I stood in the customs line. I had read accounts of Americans being detained for hours by customs officers who demanded to be paid a bribe before releasing them.

An American family of six had come to work at the Hospital of Hope a few weeks before me. Each family member had an iPad, and the parents each had a laptop and an iPhone. The customs officers accused the family of bringing the electronic devices with the intent to sell them in Togo—and charged the family hundreds of dollars in import taxes.

The missions agency told me they had arranged for my driver, a Togolese man named Massiko, to accompany me through customs so I wouldn't get hassled or detained. Then, the agency said, Massiko and I would stay at a guesthouse in Lomé for a night before making the nine-hour drive to the Hospital of Hope the following morning.

When I got to customs, I looked for a man fitting the description of Massiko that the missions agency had given me—tall, broad shoulders, early forties, holding a Hospital of Hope sign—but he wasn't there.

I grew increasingly nervous as I waited in line. Without Massiko by my side to negotiate with the officers and advocate for me, I felt incredibly vulnerable and alone.

Thankfully, when it was my turn, the customs officers waved me through without asking any questions or examining the contents of my luggage.

Once I had made it through all the checkpoints, I found myself in the airport's "lobby," which was a large open-air area with a roof, but no windows or doors. There was no air-conditioning, and the temperature was well over one hundred degrees.

I searched for Massiko inside the lobby and, when I didn't see him there, I went outside and looked for him at the passenger pickup area, and in the parking lot. There was no sign of him. With panic beginning to well up in me, I went back inside to figure out what to do next.

I didn't know the name of the guesthouse where I was staying or how to get there. I was the only white person at the airport, and the only woman traveling alone. I realized that the other travelers and the employees who ran the airport's snack shop and currency exchange stand were all watching me.

Then the man who had tried to "help" me with my bag found me, trying once again to carry my bag in exchange for a tip. I swatted him away, and then I began to perform evasive maneuvers, hiding behind concrete pillars, the ATM and the shoeshine stand to try to escape his notice.

The woman who ran the airport's snack shop kept walking over to me asking me to buy something. People selling SIM cards and phone chargers and cigarettes swarmed around me, shoving their goods in my face and insisting that I buy something. No matter how many times I said no and asked them to go away, they circled back and tried again.

The missions agency had given me a list of emergency contact phone numbers before I left the United States, but my cell phone didn't work in Togo.

I noticed a Togolese woman in her early twenties with a warm smile who was working the airport's welcome desk, helping travelers arrange transportation and hotel accommodations. I approached her and asked if she had a phone I could borrow. Without hesitation, she handed her cell phone to me.

I called the numbers on my emergency contact list, but half of them didn't work, and when I called the numbers that did work, no one answered, and there was no place to leave a voice mail.

My next idea was to email my contacts, but the airport's WiFi network was password-protected. The girl didn't know the password, but she summoned another airport employee over and asked him to enter the password in my phone so I could use the WiFi to send emails.

At first he said no, he was not allowed to divulge the password to anyone. But when he saw tears beginning to well up in my eyes, he took my phone and entered the password. I thanked him profusely. He rolled his eyes at me and walked away.

I wrote a short email to the missionaries at the hospital and to the missions' headquarters back in the United States, telling them where I was and asking what to do next. The email literally took fifteen minutes to send. In the meantime, I took a seat at a small table by the snack shop and ordered a cold bottle of Coke.

It took another fifteen minutes to be able to download the missionaries' reply. The hospital staff apologized profusely, and said they were calling pastors in Lomé to see if someone could pick me up.

As I sat at the table waiting for the missionaries to send me further instructions, the man who had tried to "help" me found me and grabbed my bag again.

This time I stood up, got in his face, and yelled, "No!"

He let go of my bag, and then held out his hand for a tip.

I shook my head. "No. I told you no at least ten times."

He started yelling at me in French. His words were so loud and so fast, I couldn't understand what he was saying, but I knew he was angry.

I left my half-full bottle of Coke on the table and, struggling with my heavy bag, made my way outside, where I sat on a bench and cried. I had been up all night, I hadn't eaten anything yet that day, I was sweating profusely, I couldn't get this guy to leave me alone, and I was at a loss for what to do.

The guy found me on the bench and continued yelling at me, holding his empty hand in front of my face, still demanding a tip for his services.

"No!" I jumped to my feet. By now I wasn't just raising my voice at him; I was screaming and shaking my finger in his face. My heart sank at the realization that I had come to show compassion to the Togolese people and instead, here I was, screaming at a Togolese person in frustration and anger.

"Sista, can I help you?" I heard a woman ask in accented English.

I turned to see a stout fifty-something woman sitting two benches down, watching what was happening. I guessed she was from Ghana or Nigeria, nearby countries whose citizens spoke English instead of French.

"Yes!" I said, thankful for her offer. "Get this man to leave me alone."

She leaped up, got in his face, and yelled at him in a dialect I didn't understand. Whatever she said to him worked because moments later, he spit at my feet, stomped away, and didn't come near me again.

"Thank you," I said to the woman, grateful for her willingness to intervene.

She nodded. Then she said, "Sista, may I ask you a question?"

"Sure," I said.

She surveyed me from head to toe, taking notice of my white skin, thin frame, and tear-and-sweat-stained face.

"Sista, if you don't mind, are you sure you're strong enough for Africa?"

I silently shrugged as I sank back down onto the bench and wiped the tears away.

I had been in Togo for less than an hour, and already I was having serious doubts.

I ENDED UP SPENDING three hours in the Lomé airport. Three hours of tears, sweat, frustration, sluggish emails, and merchants who refused to leave me alone.

Finally, the missions agency arranged for a local pastor to come pick me up.

I was sitting on the bench outside the airport when a five-foot-two-inch, paunchy man in his mid-fifties wearing dress pants and an untucked, short-sleeved white dress shirt approached me.

"Sarah?" he asked.

I nodded.

"I am Pastor LaPointe, and I am here for you," he said in accented English.

I was so relieved, I wanted to jump up and hug him, but instead I stood and shook his hand. We walked across the parking lot to his car, a small, black four-door sedan that was at least twenty years old. I noticed a well-worn leather Bible wedged between the dashboard and the cracked windshield, and a wooden cross hanging from the rearview mirror. So even though I was a single woman, alone in a foreign country, about to climb into the car of a man I had never met before, the fact that he had known my name and had a Bible and a cross in his car gave me some assurance that he was indeed the pastor sent by the missions agency to pick me up.

As we drove toward the guesthouse, where I would spend the night before traveling to Mango with Massiko in the morning, I told Pastor LaPointe about my three-hour airport drama.

"I can't thank you enough for coming to get me," I said.

"It is no problem," he said with a warm smile. He looked tired, but I didn't know if it was because of the intense afternoon heat, the demands of ministry, a lifetime spent living in a developing country, or something else.

I asked him about his life in Togo, and he told me that after finishing high school in Lomé, he had attended a small seminary in a town a few hours north, run by American missionaries, that trained local pastors. After seminary, he began pastoring a small Baptist church in Lomé, where he had served for the past thirty years.

"Do you have a family?" I asked.

His eyes lit up. "Yes!" he said. "I have a wife and three grown sons. God has blessed me with a beautiful family."

A few minutes later, we pulled up to the guesthouse, a two-story building on a dusty, dead-end side street. The exterior walls were covered in white stucco that was peeling and cracked. The property was surrounded by a six-foot-tall rusty metal fence with a wide front gate. I noticed a small courtyard just inside the gate, lined with yellow, magenta, crimson, and pink tropical flowers in full bloom, and a few slender palm trees.

The cook and the groundskeeper, two Togolese men in their early twenties, were waiting for us on the sidewalk outside the front gate when we arrived. They shook my hand as Pastor LaPointe made introductions.

Hugo, the cook, was short and thin—and very shy. He was soft-spoken and rarely made eye contact with me. Jori, the groundskeeper, was six feet tall and muscular. He was as outgoing as Hugo was shy, and laughed loudly as Pastor LaPointe told him about my airport experience.

Pastor LaPointe reached into his pocket and retrieved a few coins, which he handed to Hugo. "Go to the market and buy bottled water for Sarah," he said in French. "The water here is not safe for Americans to drink."

Then Pastor LaPointe turned to me and said in English, "Sarah, I am sorry I cannot stay, but I am very tired. I had malaria last week."

So that explains the weariness in his eyes, I thought.

"I'm so sorry," I said. Then, out of curiosity, I asked, "How many times have you had malaria in your lifetime?"

"Too many times to count," he replied with a heavy sigh.

He shook my hand, got into his car, and drove away. I stood on the curb holding my bag, waving good-bye as I watched his car disappear down the narrow street in a cloud of rust-colored dust.

For a few minutes, Hugo, Jori, and I chatted outside in front of the guesthouse. I quickly learned that they spoke no English—they only spoke French. I had taken two years of French in high school and a semester in college, but that had been more than a decade before I arrived in Togo, and my language skills had rusted from lack of use.

When I told the guys, in choppy French, that I was excited to travel to Mango in the morning, I pronounced Mango like the fruit (*Mane-go*). They quickly corrected me and told me it wasn't *Mane-go*, it was *Mon-go*. To my embarrassment, I realized I had been mispronouncing the name of the town to my family and friends for months now, and I'd have to issue a correction when I got home.

Hugo left for the market to buy bottled water for me, and Jori showed me to my room, which was on the second floor with three other rooms. He unlocked the door, and I followed him inside. The room was lit by a single, bare lightbulb attached to a rickety ceiling fan. As I surveyed the room, I noted a twin-size bed, tiled floors, and a small wooden dresser. On top of the dresser sat an old TV operated by dials rather than buttons or a remote control.

The walls looked as if they had, at one time, been painted white, but now a layer of dust and dirt covered the textured paint that was scuffed around the lower edges and peeling where the wall met the ceiling. The room's only window was above the bed. It measured no more than twelve inches wide, and it was protected by three vertical black metal bars. Next to the dresser, a narrow door led to a small bathroom with a toilet, sink, and shower stall.

The four rooms on the second floor formed a square, and the center of the square held a small patio with two chaise lounges, potted flowers, and a wooden table with four wooden folding chairs.

Jori motioned to the patio and said that it was available for guests to use, but they were having a heavier-than-normal rainy season, so there were many, many mosquitoes and a lot of *palu*.

"*Palu* is very bad for you," he said in French.

I had never heard the word *palu* before.

"In English, it is, I think, malaria?" he said.

I nodded. "Yes," I replied. "We call it malaria. And yes, it is very bad for me."

Sitting outside on the patio for a few hours as a sitting duck for bloodthirsty mosquitoes seemed like a bad idea. I was taking anti-malaria pills and I had applied insect repellent before I left the airport, but still, I didn't want to risk contracting malaria on my first day in Togo.

Then I asked him in French if it would be safe for me to go for a walk through the city. He shook his head emphatically. "You are white American woman," he said. "It would be very, very dangerous."

After he went back downstairs, I locked my bedroom door. I turned on the TV, but there were only three channels on the knob, and none of them worked. I tried to access the guesthouse's WiFi network on my laptop, but it wasn't working. It was around 3 p.m. and dinner wasn't going to be ready until 6 p.m. So for three hours I was stuck in my room with nothing to do, nowhere to go, and no one to talk to. My room was hot and humid, and the ceiling fan's sluggish blades moved very little air. I tried to open the window, but there was no latch. I realized that even if I could get it open, the window was so narrow and the bars were so thick, it was unlikely to offer much ventilation anyway.

Sweat trickled down my temples, my neck, my chest, and even down the backs of my knees. I went to the bathroom and splashed cool water on my face, changed into shorts and a T-shirt, and lay on the bed. It felt like I was on house arrest in a sauna, held captive by malaria-infested mosquitoes and a high crime rate.

O N THE SEVENTEEN-HOUR flight to Lomé, I had read all about Togo. First, I read the 250-page medical manual for the Hospital of Hope that detailed the symptoms, workup, and treatment for the most common diagnoses encountered at the hospital. The conditions included malaria, worms, parasites, tuberculosis, heart failure, kidney failure, liver cancer, malnutrition, typhoid (a virulent strain of salmonella), hepatitis, meningitis, leptospirosis, sepsis, leukemia, osteomyelitis (a bone infection), scabies, poisonous snakebites, and sexually transmitted infections.

Then I read a guide to Togo culture, written by Lana, one of the hospital's female American chaplains who had worked in the country for several years. The guide said that the majority of people in northern Togo were conservative Muslims and, in order to be culturally sensitive and appropriate, the female American missionaries were required to wear ankle-length skirts. Lana wrote that a Muslim Togolese man seeing a woman's ankles was as scandalous as an American man seeing a woman topless. Being able to see where a woman's legs part was extremely provocative, so even pants that covered a woman's knees and ankles were still considered immodest. The female doctors and nurses at the hospital couldn't wear scrubs without wrapping an additional fabric skirt around their waists.

Also, women had to wear shirts that covered their collarbones and shoulders. No low-cut, sleeveless, or spaghetti-strap tops allowed. In clinic, female Muslim patients were to be examined by female clinicians whenever possible.

The guide also said that because the Togolese people had lacked access to medical care for so long, they had turned to alternative healers, including fetishers (animists who use charms and rituals to ward off evil spirits), herbalists, and marabouts (mystical Muslim "healers" who used the Koran in their healing ceremonies—sometimes tearing pages from the Koran, burning them, and putting the ashes in potions for patients to drink).

Next, I read an article about Togo's climate and economy that I'd found online and printed out for the flight. The article talked about a mountain range in the middle of the country that separated the north from the south and changed the weather patterns. In southern Togo, the rainy season and dry season were roughly equal. Which meant that for six months a year in the south of the country, they were able to plant and harvest. Often, the rainy season was long enough that they were able to plant and harvest two cycles of crops, giving them plenty of food to last them through the dry season.

However, in the north, the rainy season was only three months long— barely long enough to grow and harvest one cycle of crops—so malnutrition and starvation rates were much higher than in the south.

That first afternoon in Togo, as I lay on the bed in my room at the guest-house watching the blades of the ceiling fan wobble in listless circles, I contemplated the obstacles, suffering, death, disease, and punishing cultural and weather climates I was about to encounter.

I thought about the countless children under age five who died each year, the women who died in childbirth, the people who died of diseases that were entirely preventable or easily treatable.

I thought about the interminable dry season, when it didn't rain for months and temperatures soared over 120 degrees and many people died of starvation, malnutrition, and dehydration.

I thought about people dying in protracted agony from poisonous snake-bites and rabies and tetanus.

Despite the heat, I shivered at the thought of entering into this level of suffering—or, perhaps more accurately, descending into this depth of hell-on-earth.

I wondered if it was possible for a place to be literally God-forsaken. Because if it was possible, then surely Togo was that place.

A FEW HOURS AFTER I arrived at the guesthouse, Hugo knocked on my door and told me softly that dinner was ready. Saying nothing and looking at the ground as we walked, he led me down the stairs, through a narrow hallway, and into the kitchen. A small gas stove sat along one wall of the galley-style kitchen. A yard-long, foot-wide, waist-high wooden table next to the stove provided the kitchen's only counter space. The kitchen had no sink and no appliances other than the stove—no refrigerator, coffeepot, toaster, microwave, or blender.

Three shelves, each about a yard long, hung on the wall opposite the stove. The top shelf was filled with five-pound bags of rice, flour, and sugar, and a gallon-size bottle of vegetable oil. The middle shelf held a cylinder-shaped container of salt, several small plastic bags of spices, a ceramic bowl with small dried red and green peppers, and a larger bowl with a dozen brown eggs. Baskets of onions, potatoes, yams, carrots, and bananas sat on the bottom shelf.

I noticed a mat and a blanket on the floor under the shelves. "Is that where you sleep?" I asked Hugo, and he nodded shyly.

Past the kitchen was a room no bigger than seven by seven feet, painted mint green and lit by a single overhead bulb. Hugo pointed to a wooden table in the center of the room and invited me to sit down. The table was only slightly bigger than a TV tray, and it had two matching wooden chairs.

I attempted to exchange pleasantries with him, using the French vocabulary that I hadn't practiced in a very long time. We made it through the basics—*How are you? How was your afternoon?* I asked if he and Jori would be joining me for dinner, and he shook his head.

And then I told him that the Internet wasn't working, and asked when it might be working again. He gave me a confused look, and I wondered if he was reacting to my question or to my American accent.

I realized later that night, when I was flipping through my pocket-size French dictionary, that I had picked the wrong verb. Instead of telling him that the Internet wasn't working properly, I had told him that the Internet was unemployed, and asked when his Internet might find a job again. So it was little wonder he had looked so puzzled. I also discovered, to my horror, that when I told Hugo and Jori I was "excited" to be heading to Mango, I used the wrong verb and accidentally told them I was sexually aroused rather than that I was anticipating the trip.

"Would you like bread with your dinner?" Hugo asked as I took my seat at the table.

Before leaving for Togo, I had read recommended food preparation guidelines for Americans to avoid getting sick from foodborne illnesses in West Africa. There were obvious suggestions—use bottled water to brush your teeth, don't eat raw vegetables, and only eat fruit that you can peel.

But the guidelines also said that if you buy bread from the market, you should bring it home and bake it again before you eat it to get rid of all the germs that might be on it from people's hands touching it at the market.

So when Hugo asked if I wanted bread with dinner, I said, "Yes, but..." and then I tried to explain the bread guidelines I'd read, except I didn't know the French words for "bake," "oven," or "germs."

So I said in French, "Yes, I'd like bread with my dinner. But you have to set my bread on fire."

He looked puzzled.

"If my bread is not on fire," I continued, "it could make me very sick."

He looked even more confused.

I kept talking.

"Bread that is not on fire could even kill me," I said.

By this point, he was incredulous. I could only imagine what he thought of me, the crazy American woman who seemed to be asking for flaming bread to be served with her dinner.

"Never mind," I said in the end, when I realized that there was nothing else I could say to get him to understand that I needed him to rebake the bread before it would be safe for me to eat. "No bread."

A few minutes later, he returned from the kitchen with a beautifully plated serving of baked white fish, sautéed peppers, tomatoes, and onions, and an artfully carved mango.

I hadn't eaten all day, and I suddenly realized how hungry I was. Once again, I attempted to use my rusty French vocabulary to communicate with him.

What I meant to say was, "Wow! I'm really hungry!" Which, in French, is, *"J'ai faim."*

But instead, I said, *"J'ai une femme."* Which means that when he set the plate of food in front of me, I exclaimed, "Wow! I have a wife!"

As he returned to the kitchen, I watched him shaking his head, trying to stifle his laughter.

Well, at least I got him to laugh, I thought as I watched him walk away.

I ate alone in the mint-green room in silence, watching moths and flies and mosquitoes flying into the bright lightbulb and, occasionally, into my food. After I finished my dinner, Hugo returned to clear my plate, and asked if I wanted dessert.

"Non, merci," I said. I was satiated by the fish and vegetables and mango, I was exhausted from my travels, and, after being embarrassed several times by my poor grasp of the French language, I was already full of humble pie.

THE FOLLOWING MORNING, I woke up at six and groggily made my way to the bathroom. In the mirror above the sink, I caught a glimpse of the deep circles under my eyes. I was jet-lagged and, because my room was so hot, I hadn't gotten much sleep the night before.

I turned on the shower. The water pressure was low, and the water that did come out was tepid, so I showered quickly. I dressed and came downstairs to find Hugo and Jori loading up an old Land Cruiser parked in front of the guesthouse's open front gate. The sun was just barely visible on the horizon, and it was already a humid ninety degrees.

Hugo had placed a small table in the courtyard and set it for breakfast. There were two plates, which each held a serving of scrambled eggs and a small baguette. A thermos of hot water, two mugs, tea bags, and packets of instant coffee sat in the center of the table. The bread had not been rebaked, or "set on fire," but I decided to take the risk and eat it anyway because it was going to be a long day, and I didn't know when I would have the opportunity to eat again.

A tall Togolese man in his forties sat down across from me and introduced himself as Massiko, my driver for the day. He spoke excellent English, with only a trace of an accent, and his voice was gentle.

He apologized for getting my arrival date wrong, and I told him not to worry about it. I was ready to forgive and forget the three-hour airport debacle and move on to today's adventure.

As we began eating, I asked Massiko to tell me about himself.

He told me he was raised in Lomé, and his parents died when he was a teenager. An American missionary named David took him in and raised him until Massiko left to attend college in Kara, a town several hours north of Lomé. After he graduated, Massiko returned to Lomé to serve as David's bodyguard.

On one of Massiko's days off, another Togolese man was guarding David when armed thieves hijacked them as they were getting into their car in a parking lot. David told the carjackers he needed to get some important papers out of the glove compartment, and then they could take the vehicle. But as David moved toward the glove compartment, the thieves thought he was reaching for a gun, and they shot and killed him. David's bodyguard escaped to alert the authorities, and to tell David's wife and children that David had been killed.

Massiko shook his head as he recounted the story. "I owe David everything," he said. "Because when I didn't have any parents, when I didn't have anything, David looked around, and David saw me."

Then it was Massiko's turn to ask me questions.

He asked what I did for a living, why I decided to come to Togo, and why I was only going to be at the hospital for a few months. Why not a few years?

I told him about Matt's compelling newsletter that had led me to volunteer as a physician assistant at the Hospital of Hope. Then I explained that in addition to practicing medicine, I'm a writer and a speaker, and I could only stay in Togo for three months because I had to return to the United States for fall speaking engagements.

"What do you write?" he asked.

"I wrote a memoir called *The Invisible Girls*," I said.

I had brought one copy of the book with me to Togo. I pulled it out of my backpack and handed it to him. He paged through it as I told him about the breast cancer diagnosis, the recurrence, the chemo, the radiation, and the infection that landed me in the ICU.

Massiko's large brown eyes filled with tears and he shook his head. "Oh, Sarah," he said.

With appreciation for Massiko's empathy and attentive listening, I continued the story, explaining that as I lay in the hospital for several weeks, I had nothing but time to think about everything that had gone wrong since my initial cancer diagnosis. Not only was I battling cancer but also, over the past few months, my boyfriend Ian had broken up with me, my friend Libby had died of cancer, and I'd had to drop out of journalism school because I was too sick to take the train into New York City for class.

I told Massiko that when I got out of the hospital, I sold everything and bought a one-way ticket to Portland, Oregon. I landed there on a rainy

Sunday night in January as a bald, scarred, bruised mess of a girl, with just a suitcase of clothes and a broken heart.

I took a sip of coffee and a bite of scrambled eggs and continued the story.

Shortly after I moved to the West Coast, I was riding the MAX—the light rail train in Portland—when I met a Somali refugee mom and two of her little girls. The three-year-old Somali girl couldn't find a seat, and so she ended up crawling into my open lap and falling asleep. I started chatting with her mom and learned that she was here alone with five girls who were ages three to nine. The mom, Hadhi, barely spoke English, and she had no job, had no money, and didn't know a soul.

I ended up going to their apartment to check on them and found them living with no furniture, no changes of clothes, no toiletries or toilet paper, and one blanket for the six of them. They were eating moldy bread dipped in ketchup because they'd run out of money and out of food, and they were now going dumpster-diving, eating whatever they could find in the trash.

I brought them groceries and clothes, and then my church got involved and we set up their apartment with everything they'd need to survive a Pacific Northwest winter.

Even after they had everything they needed, I told Massiko, I kept going to their apartment a few times a week to spend time with them. I realized that God had used me to save their lives—but God was also using them to save my life. They accepted and loved me at one of the lowest points of my life.

I started a blog about them, and then, two years later, I turned the blog into the book, weaving my story together with theirs. I designated all the proceeds from the book to go into the Invisible Girls Trust Fund to help them to go to college.

Massiko had finished flipping through the pages and was gently holding the book in his large hands when I finished telling him the story.

"How did you come to call them the Invisible Girls?" he asked.

"Because the day I met them on the train, Hadhi was crying, and her little girl was falling asleep while she was standing up because there was no place for her to sit. They were in distress, but it seemed like no one noticed them except for me. But for some reason, I noticed them. I saw them."

A smile came to Massiko's face and he slowly nodded. "Yah," he said gently. "Yah. Because love looks around."

I had never heard anyone describe love quite like Massiko did, but he was exactly right.

"Yes! It does, doesn't it?" I nodded emphatically. "Love looks around!"

The words played in my head as I took a bite of scrambled eggs and another sip of black coffee.

Love looks around.

Love looks around and sees the world with compassion.

Love looks around and sees the world through the eyes of God.

Love looks around and sees the marginalized, invisible people who are often overlooked.

Love looks around.

S PEAKING OF LOOKING around," Massiko said a few minutes later, his words bringing me back to reality, back to the humid morning in Lomé, back to my half-eaten plate of bread and scrambled eggs.

Massiko went on to brief me about the journey we were about to make. He told me there was only one road from Lomé to Mango. Part of the road was paved and went through villages and towns, but most of it was unpaved and went through very desolate and remote places.

Many armed carjackers hid out in these remote places. Sometimes they just took a car and its contents. Other times, as in David's case, they shot and killed the people inside the car.

To combat this, armed soldiers sometimes climbed into civilians' cars to form an armed caravan to travel through these dangerous areas.

"So as we're driving, look around and tell me if you see armed men with guns," Massiko said. "And also, don't be surprised if soldiers with guns stop us and get into our car," he added. "They're just trying to keep us safe."

I looked at him, wide-eyed, studying his face to find evidence that he was joking. Or at least exaggerating. But he was totally serious.

Massiko checked his watch and told me it was time to leave. We had a long drive ahead of us, and he was hoping to make it to Mango before dark. I grabbed my backpack and said good-bye to Hugo and Jori as Massiko loaded my luggage into the Land Cruiser.

Jesus, what did I get myself into? I whispered as I climbed into the backseat.

I didn't have any cell service or WiFi to email my friends and family back in the United States to ask them to pray really hard for the next nine hours. It was just me, a gentle Togolese man, and a rusty Land Cruiser, heading into rural West Africa with no means of communication and no means of self-defense. We had two liters of bottled water and five bananas. Given that the trip was so long and the road was so desolate, I had no idea when we would eat again or what we would do if we got stranded and ran out of water.

For the second time in two days, I questioned whether I had what it took to make it here in rural West Africa.

I WAS HYPERVIGILANT AS we started our drive. Massiko darted and dodged his way through the narrow dirt streets in the neighborhood around the guesthouse. Then we turned onto a larger, paved road that ran through the center of town.

I noticed that there were no markings on the pavement—no yellow lines in the center to divide lanes of traffic, and no white lines to mark the shoulders. Driving was basically a free-for-all. Mopeds zigzagged through traffic. Cars passed each other on the right and on the left, often swerving into lanes of heavy oncoming traffic before darting back into their own lane, avoiding head-on collisions by mere inches.

Narrow, top-heavy vans with mounds of suitcases and furniture and goats strapped to their roofs sped through the streets, looking as if they might tip over at any moment. Massiko told me that van drivers were paid per passenger, so they crammed up to twenty people in vans that were only made to fit ten.

As Massiko and I made our way through Lomé, I noticed small stores scattered through the city. Most of them were made of cinder block and were marked by faded wooden signs hand-painted in French. Wooden stands lined the roads, with merchants offering everything from mangoes to SIM cards to sandals.

The other vehicles on the road were driving erratically, which meant Massiko also had to drive erratically to avoid crashing into them. We had several near misses, and each time I instinctively closed my eyes and tightened my grip on the door handle. Because time was of the essence, I prayed the shortest prayer I knew. "Jesus, Jesus, Jesus!"

Twenty minutes after we left the guesthouse, we arrived at the outskirts of Lomé, where the city dump was located. Garbage was piled at least six feet high and extended across a dozen city blocks. I counted three bulldozers in the dump, driving across the garbage, tamping it down to create room for more. In other parts, pillars of gray smoke rose from burn piles, with rancid ash billowing toward the sky.

At least a dozen stalls had been erected at the entrance of the dump, where people sold objects they'd picked out of the trash.

Just past the dump, we made a right turn onto a paved two-lane highway that led north. I turned around in my seat to get one last glimpse of Lomé, but a gust of wind had blown across the dump, and all I could see was smoke.

A T BREAKFAST, MASSIKO had asked me to look around, but a few miles outside of town my exhaustion overcame my fear of carjackers, and I fell asleep with my head resting against the window.

An hour later, I was abruptly woken from my nap when Massiko hit a pothole. Even though I was wearing my seat belt, the jolt threw me forward and I almost hit my face on the back of the headrest in front of me.

I looked out the window to see that the paved road had ended, and we were now bouncing along a red dirt road. It wasn't a smooth dirt road with occasional potholes. It was all potholes with occasional patches of flat road in between.

"We are okay, Sarah," Massiko said, seeing my startled face in the rearview mirror.

For almost three hours, we bounced along the road. During that time, the land around us was a flat savanna covered with tall grass that was a faded shade of green with withered brown edges. I saw a smattering of short, broad trees in the distance to the east and west. Flat, grass-covered terrain stretched out ahead of us as far as I could see.

Every few miles, we passed through a small village. If we stopped for traffic or for a pedestrian crossing the road, women with baskets on their heads swarmed our vehicle, knocking at the window, offering to sell us bananas or roasted peanuts or baguettes or pineapples or glass bottles of warm Coke.

In between the villages, women walked along the road with baskets of food or buckets of water on their heads. Children walked along the roadside, sometimes with their mothers and sometimes on their own, balancing branches and buckets on their heads. The littlest children looked like they might be three or four years old.

As we continued to drive north, encountering new villages and new people and new terrain, Togo unfolded before me like pages of a book I'd never read. I was grateful for the pothole that had woken me up from my nap, because I spent the rest of the day looking out my window, learning Togo's landscapes and seeing its Invisible People.

Love looks around, I thought as I watched men trudging through dusty fields in bare feet, as I watched laughing children walking together down the road, as I watched mothers carrying babies on their backs and baskets on their heads.

Love looks around, I thought as I prayed a blessing over the people I saw.

Love looks around.

FIVE HOURS INTO our drive, Massiko looked in the rearview mirror and said, "Sarah, are you hungry?"

I nodded. We had talked so much during breakfast, I hadn't finished my scrambled eggs and bread, and my stomach had been growling since I woke up from my nap.

"Do you like peas?" he asked.

"Peas?" I asked, wondering if I'd heard him correctly.

He nodded. "Yah, peas," he confirmed.

"Yeah, I guess," I said. I mean, I didn't dislike them.

A few minutes later, we arrived at a small town. The main street was lined with dozens of wooden booths where merchants sold soap and dishes and batteries and produce and fabric.

Massiko pulled into a gas station and filled up the Land Cruiser's tank. Then he parked the car on the side of the gas station, and we got out and ran across the street to a small café.

The café consisted of a square, raised wooden platform with a canvas roof, and ten small tables with plastic chairs. There were no walls and no overhead lights.

A woman brought us laminated menus written in French. I scanned the menu, using my limited French to interpret my options.

Every single item on the menu was a large plate of peas, paired with a different side. Peas with bread, peas with chicken legs, peas with steak, peas with *pintade*.

"What's *pintade*?" I asked Massiko.

He thought for a minute, then shook his head. "I don't know how you say it in English."

I'm an adventurous eater, so I ordered peas with *pintade*, and a bottle of water. I found out later that *pintade* is French for "guinea fowl," a bird that is smaller and leaner than a chicken, and is ubiquitous in Togo.

A few minutes later, the woman placed a plate in front of me that was heaped with steaming petite peas tossed in oil and curry sauce, and a piece of meat that looked like a roasted chicken thigh.

I tried to cut into the meat with my plastic knife, but it was so tough, the knife snapped in half. So I picked it up with my hands and bit into it. It tasted more like duck than chicken, and it was almost too tough to chew.

The peas were flavorful, but I could only eat half the plate. I was used to peas as a side dish, not an entrée.

Massiko ate his plate of peas and chicken in less than five minutes, and washed it down with a bottle of fruit juice.

"If you're still hungry, you can finish mine," I said, sliding my plate toward him. "I'm full."

He ate all my peas, and then proceeded to put the whole piece of guinea fowl in his mouth. He chewed for a while, and in the end spit out two small bones. He'd managed to use his mouth to get all the meat off the bones.

When we finished eating, Massiko paid the tab, and then, as we were leaving the café, he looked up at the overcast sky.

"Run, Sarah, run!" he said. "It's going to rain."

We ran across the street, climbed back into the Land Cruiser, and began driving again. Minutes later, a torrential rain began to fall. Even with the windshield wipers going at full speed, Massiko had to hunch forward over the steering wheel to see the road ahead.

We drove that way for half an hour. I was clutching my door handle, praying hard that we wouldn't run off the road or encounter carjackers in the deluge.

The rain finally began to taper off, and Massiko relaxed back into his seat.

Soon after the rain ended, we drove out of the flat, grassy savanna of southern Togo and into the mountains in the middle of Togo.

All of a sudden, the brown savanna grass ended, and as the road ascended into the mountains I began to see vibrant green grass and dense groves of flowering trees.

The temperature dropped about ten degrees, the air became less humid, and I began to see lots of fields with green shoots popping out of the red soil.

I rolled down the window and let the cool air blow through my hair as we continued to make our way north, every mile taking us closer to where I would be spending the next three months of my life.

NINE HOURS, A dozen villages, countless potholes, a plate of peas, and a torrential downpour later, we arrived in Mango.

There was one paved road that ran through town. Red dirt paths ran perpendicular to the paved road, lined with clusters of single-room homes. Some were mud houses with thatched roofs. Others were made of cinder blocks. Others were made from wood and corrugated tin.

All of the buildings in town were one-story with the exception of an eight-bedroom, two-story home built for the minister of education. I learned later that because building codes aren't enforced in rural Togo, people build only one-story homes so there's less chance of a structure collapsing.

At the center of town was a market with dozens of stands where merchants were selling fabric, produce, housewares, jewelry, eggs, and tools.

Goats, sheep, guinea fowl, chickens, and stray dogs roamed the streets.

The town's largest mosque was next to the market. Smaller mosques were scattered throughout the town, with loudspeakers attached to the top of their minarets. Massiko told me that calls to prayer were made five times a day—at dawn, noon, midafternoon, sunset, and nighttime.

The town was surrounded by acres and acres of fields where farmers were growing corn, green beans, yams, onions, tomatoes, lettuce, and peppers. The rainy season had just begun, so crops were only a few inches high.

The Hospital of Hope was a mile past town. I breathed a sigh of relief when I saw the large sign at the front entrance. Massiko and I had successfully completed the nine-hour drive with no car trouble, accidents, or carjackings.

We drove past the sign and the guard shack, and into the walled hospital compound, which had taken more than a decade of planning and three years of construction to build. The cinder-block wall that surrounded the hospital was only four feet tall. Massiko explained that it was built to keep out poisonous snakes, not people.

The compound contained an outpatient clinic, the hospital, six houses, five guest rooms, a recreation/dining room, a pool, a maintenance shed, and a water tower. Next to the guard shack was the Cuisine. Built of cinder blocks, it was a barn-like building with twenty "stalls" where families whose relatives were in the hospital could stay until their loved one was well enough to go home.

Each stall had a mosquito net and a small metal cooking stove that looked something like a hibachi grill. Outside were two water pumps and two fire pits. Past that was the latrine, which contained hole-in-the-ground toilets as well as a handful of showers.

Massiko told me that hospitals in much of the developing world don't have cafeterias or kitchens, so patients rely on friends and family members to bring them water and food.

Unlike other hospitals in rural Africa, the Hospital of Hope did provide linens, pillows, and beds for patients. And unlike many other hospitals, it was clean. A full-time housekeeping staff mopped the floors, disinfected the equipment, emptied trash cans, and cleaned the bathrooms at least twice a day. Although, as I would discover in my three months there, despite the housekeepers' best efforts, there were lots of mosquitoes, flies, frogs, and spiders that got inside the hospital anyway—as well as one scorpion and two poisonous snakes.

In the back of the property was half an acre of land called the Farm where a French agricultural expert named Marc was experimenting to see the most nutritious plants Togolese people could grow in that climate. He was growing Moringa trees, also called Miracle Trees. Indigenous to West Africa, their leaves contain nine times the protein of yogurt, ten times the vitamin A of carrots, fifteen times the potassium of bananas, seventeen times the calcium of milk, twelve times the vitamin C of oranges, and twenty-five times the iron of spinach.

Marc was growing Moringa trees as close together as possible, then crushing the leaves into a powder that could be added to infant formula, tea, or oatmeal for patients who were malnourished.

The Farm also had a pen containing sheep, goats, a mule, and chickens, all given to the hospital by patients in lieu of cash to pay off their medical bills.

The compound's perimeter measured exactly one mile, and everything inside made up the Hospital of Hope.

I couldn't think of a better name for a hospital that was located in an arid, remote corner of the least happy country in the world.

MASSIKO PULLED UP to the guesthouse and three American women came to meet us. I met Beth, a woman in her forties whose husband, Todd, was a surgical physician assistant and the medical director of the hospital. Beth's sandy-blond, chin-length hair framed her petite facial features. When she smiled, her blue eyes sparkled, and I noticed well-worn creases at the corners of her eyes, indicating the smiles and sunshine that had graced her face during the decade she and Todd had spent in Togo. She shook my hand with a vise-like grip, and I noticed her well-defined forearm muscles. She was kind, and incredibly strong. I found out later that in addition to walking several miles a day, she also did workout DVDs at home five mornings a week. She and Todd had four sons, ages nine through fifteen, who volunteered at the hospital during the summer.

Charity, a woman in her early thirties whose husband, Matt, was the hospital administrator, had her fourteen-month-old boy strapped to her back in typical Togolese fashion. She was soft-spoken and had curly, shoulder-length brown hair that was pulled back into a ponytail and tied with a strip of fabric that matched her skirt.

Then I met Hazel, a short, stout, gray-haired woman in her mid-sixties who ran the guesthouse with her husband, Fred.

They were all wearing short-sleeved shirts and ankle-length skirts. As I climbed out of the Land Cruiser, I was glad I'd remembered the guidelines and worn a T-shirt and long skirt for the drive up.

I had expected the guesthouse to be a multistory hotel like the one in Lomé, but this one was more like a five-room motel attached to the large dining hall/common area.

Hazel showed me to my room, a twelve-by-fourteen-foot space with a stone floor, a twin-size bed, and a small table. On the table was a plastic gift basket that contained a variety of supplies. "We bought you some things at the market that often come in handy here," she explained.

Next to the basket was a black three-ring binder. "This has some information about the town, as well as the rules of the compound," she said. "You'll want to read that. Also," she added, "the hospital has its own water filtration system, so tap water within the compound is safe to drink."

I nodded as she continued to show me around the room.

An alcove with a wooden shelf, a metal bar, and ten plastic hangers served as the closet. Next to the closet was a small bathroom with a shower stall. I was disappointed that there wasn't a tub, because when I finished a hectic shift in the ER, I'd often take a long bubble bath to relax before going to bed.

The room had one window along the front wall, next to the door, that looked onto the hospital, and a window along the back wall that faced the back of the compound. An air-conditioning unit was mounted above the window on the back wall, and Hazel told me I'd be charged a dollar per hour to use it.

"Okay, I think that's it!" Hazel said when she'd finished showing me around. "I'll come get you when dinner's ready."

After she left, I sifted through the basket and found bottles of water, packages of crackers, two packets of antibacterial hand wipes, a cloth grocery bag, a flashlight, and a six-foot-long piece of thin white rope. Everything made sense except for the rope. *How, why, and when would I need that?* I wondered.

As I began to unpack, tears welled up in my eyes. In addition to being exhausted, I felt alone and isolated here in this compound within a foreign country, staying in an austere room that felt anything but homey. The mattress was hard, covered by coarse tan sheets. There were no blankets or comforters, no rugs or lamps or art pieces or nightstands or books to make the space feel more inviting.

All I could think as I arranged my shirts on the shelf and hung my skirts in the makeshift closet was that for the next three months of my life, I was going to be staying in a room that looked and felt more like a jail cell than a guest room.

Maybe, like a despondent inmate, jail would prove too much for my sensitive soul.

And maybe this was what the rope was for.

A N HOUR LATER, Hazel knocked on my door to tell me dinner was ready. I gave myself a gentle, positive pep talk in the bathroom mirror as I splashed water on my face and ran a brush through my dusty, tangled long brown hair.

As I left my room, I noticed it was starting to get dark outside. The patients' families who were staying in the Cuisine were making fires to start cooking dinner, and the air was filled with aromatic smoke.

The dining hall was a large room with a concrete floor and ten long tables that were lined with metal folding chairs. In the far corner was a stack of board games, a bookshelf with several dozen paperback books, a Ping-Pong table, two mismatched couches, and a handful of stuffed armchairs.

Dinner that night was sloppy joes, potato salad, chips, and red Kool-Aid, served buffet-style on the counter between the dining hall and the kitchen.

I felt like I was back at the summer camp I attended when I was growing up. Substitute staff houses for cabins, the Cuisine cooking area for a bonfire, and patients for campers, and the hospital compound was just like summer camp—if summer camp had poisonous snakes and malaria, and if half the campers died.

I fixed myself a plate of food, poured myself a cup of water, and sat down across from a couple who had already started eating. They introduced them-selves as Wade and Patty, and told me they had arrived from Indiana a few days before me.

Wade was a large, gregarious man with a giant mustache who used to be a firefighter before he became a nurse. His wife, Patty, was a quiet woman with chin-length gray hair who was doing accounting for the hospital.

"How long are you here?" I asked.

"Six months!" Wade said with enthusiasm.

Patty explained that their two children were grown and out of the house. A missionary had come to their church a few months back and given a talk about the Hospital of Hope, the suffering of the people of Togo, and the need for volunteers.

"So we prayed about it for a few weeks, and we both decided Togo's the place for us!" Wade's voice boomed.

When we had finished eating, we cleared our plates and stepped outside to return to our rooms. It was 7 p.m. and already it was pitch black outside. The mosques were issuing the evening call to prayer, which sounded like a mournful chant sung in a minor key.

Wade and Patty were staying in the room next to mine. I waved good night to them, unlocked the door to my room, and flipped on the light. A quarter-size spider scurried across the floor in front of me. I quickly stepped on it, wiped it off the sole of my shoe with a wad of toilet paper, and flushed it down the toilet.

Then I sat on the edge of my bed in silence, wondering what to do for the rest of the evening. I turned on my laptop to find that the Internet wasn't working. The shops in town were closed. All the missionaries were either working, resting, or putting their kids to sleep.

I tried to remember what I did at home when I was bored. I usually called or texted a friend, read articles online, retrieved a book from the library, returned emails, or downloaded a movie. But none of those options was available to me here.

I remembered seeing a bookshelf in the dining hall, so I grabbed a flashlight and went to find something to read. A lot of the books were about theology, which I don't like to read for entertainment. I finally settled on a yellowed paperback copy of *Anne of Green Gables*.

I read the entire book that night. *Only eighty-nine more nights to go*, I thought as I turned out the light and fell asleep to the sound of crickets and frogs just outside my door.

BETH HAD TOLD me that the non-nursing clinical staff—doctors, nurse practitioners, and physician assistants—met in the dining hall for staff devotions at 7 a.m. every Friday.

On my first Friday in Mango, I woke up at 6 a.m. and spent half an hour journaling, trying to record my travel adventures and first impressions of the hospital before I forgot the details.

Then I climbed out of bed and started to get ready. I had bought five ankle-length skirts at a consignment store before I left the United States. I picked the teal one, plus a white T-shirt, and a pair of flat black Mary Jane shoes as my outfit for the day. I pulled my long hair into a ponytail. I started to put on makeup out of habit—not much, just enough to subtly accent my facial features and hide some freckles—but then I stopped myself.

What if makeup, like ankles and kneecaps, was taboo in this culture? I usually only wore light foundation, eye shadow, and clear lip gloss when I went to work in the United States. But was that too much? I didn't know the answer, so I decided to go without makeup that day, just to be safe.

When I walked into the dining hall, Beth's husband, Todd, the hospital's medical director, greeted me. I had corresponded with him via email, but this was the first time we were meeting in person. He was well over six feet tall with broad shoulders and a thick build, wearing light-blue scrubs and flip-flops. He had short blond hair and blue eyes. I held out my hand to shake his, but instead he wrapped his arm around my shoulders and gave me a strong squeeze.

"We're so glad you're here!" he said enthusiastically. "I'm always glad when we have PAs come—of course, I'm kinda partial."

"I'm glad to be here," I said. I forced a smile, trying to hide how overwhelmed, trepidatious, and exhausted I felt.

There were sixty American missionaries at the Hospital of Hope, but only seven of us, including Todd, were full-time doctors or physician assistants.

When I arrived that morning, they were all sitting at a round table. I walked around the table with Todd as he made introductions.

Tanya, a thirty-five-year-old pediatrician from Kentucky, was a "lifer," a missionary who planned to spend her life overseas. She was also the hospital's chief of staff. She had black hair, an athletic build, and a loud, piercing voice.

Betsy, also a pediatrician, also in her thirties, was in Togo for two years. Her voice was as quiet as Tanya's was loud. She had pale skin and freckles, and that morning she wore her long, curly black hair in a thick French braid.

Emilie, an internal medicine doctor from France, was married to Marc, the agricultural expert who ran the Farm. They were the only non-American missionaries, and they were lifers. Emilie was a petite woman in her thirties with chin-length, curly blond hair and a thick French accent.

Laura was a redheaded internal medicine doctor whose husband, Chad, was the hospital's accountant. They, along with their four young boys, were lifers, too.

The last person I met was Paul, a lanky forty-five-year-old general surgeon from Michigan who was volunteering in Togo for a few months.

I smiled and shook hands with each of them as Todd introduced us. Then I poured myself a cup of coffee and took a seat next to Todd at the table.

"Well, I asked Paul to lead our devotions this morning," Todd announced.

Paul read a ten-minute devotional about the biblical story of Nehemiah, who led the Israelites in rebuilding the crumbled walls of Jerusalem. Nehemiah and his workers refused to give up, despite the seemingly impossible task, and despite the fact that while they were working they were taunted by their enemies. The devotional concluded by encouraging Christians to never give up in the task God was calling them to do, no matter how overwhelming it seemed, and no matter how many people doubted along the way.

Paul closed the devotional, laid it on the table, and folded his hands on top. "I think these are appropriate words for today," he said, "especially after the week we've all had."

I looked around the table. Except for Todd, who brimmed with energy, the other clinicians looked weary, with drawn faces, dark circles under their eyes, and large cups of coffee in their hands. They all nodded as they absorbed Paul's words and remembered the story of Nehemiah.

"Let's pray," Todd said. One by one, we went around the table and each prayed out loud. Tanya prayed for the "eternal salvation of souls" at the hospital. Betsy and Laura prayed for specific patients they'd cared for that week by name. Emilie prayed in French, and she spoke so quickly, the only words I understood were *Notre Père*, Our Father.

Paul prayed for wisdom and stamina, which he and Todd would need in spades since they'd be in the OR for at least twelve hours that day.

Todd prayed for the same. He also prayed that God would keep the team healthy, unified, and determined so they could accomplish the work they had come to Mango to do.

Then it was my turn to pray. "Jesus, please heal our patients and let them experience your love through us. We love you. Amen."

"Amen," the team echoed as I concluded my brief prayer. Everyone got up from the table and refilled their coffee cups, anticipating another long day of patient care.

Todd suggested I spend the morning shadowing Tanya in the hospital, and the afternoon shadowing Betsy in the outpatient clinic.

So with my stethoscope around my neck and the hem of my long skirt brushing along the red dirt path, I walked across the compound to begin my first shift at the Hospital of Hope.

TANYA GAVE ME a tour of the hospital before we started rounding on patients that first Friday morning.

In front of the hospital was an outpatient clinic with ten exam rooms, a registration office, a lab, a pharmacy, and a cashier's office. There were long, backless wooden benches in front of the clinic rooms where patients waited their turn until the provider was ready to see them.

The inpatient part of the hospital was the size and layout of a small US emergency room, with a nurses' station in the center, and patient wards along the periphery.

When we walked in the front door, what hit me first was the smell. Or rather, the stench. The hospital wasn't air-conditioned, and the ceiling fans scattered around did little to move or cool the humid, stagnant air inside. The smell of feces, urine, vomit, and body odor was so strong, it made me sick to my stomach. I tried breathing through my mouth instead of my nose to see if it would lessen the stench, but that made it even worse, because then I wasn't just smelling the odor; I was tasting it.

The smell transported me back to grad school, when I spent three hours a week in anatomy lab dissecting a cadaver. The smell of formaldehyde and decaying flesh in the lab was so sickening, I kept Vicks VapoRub in my locker and filled my nostrils with it at the beginning of every session. When that didn't sufficiently block the smell, I started smearing Vicks on the inside of a surgical mask and tying it over my nose and mouth as tightly as possible.

That first Friday morning, as Tanya showed me around the Hospital of Hope, I didn't have Vicks or a surgical mask with me. So when the smell became too much, I lifted the inside of my wrist to my nose and took a few whiffs of the perfume I'd applied earlier that morning.

The nurses' station had cabinets of pills and IV medications, two hand-washing stations, several trays with IV-starting equipment, a large screen to view digital X-rays, and two computers.

Tanya explained that half the nurses and medical assistants were American, and half were Togolese. When construction began on the hospital five years ago, Todd and Matt hired local Togolese carpenters, bricklayers, and contractors to build the facilities. Instead of letting them go once the hospital was ready to open, Todd and Matt offered them free job training to become medical assistants and surgical techs.

Tanya pointed to a tall, muscular Togolese man in his mid-thirties in blue scrubs who was measuring the temperature of a four-year-old patient in pediatrics. "That's Darvesh," Tanya said. "A year ago, he was pouring concrete to build the hospital, and now he's one of the most intelligent, capable medical assistants we have. The Togolese nurses started their training three years ago at our sister hospital five hours south of Mango," she continued. "They were allowed to attend the nursing school for free, on the condition that they would move to Mango when this hospital opened in March."

"That's so great!" I said. "Now all we need is a PA program or a medical school in Mango to train locals to become clinicians, and we will have worked ourselves out of a job!"

Tanya gave me a confused look, as if the idea that the Hospital of Hope could be run entirely by Togolese clinicians had not occurred to her before.

"Which employees does the hospital pay?" I asked, changing the subject.

"Only the Togolese staff," she said. "They get paid from the funds the hospital collects from patient fees. The Americans are all volunteers—they raise support from family and friends in the United States to cover their travel and living expenses."

"Are all of the clinicians Americans?" I asked.

"All but two," she said. "Emilie's from France. And then there's François, a Togolese physician assistant who graduated from a PA program in Lomé. He works full-time in the clinic, and he's the only clinician on the hospital's payroll."

Tanya and I left the nurses' station and started walking around the wards. We walked past an alcove with three beds. Each bed had a cardiac monitor mounted on the wall above it, and they were reserved for the sickest patients. Perpendicular to the wall with the alcove was a wall with three doors labeled ISO 1, ISO 2, and ISO 3, isolation rooms reserved for patients with contagious illnesses.

The third wall had an alcove with four gurneys that made up the "emergency room" for patients with urgent conditions who didn't necessarily need to be admitted overnight. Along the fourth wall was an open room with twelve cribs that served as the pediatrics ward.

A short hallway led to a twelve-bed ward for women with medical or surgical issues. Across the hallway from the women's ward was a four-bed maternity ward for women who were in labor or had just delivered a baby.

While Tanya loudly greeted the Labor & Delivery nurses, I peeked behind the curtains and found that in each bed, there was a woman in active labor. Even though the women had not been given any pain medication or epidurals, the ward was quiet, without so much as a moan or a groan. I wondered if it was possible to measure the pain tolerance of a woman in active labor, seven centimeters dilated, lying motionless and silent in a room that was at least ninety degrees, without ice chips or an epidural.

On the opposite side of the hospital, down a short hallway from the nurses' station, was a twelve-bed men's ward for male patients admitted with medical or surgical issues.

We walked down a long corridor behind the ISO rooms, and Tanya showed me the radiology suite, which held an X-ray machine and an ultrasound machine. Across the hall from radiology, double doors led into the surgery department, which had a large closet of sterile surgical supplies, men's and women's locker rooms, and two deep stainless-steel sinks where surgeons scrubbed in before entering one of four sterile operating rooms.

The only part of the hospital we didn't tour was the morgue. Tanya pointed out the back door to a cinder-block building the size of a two-car garage that was fifteen yards from the hospital. She said that while the structure was technically designated as the morgue, it wasn't air-conditioned, so it wasn't used often. Plus, Muslims were supposed to bury the body of a deceased loved one before sunset the day the person died. There were no autopsies, funeral parlors, embalming, caskets, cemeteries, or hearses in rural Togo.

When a patient died, most families took their loved one's corpse home right away, wrapped the body in cloth or cardboard, and buried it in a hand-dug grave in their yard.

"What if the patient is too heavy to carry?" I asked Tanya.

"Sometimes they put dead bodies on the back of their mopeds and drive them home. You'll often see a mummy strapped to a moped driver's back. If the dead person is really tall, sometimes their feet will drag on the ground behind them as the moped drives away."

I looked to some American nurses nearby who were listening to our conversation, and they nodded to confirm that Tanya wasn't joking.

As we walked over to the nurses' station, I thought about the morgue and mummies and mopeds. Togo was getting stranger—and sadder—by the minute.

Tanya and I pulled up two chairs in front of a computer. She handed me a slip of paper. "Here's your username and password," she said. "Log in here and see if it works." She pointed to the lab icon on the computer screen.

I made notes as Tanya showed me how to order labs and find the results.

"Now log in here." Tanya pointed to the radiology icon.

I logged in, and she showed me how to order X-rays, and how to zoom in, zoom out, and increase or decrease the contrast to see an image better.

A rack of clipboards sat on the counter next to the computer. "These are the charts," Tanya said. "Everything besides labs and imaging—progress notes, medications, consults, and other orders—is handwritten here."

She pulled a chart from the rack to show me where to write notes and orders, and where to find the vital signs and nurses' notes.

The chart she pulled happened to be for an eleven-month old pediatrics patient who had been admitted two weeks before with severe dehydration and malnutrition.

"The front page is always the admissions H&P," she said. I knew that an H&P, or History and Physical, is an extensive note that records the reason for a patient's admission, any medications taken, allergies, past medical history, past surgical history, social details such as living arrangements, and, in adults, any tobacco, alcohol, or drug use. An H&P also includes a detailed exam, vital signs, an assessment that lists a patient's problems and likely diagnoses, and a plan for how to treat the patient.

I skimmed the child's H&P and found that when he was admitted, he had been only ten pounds—the average weight of an eleven-month-old is twenty-one pounds. His eyes had been sunken, he hadn't urinated for more than a day, hadn't passed any stools in a week, didn't produce any tears when he cried, and was so weak he could barely move.

"Why was he so dehydrated and malnourished?" I asked Tanya.

"His mother had been breast-feeding him, but their village ran out of food and the cisterns ran out of water, and the mother's milk dried up. Instead of supplementing with formula or bringing the baby to the hospital, she followed her village's tradition and took the baby to a fetisher instead. The baby arrived here with charm bracelets on his ankles and a sacred ribbon with bird feathers wrapped around his waist. When the fetisher didn't work, the mother took him to an herbalist, who crushed herbs in water and gave it to the baby to drink, but thankfully, he refused it. Sometimes the herbalists send patients into kidney or liver failure with their remedies," Tanya said.

She continued, "After the herbalist, they took him to a marabout, who performed several ceremonies to cast out the evil spirits that were supposedly draining the baby's life out of him. Finally, in an act of desperation, the mother brought the baby here. The hospital was their last resort."

We read through the rest of the note. Under the "Plan" section, Tanya had ordered labs to check the baby's electrolytes and screen for HIV, hepatitis B and C, anemia, and malaria. She had ordered a nutrient-rich formula to be delivered via an NG (nasogastric) tube that ran from the baby's nose down into his stomach. She also ordered daily weights to measure his progress. And she ordered IV fluids to rehydrate the baby. For the last step of the plan, Tanya had written in all-caps, "NO FETISHERS, HERBALISTS or MARABOUTS!!!"

When we had finished reading the note, Tanya shook her head. "The family spent all their money on alternative healers," she said. "They have no money left to pay their child's hospital bill. If they had spent their money on formula, all of this could have been avoided."

MY ORIENTATION WITH Tanya was interrupted when two hospital security guards came bursting through the front door, carrying a teenage boy between them, yelling in French, *"Urgence! Urgence!"* Emergency! Emergency!

The boy was half conscious, and blood was pouring out of a large wound on his lower right leg, leaving a trail on the floor. The security guards raced to an empty ER bed and laid him down. I followed Tanya as she ran over to assess the patient.

The security guard explained in rapid French that the boy had wrecked his moped and broken his leg. Tanya quickly put on gloves and turned on the bright, round overhead light to reveal that the boy had a compound fracture. He had broken his ankle, and the bones were protruding through the skin. He had also likely severed an artery, because instead of oozing from the wound, blood was spurting out, spraying several inches upward before spattering the gurney and the floor.

By now, there were two nurses and two medical assistants at the bedside. Tanya gave quick orders in French.

"Type and cross two units, SAT, VAT, a CBC, two large-bore IVs, ten of morphine IM, and page Todd!" she yelled.

In less than five minutes, the IVs had been started, the lab was cross-matching blood to find two units that were compatible with the patient's blood type, he had been given injections of SAT, VAT, and morphine, and Todd had arrived at the bedside.

After quickly examining the patient, Todd picked up a phone at the nurses' station and called down to the OR. "STAT ORIF of a compound distal tib/fib fracture of the right ankle," he said, alerting the nurse anesthetist and the surgical tech that they needed to be ready to start operating on this patient as soon as possible.

And then, just minutes after he had arrived at the hospital's front gate, the patient was on his way to the OR, with two IVs running fluid into his arms at full speed.

As the medical assistants cleaned up the tubing and packaging that was strewn across the floor and a housekeeper mopped up the blood, Tanya and I washed our hands in the sink at the nurses' station.

"Whew!" she said as she fell into the chair she'd been sitting in before we'd been interrupted. "Did you get all that?"

My heart was still racing with adrenaline, and I was still processing what had just happened in what seemed like a blink of an eye.

"I got most of it," I said.

I knew that a compound tib/fib fracture was a break in both ankle bones—the tibia and the fibula—with the bones protruding through the skin. I had recognized the spurting pattern of an arterial bleed. I knew that a type-and-cross determined a patient's blood type and selected donated blood that was compatible. And I knew that an ORIF was an orthopedic procedure—Open Reduction Internal Fixation—in which a surgeon used screws to stabilize a broken bone that was out of place.

"The only thing I didn't recognize was SAT and VAT," I admitted.

Tanya explained that regular immunizations didn't exist in Togo, which meant that patients weren't immunized against tetanus. If patients had an open wound—like a compound fracture, a laceration, or a burn—they needed to receive a long-acting tetanus shot that would give them immunity for the next five years, as well as a short-acting serum that would boost their immunity against tetanus over the next few days.

I pulled out a small notebook from my messenger bag and made a note of what *SAT* and *VAT* stood for, as well as the standard adult dosing.

Before I left for Togo, I'd considered myself a competent, intelligent clinician. I had graduated from an Ivy League PA program, scored high on my board certification exam, and practiced medicine for more than a decade.

But as I discovered that first day at the hospital—and in the days and weeks that followed—when it came to practicing medicine in the developing world, there was so much I didn't know, so much I hadn't needed to know in the United States, either because the disease had been eradicated, as in the case of polio, or because the problem simply didn't exist in the US, as in the case of typhoid and malaria.

Within a week of arriving at the Hospital of Hope, I had filled my notebook with everything I didn't know about practicing medicine in Togo.

AFTER THE PATIENT with the ankle fracture was rushed off to surgery and the ER bay was clean, the hospital settled back into its normal rhythm. Nurses hung IVs, aides checked and recorded vital signs, and two surgical techs wheeled a bandage cart through the wards and changed the dressings of all the surgical patients. The sounds of beeping monitors, whimpering pediatric patients, and squeaky gurneys being rolled down the hall blended together to create a familiar hospital din.

Tanya continued to patiently answer my questions. I was curious to know how the hospital was funded. Was it considered a "charity" hospital that offered free care, or did patients have to pay? And if patients had to pay, how did they afford their care?

She explained that the hospital was structured like the hospitals run by the Togolese government. Togo doesn't have health insurance, so all patients paid out of pocket for their care. Before they were discharged from the hospital, patients had to pay their bill in full. If they didn't have the money, they could borrow from family and friends, or sell livestock or other goods. In some cases, they were allowed to give livestock—a chicken or a sheep or a goat—to the hospital in lieu of cash. Patients who had had surgery or other expensive procedures donated larger animals, like mules and cows.

In addition to performing agricultural experiments, Marc took care of the donated animals on the Farm. Often, the animals would breed, producing offspring that the hospital could sell at a profit. It was the livestock equivalent of earning interest on an investment.

The government hospitals had an even more extreme pay-as-you-go system, Tanya said. Patients had to pay cash for each step of their treatment. Before the nurse started an IV, or a doctor ordered a blood test, they demanded payment. If a patient couldn't pay, nothing further was done, even if the patient was dying.

Tanya told me that a few months before the Hospital of Hope opened,

Matt had visited a government hospital in southern Togo. There was a man sitting outside the hospital's front gate with an open femur fracture. His thigh bone was broken and sticking out of his skin—and the doctors and nurses just walked around him, totally ignoring him, because he couldn't afford to pay. Matt was so appalled and angry, he carried the man inside, demanded that the staff care for him immediately, and paid the man's bill himself.

Unlike the government hospitals, the Hospital of Hope performed any lifesaving treatments regardless of whether a patient could pay, and sorted the cost out later. If patients couldn't come up with the money to cover their bill before they were discharged, and didn't have any livestock to sell or donate, the hospital either arranged a payment plan for them or, in the poorest cases, used its Benevolence Fund to write off the entire cost.

Tanya encouraged me to be very cost-conscious when prescribing medications or ordering tests on patients. "Only order what is absolutely necessary," she said.

"How much does a blood test cost?" I asked.

"Each test costs three thousand CFAs," she said.

The CFA (which, in French, stands for "Communauté Financière d'Afrique") is the currency of Togo and other West African countries that were colonized by France. Instead of pronouncing each letter of the acronym, C.F.A., most people made a word out of the three letters and pronounced it *see-fuh*.

When I was in Togo, the exchange rate was roughly five hundred CFAs to one US dollar. I did the math. A blood test was only six dollars US, a bargain compared with the price of labs in the United States.

"That's not bad," I said with a shrug.

"Let me put it to you this way," Tanya said. "In the village, you can buy a plate of food that will feed two people for two hundred CFAs."

When she put it like that, suddenly the cost of care seemed exorbitant.

In the United States, I rarely considered the cost of tests and medications and procedures because most things got billed to insurance companies that paid vastly different rates depending on a patient's plan and level of coverage. The billing process took a long time, and the total cost of care wasn't settled until months after I'd seen the patient.

I made a mental note to look up the cost of the labs and medications the

Hospital of Hope offered so I could save patients as much money as possible, though I realized that scaling back on labs and imaging would mean I would have to up my game as a clinician. The less objective data I had, the more I would have to use my clinical skills and intuitive judgment to determine diagnoses and treatment plans.

Treating patients without the labs needed to confirm their diagnoses was like pilots having to land planes with manual controls instead of automated ones. It was the clinical equivalent of flying blind.

A T NOON, TANYA and I walked to the dining hall for lunch.
On our way over, Tanya told me that the Togolese women who worked in the kitchen only made breakfast and dinner for the people staying in the guesthouse, but they made lunch for the entire team.

I walked into the dining hall expecting it to look like a hospital cafeteria in the United States at mealtimes, when people from all departments stopped by to grab a bite to eat. But to my surprise, instead of being a cross section of the hospital, there were only white Americans at lunch. I learned that Togolese staff went to the men's or women's locker rooms to eat their meals, which they either brought from home or purchased from vendors who sold food at the hospital's main entrance.

During my time in Togo, I learned that the Togolese staff weren't invited to the dining hall for lunch because the meal cost five dollars per person which was reasonable for the Americans but prohibitive for the Togolese. Especially considering that in the village, two hundred CFAs bought you a plate of food big enough to feed two people, asking them to pay twenty-five hundred CFAs for one meal in the dining hall was absurd.

But the longer I was in Togo, the more I realized that it wasn't only money that separated Togolese and American staff. The Togolese weren't invited to attend our Sunday-evening church services, either—which, of course, were free. And instead of adapting to the Togolese diet and eating locally grown food, Hazel insisted on sending Massiko to Lomé for cheese and beef and milk and sour cream and other ingredients needed to make "American" food that weren't available in Mango.

Every four years, the lifer missionaries returned to the United States for a yearlong furlough in which they traveled around to give updates to the churches that supported them financially, reconnected with extended family, and rested. I have never been a lifer missionary, so I'm not an expert on the best approach. Maybe the idea of a regular furlough is a time-tested tradition worth keeping. Maybe it's the thing that creates longevity and sustainabil-ity for Americans who are serving overseas. But seen through the eyes of the Togolese people, it could very easily seem that Americans lived in Togo for four years, and then they went back to their *real* home in America.

When they were viewed together, these practices smacked of imperialism, in which a dominant (usually white and Western) culture deigned to bring subjects (who were usually impoverished, less educated, and black) under the Westerners' umbrella of authority, provision, and control. To use a domestic example, it seemed like the Hospital of Hope was a modern form of the *Plessy v. Ferguson* ruling, which concluded that "separate but equal" facilities were sufficient.

Plessy v. Ferguson was overturned in 1954 by the *Brown v. Board of Edu-cation* ruling, when the Supreme Court ordered the desegregation of public schools. But in Togo, the missions agency perpetuated the same behavior and assumed the same posture toward people of color living in the develop-ing world as whites did toward blacks in the early twentieth century (and beyond). Though no one in Togo ever said it out loud, the actions of the white missionaries suggested a sense that they were not only different from, but superior to, their Togolese colleagues and patients.

Missionaries were not only Christians, but fundamentalist Baptists, who claimed to have an exclusive handle on God's Truth.

Missionaries were whites who had the resources to "help" the less fortu-nate black people.

Missionaries were the educated, English-speaking Americans who had parachuted into the African bush to rescue the people who were physically, and spiritually, perishing there.

Missionaries were the classic White Saviors, here to save black people's bodies and souls.

I wondered how to be part of a team whose approach to Togo I didn't like or agree with. I wondered how to practice medicine as a white American without perpetuating negative stereotypes. I wondered how to help the Togo-lese people without doing more harm than good. I wondered how to care for Togolese patients without robbing them of their dignity and autonomy.

I had faced similar questions when I was interacting with the Invisible Girls, and later writing the book about us. Was I just going to be another privileged white woman helping poor black people? A reincarnation of Eugenia Phelan from *The Help* or Leigh Anne Tuohy from *The Blind Side*?

As I worked with the Somali girls, I came to several realizations. First, I realized that it had to be a reciprocal relationship. Not a vertical relationship where I was reaching *down* to them to help them up to my level, but a horizontal relationship, where we were giving to and receiving from each other. I was able to give them financial help, clothes, furniture, food, transportation, and knowledge of American culture. And in return, Hadhi and the girls were able to give me acceptance, love, hospitality, friendship, and entrance into Somali culture.

Second, I realized that my efforts to help the Invisible Girls would only be healthy and sustainable if my motivation for helping them was to imbue them with *dignity* and *empowerment*. If I was motivated by guilt, pity, obligation, self-righteousness, or pride, it wouldn't be healthy for me or for them.

I had learned so much from the Somali refugee family I met in America. Now I had to figure out how to translate that wisdom into Togo, into a hospital setting, into French.

O N THAT FIRST Friday in Togo, lunch was lasagna, salad, garlic bread, chocolate cake, and more red Kool-Aid.

I found a seat near Matt and, as we were eating, I asked him how the hospital had been doing since the April newsletter that had gotten me here.

He said that now, there were close to six hundred patients showing up at triage every morning. The longer the hospital was open, the more the word got out that we were there. Patients in neighboring countries of Burkina Faso, Ghana, and Benin hired vans to drive groups to the hospital. They would make the long drive the day before, and sleep outside the hospital that night. Then, at four thirty the following morning, they would line up to be triaged, even though the clinic didn't open until eight.

Matt told me he arrived at the hospital at 6:30 every weekday morning and did the triage himself. He didn't have any formal medical training, but Tanya and Todd had taught him the basics of triage to determine who needed to be seen that day and who could wait. Matt had a medical assistant go through the line with him and measure everyone's vital signs, and then Matt made the final call about who got an appointment that day.

All pregnant women and children who showed up got seen automatically. Then the remaining appointment slots were given to the sickest patients. If patients had normal vital signs and no acute symptoms, they were given a slip of paper called a *rendez-vous*, guaranteeing them an appointment in two or three months, when, theoretically, the triage line would be shorter and the clinic staff would have time to see them.

Matt told me about one of his favorite patients—a man in his fifties from Burkina Faso who had never been to a hospital in his life, and had no idea how the medical system worked. The man walked for three days to get to the Hospital of Hope, got in through an unlocked side door, found an empty bed in the men's ward, and lay down. Instead of kicking him out and making him stand in the triage line, Matt said, "Get this man some water!" and, as the man gulped down liter after liter of cool, clean water, Matt washed the man's dusty, callused feet himself.

Other patients were not so endearing, Matt said. Because of the number of patients, and the limited number of appointment slots, triage became competitive. Patients became aggressive, elbowing each other—and sometimes getting into fistfights—in line. Others began faking symptoms to be seen. They would fake seizures, they would fall to the ground yelling in exaggerated pain, or they would strip naked to show off a small patch of skin with a rash.

Sometimes the patients—usually middle-aged men—who couldn't get an appointment that day remained persistent, sitting in the reception office glaring until the staff agreed to bend the rules and add them to that day's patient schedule.

Other patients were not insistent enough. The week before I arrived, one woman in the triage line didn't tell anyone she was in labor, and delivered a baby on the floor outside of triage, with two hundred patients looking on. The baby died an hour later. The mom died the next day.

Then, Matt said, the day before I arrived, there was an elderly woman who came and stood in the triage line. Her vital signs were normal, but because of her advanced age, Matt gave her an appointment. She lay down on a bench outside the exam room to wait her turn. By the time the provider called her name a few hours later, the woman was dead. No one knew why she had died, or exactly when.

She had just quietly slipped away.

Aᴄᴛᴇʀ ᴍᴀᴛᴛ ᴇxᴄᴜꜱᴇᴅ himself to return to the office, I introduced myself to the nurses around me. There were eight white American women in their mid- to late twenties. They were all single, and they lived together in an eight-bedroom house two miles from the hospital—the two-story home owned by the minister of education—and commuted to and from the hospital by moped or bicycle.

Their shifts were twelve hours long—either 7 a.m. to 7 p.m., or 7 p.m. to 7 a.m. Every five weeks, they rotated between day shift and night shifts, and they rotated among all the departments of the hospital. Half of them were in Togo for one year, the other half of them were in Togo for two years.

They had all resigned their jobs in the United States and gone from making good salaries to making nothing at the Hospital of Hope. They had all had malaria at least once and, when one of them was sick, the others pitched in and worked more than their scheduled hours to cover all the shifts. They also donated a pint of their own blood to the hospital's blood bank every few weeks because, given all the trauma and surgical patients the hospital cared for, there was a chronic shortage of blood.

Ginny, a nurse who was often assigned to the maternity ward because she had worked in Labor & Delivery in the United States, said that the week the hospital opened, a woman had a life-threatening postpartum hemorrhage after delivering her baby. The hospital didn't have the woman's blood type in the blood bank, but Ginny was O negative, called the "universal donor" because anyone can receive O-negative blood. The situation was so dire, they didn't have time to draw Ginny's blood, run it through the usual lab process, and then transfuse it into the patient. So as they were prepping the OR to do emergency surgery, Ginny lay down next to her patient while another nurse started an IV to transfuse blood directly from Ginny's vein into the patient's. The patient ended up needing an emergency hysterectomy, but she and her baby survived.

As I listened to the nurses tell me more about the intense work they did at the hospital, all they had sacrificed to leave their families and jobs in the United States, and everything they continued to sacrifice now that they were here in Togo, I was in awe of them. They were tenacious, the Navy SEALs of nursing.

Even though I didn't agree with all of the team's approaches to Togo, I was proud to be part of this Hospital of Hope team because, other than Todd, one male nurse, and occasional visiting doctors, the American medical team comprised all female clinicians and nurses—and only two of them were married. Which meant that basically the hospital was run by single women.

As a single woman in America—especially a single woman in the church—I often felt like I was in the minority. I was excluded from marriage classes, couples retreats, and the weekly moms group at my church. I felt isolated and less-than, invisible, continually struggling to find my place in a community that comprised mostly married couples with kids.

But here, as a single woman in Togo, for the first time in my life I was in the majority. I was part of the team of indomitable women who staffed the hospital, cared for patients, and saved lives.

It was especially ironic—and satisfying—to be a single, female clinician here in northern Togo, here in this very conservative culture where men called the shots and made the rules, here where it was so shameful for a woman over eighteen to be single that the country allowed a man to take up to four wives.

And yet it was here, in the midst of this male-dominated, conservative Muslim culture, that Christian single women were almost single-handedly running the hospital that saved the lives of Togolese women, children, and the chauvinistic, misogynistic men who ruled them.

AFTER LUNCH, I walked over to the clinic with Betsy, and for the rest of the afternoon I sat in a chair in the corner of the small exam room and watched her see patients.

She spoke fluent French, but even so she needed to use a Togolese translator for at least half the patients she saw because so many of them only spoke local languages.

The first patient of the afternoon was a three-year-old girl who'd had a fever and been vomiting for the past two days. Her malaria test came back positive, so Betsy prescribed Coartem, a pill with two anti-malaria medications that the mom was to give her daughter twice a day for three days. In seventy-two hours, this little girl would be cured of malaria, and would avoid becoming one of the six million children under age five who died each year in the developing world from malaria and other preventable causes.

The little girl's mom was also there to be seen as a patient, because she'd gone three months without a period. Her urine pregnancy test came back positive, so Betsy prescribed her a prenatal vitamin and made her an appointment for the following week at the hospital's prenatal clinic, which was run by a nurse midwife from the United States.

As I watched Betsy deftly diagnosing and treating conditions, patient after patient after patient, I thought about what would've happened to these people if the Hospital of Hope hadn't been there.

I thought about the small children with malaria who might have died of the disease if they hadn't been treated with Coartem promptly. I thought about the birth defects, the premature deliveries, and the mothers who might have died in childbirth if the Hospital of Hope hadn't been there to provide prenatal, labor and delivery, and postpartum care.

I was looking forward to the rewarding experience of being a clinician here—dispensing diagnoses and treatments to not only help Togolese patients become more healthy, but to also literally save their lives. The Hospital of Hope was like an oasis in a desert for people whose bodies otherwise would've died from lack of medical care. And didn't Jesus say, "Whoever gives a cup of water in my name..."?

Lots of the patients we saw that afternoon were relatively straightforward, but there were some challenging cases, too, like the seventy-year-old woman who came in with three months of intense pain in her left shin.

When Betsy questioned her, the woman said she'd had no trauma to her leg, and she denied having any fever or chills. She just had pain in her shin when she walked, which went away completely when she sat or lay down.

Betsy sent her for an X-ray, which showed a large circle of decaying bone in the center of her shinbone, the tibia. "I think it's osteomyelitis," Betsy said as we looked at the digital image on the computer in the exam room. "But let me have Todd take a look at it just to make sure."

I had seen cases of osteomyelitis, a bone infection, in the United States. Usually it happened because someone sustained a wound from stepping on a nail or cutting themselves with a knife, and the underlying bone got infected. But this woman hadn't had any injury, and there was no visible break in the skin.

Betsy called Todd, and a few minutes later he came to the exam room and studied the X-ray images with us.

"That's osteo, all right," he said.

Then, in French, he had a conversation with the woman and her son about what it would take to fix her leg. A series of three surgeries would be needed to carve out the rotted bone, graft new bone in its place, and then seal the wound. The process would take months, and would cost hundreds of thousands of CFAs.

The son asked Todd what would happen if his mom didn't have surgery.

Todd shrugged. "Well, she'll continue to have some pain, and she'll walk with a limp," he said. "But it's not likely to spread anywhere else."

The son said they didn't have the money to pay for the surgery, and Todd told him that if his mom's condition worsened, she should return to the hospital.

Betsy wrote the woman a prescription for some paracetamol, the European equivalent of Tylenol, and they left.

I asked Todd how the woman could've gotten a bone infection if there was no overlying injury.

He said it was because the Togolese people didn't have toothbrushes.

At first, I was confused. What did dental hygiene have to do with a shinbone?

Todd explained that because Togolese people didn't brush their teeth, they had a lot of bacteria in their mouths. The bacteria got into their bloodstream through their gums, and traveled to various parts of their bodies. Sometimes it settled in their heart valves, and sometimes it settled in their bones.

I asked Betsy why she had to write a prescription for paracetamol when, in the United States, these types of painkillers are available over the counter, with no prescription needed.

Betsy explained that in Togo, there was nothing like the FDA to regulate the quality of over-the-counter medications. So often at the market, vendors sold medication that was expired, had a less-than-promised level of active ingredient, or wasn't the same medication at all.

"It happens a lot," she said. "People tell me the paracetamol they buy at the market does nothing, and then they get the prescription from our pharmacy, and it actually works."

Toothbrushes and Tylenol.

The words echoed in my head all afternoon.

Patients drove for hours to get to the hospital, waited in the triage line overnight, and paid several days'—or even weeks'—worth of wages for an appointment and a prescription, all because they didn't have access to toothbrushes or Tylenol.

THE NEXT PATIENT we saw was a twenty-eight-year-old woman who had pelvic pain and vaginal discharge. Betsy asked her a series of questions. How long had she had the symptoms? When was her last period? How many times had she been pregnant? How many live births had she had? And lastly, how many wives did her husband have?

The woman had been symptomatic for three weeks. Her last period was a week ago. She had been pregnant nine times. Three of the pregnancies ended in miscarriages. She'd had six live births, but two of those babies had died in infancy. And her husband had two other wives.

Betsy did a pelvic exam on the woman, then prescribed her antibiotics to treat her for gonorrhea and chlamydia.

After the woman left to fill her prescriptions, I asked Betsy, "How did you know to ask her how many wives her husband had?"

"It's considered more shameful for a woman to be single than to be in a polygamous marriage, so many married women in northern Togo are in polygamous marriages," Betsy explained.

"What's the normal marrying age?" I asked.

"I haven't met an unmarried woman older than twenty," she said. "And as far as legal marrying age, there isn't one. In fact, a few months ago, a twelve-year-old girl's parents arranged her marriage to a fifty-year-old man, and she's already pregnant."

Betsy shook her head, grabbed the next chart from the stack on the counter, and called the next patient.

LATER THAT AFTERNOON Betsy and I saw a fourteen-year-old Togolese boy who shuffled into the exam room, accompanied by his older brother. I startled at my first glimpse of the patient's appearance. He was a little over five feet tall with a thin frame that was distorted by massive swelling in his lower body. His belly was distended, as if he were five months' pregnant, and his legs were so swollen that when Betsy pressed her thumb into his shin, the imprint stayed. In medicine, it's called pitting edema. The boy's brow was furrowed. When he glanced at me, I could see the fear—and the jaundice—in his eyes.

The boy's name was Felix. His brother, about five years older and a foot taller, was Lucien. They were both wearing dress pants and short-sleeved, collared shirts, but even though they had made an effort to dress up to come to clinic, the stains on their plaid shirts and the threadbare patches on the knees of their pants hinted at their financial situation.

When Betsy asked him to explain his symptoms, Felix shyly studied the floor. Lucien elbowed him and whispered something in his ear, and Felix started talking. He'd had abdominal pain for a few months. Last week the swelling in his abdomen and legs had begun, progressing every day until there was so much swelling in his belly, it was difficult for him to breathe. This morning he'd woken up with yellowed eyes, and his urine was dark brown. His parents worked all day—his mother sold spices at the market and his father herded cattle—so it fell to Lucien to walk two miles with Felix to bring him to the clinic.

Betsy sent Felix to get blood work and an ultrasound. An hour later, the results were back. Felix's hepatitis B test was positive. In the United States, babies are immunized against the disease in infancy, but Togo doesn't have pediatric immunizations, so many young people contracted hepatitis, and many of them, as in the case of Felix, went on to develop liver cancer in their teens or early twenties.

Todd had performed the ultrasound and in the chart note he wrote that the patient had a large hepatocellular carcinoma—inoperable, terminal liver cancer. "Call the chaplains," Todd wrote, just above his signature.

I saw those words a lot over the next three months. Call the chaplains was shorthand for "This patient has a terminal diagnosis, we have no interventions to offer, and in very short time their soul will pass from this world to the next."

The hospital had eight chaplains. Four were Togolese and four were American. There were a total of three female chaplains and five male chaplains. Every morning, they walked through the hospital and prayed for each patient and their family members. They showed Christian movies, dubbed in French or a local dialect, on TVs mounted in each hospital ward, and they had conversations with patients who were interested in learning more about the Christian faith.

In addition to providing spiritual resources, the chaplains also served as social workers, providing emotional support to patients and family members and helping them arrange practical logistics, like lodging, transportation, and finances.

The afternoon I was in clinic with Betsy, we did "call the chaplains," as Todd suggested, but none of them was available to come to the clinic.

Betsy explained the diagnosis to the patient and his brother in slow, deliberate French.

"What can be done?" Lucien asked.

"Nothing," Betsy said quietly. She explained that the liver cancer would soon cause the patient to go into liver failure. He would probably have quite a bit of pain, and the swelling in his abdomen and legs would increase. She could prescribe him pain medication and diuretics (water pills) to alleviate the symptoms, but beyond that, there was no further treatment she could offer. And unfortunately, there was no cure. In a few weeks or months, he would likely die from his disease.

Betsy asked Felix and Lucien if we could pray for them, and they nodded.

Betsy turned to me. "Would you pray, Sarah?"

I leaned forward and gently took Felix's sweaty, tense hands in mine. There was panic in his eyes. I tried to soothe his anxiety by rubbing the back of his hands with my thumbs.

I closed my eyes to pray, and I felt his tears dripping down, seeping through the cracks of our interwoven fingers.

I was not prepared to pray for a fourteen-year-old who had just been given a terminal diagnosis—especially a diagnosis that was completely preventable in the United States.

I didn't know how to swallow the anger that surged through me at the thought that a fourteen-year-old boy—*he's just a child*, I vented to God later—was going to die from a disease that could've been avoided with a three-vaccine hep B series.

Never in my life had I felt so conflicted about God. Wasn't the God to whom I was praying for comfort on behalf of this boy and his family presumably the same God who had let this happen?

How do you rail against God and petition him at the same time? How do you simultaneously question his judgment and throw yourself on his mercy?

I had no idea when I walked into the exam room that afternoon that I would encounter any of these emotions, let alone all of them, all in the same moment, all because of one boy—a boy I had never seen before and would never see again.

As I prayed out loud in English, and Betsy translated in French, I instinctively tightened my grip on Felix's hands, wanting to rescue him from his terminal diagnosis and keep him here with us in the land of the living.

But deep down, I knew that there was nothing else I, or anyone, could do to make him stay. All too soon, the angry, aggressive cancer cells in his liver would eat through the cord that tethered Felix to this world, and his fragile soul would fly away.

AFTER BETSY SAW the last patient of the day, she finished writing her chart notes and put her stethoscope and treatment manual into her backpack.

"Do you have any questions?" she asked.

I shook my head, and asked if I could stay awhile longer to look over the notes I'd made in my notebook that afternoon. I also wanted to do some reading on the conditions we'd seen that I was less familiar with.

"Sure," she said. "Just lock the door when you leave."

I sat alone in the clinic room for a while. After a chaotic afternoon, punctuated by some treatment successes and, as in the case of Felix, some significant failures, I needed time to let all the thoughts and emotions I had been keeping at bay wash over me.

How could one tiny exam room, in the course of one afternoon, simultaneously contain so many successes and so many sorrows? As a clinician, how was I supposed to celebrate so many wins and mourn so many losses at the same time?

How do you ride that emotional up-and-down roller coaster for days, weeks, months without getting emotionally dizzy and disoriented?

With more questions than answers, I turned off the fan and the light and left the exam room, locking the door behind me.

I walked around the corner to find Todd, Tanya, and Paul sitting on one of the long benches outside a clinic room, resting after a long day of work.

I sat down next to Tanya, removed my stethoscope from my neck, and took a deep breath. The sun was low in the sky, and a faint, cool breeze was blowing across the compound.

Suddenly Todd looked up and said, "There's my man!"

At the end of the sidewalk that spanned the length of the clinic, about ten yards from where we were sitting, there was a ten-year-old boy supporting his weight on handmade wooden crutches, grinning.

"Show us what you've got, Matisse!" Todd called to him in French.

With a glimmer in his eyes, Matisse began taking steps with his crutches, one slow swing-through-and-step at a time, until he reached the bench where we were all sitting. He gave all of us high-fives before taking a seat next to Todd, who put his arm around the boy's shoulders.

Todd beamed more like a proud father than an accomplished surgeon as he told me the boy's story.

When Matisse was a toddler, he developed severe osteomyelitis in his legs that left him unable to walk. Because he also had extensive osteomyelitis in his forearms, he couldn't even crawl. Wheelchairs were scarce, and the mom didn't have enough money to buy one anyway, so for the past eight years she had been carrying her son on her back. In April she heard a rumor that a new hospital had opened in Mango, and she carried Matisse for fifteen miles to bring him here.

Matisse's initial X-rays showed the worst osteomyelitis Todd had seen in his surgical career. Luckily, an orthopedic surgeon from the United States was scheduled to arrive in Mango a few days later. The surgeon looked over the X-rays with Todd and agreed that they should operate to try to salvage at least some of the boy's bones—but if the surgery was unsuccessful, they would probably have to amputate some, if not all, of Matisse's limbs.

They explained the pros, cons, benefits, and risks of the surgery to the mother, who begged them to at least try to save her son's limbs, even though she and her son would have to live in the Cuisine for six months or more, and the cost of the surgeries would take her a lifetime to pay back.

Todd and the orthopedic surgeon operated on the boy's forearms first, carving out the decayed, infected bone and then, several weeks later, filling in the holes with healthy bone they had grafted from his pelvis. When the boy's arms had healed, they operated on his legs, one at a time, going through the same painstaking process of removing the corroded bone and then, weeks later, filling in the gaps with grafts of healthy bone.

Matisse and his mother lived in one of the "stalls" in the Cuisine, where she cooked for him, washed his clothes by hand, and gave him sponge baths because he couldn't risk getting his incisions wet in the shower. Every morning, they arrived at the surgical clinic and sat on the bench outside, waiting sometimes for hours until it was Matisse's turn to see Todd and have his bandages changed.

Now, three months later, Matisse's arms and legs had not only been spared amputation but had almost completely healed. For the first time in years, his mother didn't have to carry him wherever they went. Next week, if everything continued to go well, he would begin walking without crutches. And the week after that, Matisse and his mother would be able to return home to their village.

When Todd finished telling me the story, he simply said, "This," and gently squeezed Matisse's shoulder. "Ten years of planning, three years of construction, millions of dollars of fund-raising, eighteen-hour workdays, years of sleepless nights...and we do it all for this."

THE HOSPITAL'S OUTPATIENT clinic was closed on the weekends, so every Saturday morning the staff had a tradition of gathering at Laura and Chad's house for waffles. On my first Saturday in Togo, I walked over to their house, which was on the opposite side of the compound from the guesthouse.

Over waffles that morning, I was introduced to more missionaries. Some worked in maintenance, some in accounting, and three of them were teachers who taught the missionary kids. Everyone I met was white, and they were all American.

While we were eating, the phone in the bedroom rang and Laura answered it. Because cell service was so unreliable, there were landline telephones installed all over the compound—three at the nurses' station, two in maternity, one in each exam room, one in the dining hall, one in each room at the guesthouse, and one in each home on the compound. There were also phones installed in registration, radiology, and the pharmacy.

Most of the doctors had homes on the compound so they could get as much rest as possible in between shifts, and so they could respond quickly in case the hospital was overwhelmed by a mass trauma or other unforeseen emergency. Tanya and Emilie were the only doctors who lived in the village.

Anyone who was scheduled for an on-call shift, whether they lived on the hospital compound or in town, slept in the doctors' lounge at the hospital because in life-threatening emergencies, seconds mattered. The lounge was a small room down the hall from the main hospital with several shelves of medical books, a futon, and an oscillating fan. A small wooden stand next to the futon was supposed to hold a computer, but there wasn't enough money to buy one, so the stand was empty except for a landline telephone.

Moments after Laura answered the phone, she emerged from the bedroom with her stethoscope. She whispered something to Chad and hurried out the front door toward the hospital.

Chad was standing in the kitchen when I went to refill my coffee cup, and I asked him where Laura had gone.

He whispered that one of the women who was in labor yesterday—one of the women I'd seen when Tanya was giving me the tour—had spiked a fever during the night, and her malaria test came back positive. The baby's heartbeat had suddenly accelerated, indicating that the baby was in severe distress. Tanya and Paul had done an emergency C-section around 4 a.m., but by the time they got the baby out, he was dead, and despite attempting to resuscitate him for more than an hour, they couldn't bring him back.

Laura had trained as an adult internal medicine specialist, but when she was on call at the hospital, she would be the only physician there, so she needed to be able to treat pediatric patients as well. Tanya had called Laura to come to the hospital to practice intubating an infant.

"They're practicing intubation on a dead baby?" I whispered to Chad.

He nodded reluctantly and glanced around to make sure no one had overheard.

The American doctors were practicing intubation on a dead Togolese baby. I wondered how the mom would feel if she knew.

I didn't know why that bothered me so much. After all, in PA school I'd done dissection on a cadaver.

Maybe sometimes you have to use death as a tool to learn more about life. Didn't Jesus say something like that—that a kernel has to die and fall to the ground in order for new life to come? Maybe that meant that what Tanya and Laura were doing now—and what I had done in grad school—was not only justifiable, but necessary.

Maybe.

For the rest of breakfast, I said very little. I was thinking about the dead baby and his mom and about Bernie, the eighty-six-year-old cadaver I'd dissected in anatomy lab in grad school more than a decade before.

BERNIE DIED OF a stroke that affected his right side and caused permanent contractures of the muscles in his right arm. He perpetually looked as if he were raising his hand. As if he were patiently waiting for a teacher to notice him so he could finally ask his question. I always wondered what question he would ask if he could speak.

Our anatomy professor often reminded us to be grateful for these people who had "willed their bodies to science." As I cut through Bernie's skin, tendons, muscles, and organs, I used to think about how odd it would be as a family member of a deceased person who had willed his body to science, sitting in the attorney's office as the will was read aloud. "Sam gets Grandpa's pearl-handled revolver, Marcy gets Grandpa's mug collection, and the medical school gets...well, the medical school gets Grandpa."

When these people died, their bodies were drained of blood, pumped full of formaldehyde, and taken to the anatomy lab, which was on the third floor of the Yale Med School building. The lab was a large room with several dozen steel tables. Each table had a cadaver in a black body bag, and was lit by a bright, round overhead light.

Our class was divided into groups of six, and each group was assigned to a body. Every week we'd gather around the body and dissect one portion of it, methodically following an anatomy guidebook that explained every structure we encountered as we cut deeper and deeper and deeper.

Soon after the semester started, as my five classmates and I gathered around the table and began to prepare for that week's dissection, Dustin said, "I think we should call him Bernie."

"What?" I asked.

I knew some of the other groups had named their cadaver so they could refer to it as something other than "the body" or "the deceased." But our group hadn't talked about naming our cadaver.

Dustin said, "Well, last night I was talking to my father-in-law and he asked how Bernie was doing. When I asked him who Bernie was, he said, 'You know, Bernie. The dead guy.' So I thought maybe that's what we could call him."

My classmates and I looked at one another, then nodded in assent. And so for the rest of the semester, we dissected Bernie. The dead guy.

EVERY WEEK WE opened our anatomy guide to see which of Bernie's body parts we were dissecting next. One week we cut his chest open and examined the lungs, as well as all the vessels and valves and chambers of the heart.

One week we dissected the spine and saw the vertebrae and disks and facet joints, and the ligaments that held them all together.

On the day that we were to dissect Bernie's arms to see the muscles and blood vessels and bones that made up the upper extremity, we had a problem. Because he'd had a stroke before he died, the muscles in his arm were contracted so that his elbow was at a ninety-degree angle, and his hand was frozen into a rock-hard claw.

We called our professor over to our table and asked what we were supposed to do, because we couldn't dissect the arm or hand in their current position. The professor tugged on Bernie's elbow and tried to get the arm to fully extend, but it wouldn't budge. Next, the professor tried to gently open the fingers, without success. They were clenched shut.

He took a step back and shook his head. "You might want to cover your ears," he said. "This is going to be disturbing."

Then he put one hand on Bernie's shoulder and the other hand on Bernie's forearm and with one swift, strong movement, he broke Bernie's elbow. A loud cracking sound resonated through the lab, like the sound of a snapping branch in a winter forest.

I almost threw up.

Five smaller cracks followed as the professor broke all of Bernie's fingers. When he had laid the arm and fingers flat, he stepped back. "There you go," he said.

The following week, the anatomy lesson was on genitalia. The guidebook instructed us to sever the penis at the base of the shaft so we could look at a cross section and see the conduits for urine and semen and blood.

Every week, a different person in our group was responsible for wielding the scalpel, because we all needed to get used to the sensation of slicing through human flesh.

Dustin was supposed to operate the scalpel the week we were doing the genitalia dissection. He held Bernie's penis in one hand and the scalpel in the other.

"I'm just supposed to—so I just, just—like, seriously, slice it off?"

Nikki, the classmate who was reading the instructions aloud from the anatomy manual, nodded. "Take the scalpel and cut the penis off where the shaft meets the suprapubic area," she repeated, holding the anatomy book up so Dustin could see the instructions for himself.

He stood there, poised to act, when suddenly he lost his nerve. Shaking his head and laying down the scalpel, he said, "I can't do it, Bernie. I just can't cut your member off, dude."

One of my female classmates did it instead. I thought it was the most disturbing thing I'd ever seen.

Until the final week of the semester, when we had to saw off his head.

I HADN'T THOUGHT ABOUT dissecting Bernie for a long time, until I was sitting at Saturday Waffles in Togo that morning, thinking about the doctors practicing intubation on a dead baby.

I was too preoccupied to eat, so I excused myself from breakfast and walked over to the hospital. By the time I got there, Tanya and Laura were outside OR 2, taking off the masks and gloves they'd worn to practice intubation.

Tanya got a page and rushed off to check on a patient. Laura was standing at the deep stainless-steel sink, washing her hands.

I really wanted to see the baby, though at the time I couldn't even explain to myself why. To verify that the baby was dead? To test my reaction to death to see if I could still handle it? To encounter death in a tiny body before I encountered an adult-size Togolese body?

It felt like a strange request, and I was worried Laura would somehow be offended or say no, but, with my voice barely above a whisper, I asked, "Can I see the baby?"

"Sure," she said, without looking up, nodding her head toward the OR door.

I donned a pair of gloves and then slipped into the operating room. The door silently closed behind me.

The lights had all been turned off, and the resuscitation equipment had been powered down. The room was cool and dim and still.

It was very, very still.

An empty operating table sat in the center of the room, with a ventilator and a tray of sterile supplies at the head of the bed. At the far corner of the room stood a large wooden cabinet with glass doors that contained sterile surgical trays, gloves, gowns, masks, and sutures. Against the near wall, just to the right of the door, was an isolette—the kind that hospitals have in delivery rooms, where they lay a baby immediately after it's born to clean it, suction it, and check its Apgar score—an evaluation done on a newborn at one and five minutes after birth to see how the baby had tolerated the birthing process, and how it was adjusting to life outside the womb.

In the middle of the isolette there was a baby swaddled in a clean white blanket. He had a cone head, indicating he'd been wedged head-down in his mother's birth canal for a long time.

Black babies are often light in color when they're born—their skin darkens as they get older—but this baby's pale-brown skin had a sickening sallowness to it. He had curly black hair, and his tiny pursed lips still had a twinge of pink in them. He looked peaceful. If I didn't know better, I would've thought he was sleeping. Simply sleeping.

I approached the isolette as quietly as possible, tiptoeing so as not to break the nearly palpable stillness that had fallen over the room like a tender, sacred spell. I stood before the isolette in silence, wondering how death, so haunting and horrific, could also feel so holy.

And then the baby's left eyelid twitched—or at least, I thought it did. And my heart began to race. What if God had changed his mind? What if this baby was coming back to life? What if I was witnessing a miracle? A resurrection?

I quickly unwrapped the blanket he was swaddled in and placed my hand on his chest to see if I could feel a heartbeat. There were faint bruises on his chest from where Tanya had attempted chest compressions.

There was no heartbeat. His body was ice-cold. He had been dead for several hours now. The eyelid twitch had been all in my imagination. Like Thomas, who wouldn't believe Jesus had been resurrected until he touched the nail prints in Jesus' hands and the spear-shaped scar in his side, I searched this baby's body with my own eyes, my own hands, and finally, I accepted that he truly was gone.

I acknowledged the reality that within a few hours, his body would stiffen, and in a few days it would start to decompose. As he lay beneath the dirt in his family's backyard, crumbling to pieces in the ground, his body would undergo the opposite of a resurrection.

What was the opposite of resurrection? *Is it surrection?* I wondered.

No, I realized, because *to surrect* means "to rise." And re-surrecting means "to rise again." In that case, to be born—to come alive for the first time—is to surrect. This baby had been dead before they could deliver him by C-section, which meant he had never surrected in the first place, so it was impossible for him to be re-surrecting now.

Instead of rising up into life, this baby had fallen down into death—which, I remembered from anatomy class, is what the word *cadaver* means. It means "to fall."

In the end, each of us falls dead. We teach that inevitable truth to children from the time they're old enough to sing "Ring Around the Rosie," a song written about the bubonic plague that hit London in 1665.

Ashes, ashes, we all fall down.

Yes, it's true, we all fall down—but some falls seem particularly untimely and unfair.

Standing before the isolette, a thousand questions poured out of me as half accusations, half prayers.

God, why do you let some souls live for a lifetime, and others only for a second or two?

Why do you give life only to take it away in seconds?

Why is the deck stacked against souls born into rural West Africa and other parts of the developing world?

Why did this baby's mother have to labor for days, only to lose her baby in the end? Why did she have to endure that much pain in vain?

Why did some mothers come to the hospital in labor and leave the following day with a perfect baby in their arms, while others left holding a tiny corpse?

Anger, frustration, and helplessness welled up in me as I realized my questions led only to more questions. There weren't any satisfactory answers.

A few days before, as I lay on my bed at the guesthouse in Lomé thinking about the poisonous snakes, infant mortality, suffering, and death in Togo—the world's least happy country—I had asked if it was possible that there was a place on earth that could literally be God-forsaken.

Standing in front of that isolette, I thought of Jesus, who asked in anguish on the cross—"Eli, Eli, lama sabachthani?"

My God, my God, why have you forsaken me?

Was it possible for a place to be literally God-forsaken?

If the experience of Jesus and the suffering in Togo were to be taken literally, then maybe God's answer was yes.

A resounding, terrifying yes.

I LAID MY HAND on the baby's forehead and prayed for the angels to swiftly carry his soul to Jesus, and to comfort the mother in her grief.

And then I wrapped him back up in the blanket so when Tanya and Laura gave him to his mother to take him home and bury him, she wouldn't have to see his bruised chest, his pulseless limbs, and his cyanotic toes. Plus, in the meantime, I didn't want the baby to be cold.

In high school literature class, I learned the word *anthropomorphize*, which means "to attribute human form or personality to things not human."

Because I'm a very empathetic soul, I often found myself anthropomorphizing the world around me. When I was little, I believed grass felt pain when it was mowed. I believed that when wind was especially gusty, it was trying to get my attention.

Even though I knew it was scientifically impossible, I secretly worried that Bernie and the other cadavers in the anatomy lab got cold or lonely or afraid at night, when all the lights in the lab were off and all the students had gone home. I wondered if they somehow knew what we were doing to their bodies, and if they regretted their choice to donate their body to science.

One afternoon, when all my classmates had left the lab, I was putting Bernie back into the body bag. Well, to be more accurate, I was putting the pieces of Bernie back into the body bag, because we had amputated his leg, castrated him, and disemboweled him by that point. I leaned down close to his ear—which we would be severing, along with his nose, the following week—and I whispered, "Bernie, I am so sorry. I hope you can forgive me."

And then I zipped the body bag closed and walked out of the lab. But I left the light on.

Just in case.

SEVERAL MONTHS AFTER I finished anatomy lab, I began rotations at the hospital, where I encountered more dead bodies.

A ninety-four-year-old woman died in her sleep in the geriatrics ward one afternoon. She was DNR, Do Not Resuscitate, so when the nurses found her unconscious, not breathing, and pulseless, they didn't start CPR. They simply called the attending physician. He happened to be the physician who was supervising me on that rotation, so when he got the phone call, he took me with him to "declare her"—to verify she was dead and sign the death certificate.

We walked into the room to find a wrinkled, bony elderly woman curled up in bed beneath the blankets. She had very little hair, but the hair that did remain was wispy and white. Her eyes were closed, her cheeks were sunken, and her mouth was slightly open.

Without putting on gloves, the attending approached the body and pulled back the sheet. He put his fingers on the woman's neck and waited for a few seconds. Then he tried to pick up her arm—but it was stiff and immobile.

"Oh yeah, she's gone," he said as he signed paperwork that the nurse had handed him on a clipboard.

The staff had already called the funeral home to come pick up the body. While we waited, the attending talked to me about death certificates, declaring someone dead, and rigor mortis, topics that I was not interested in because I had gone into medicine to learn how to prevent death, not how to acknowledge, certify, and document it.

The doctor held the woman's face in his hands and used his thumbs to try to close her jaw, but it wouldn't budge. Then he tried to uncurl her arms and legs, but they wouldn't move, either. He said she had likely been dead for several hours before the staff discovered her, because she was already in rigor mortis.

Next, the doctor taught me how to declare someone. You can order an

EEG to look for brain activity, he said, but most of the time that test took too long, it was expensive, and there were other, faster, cheaper ways to verify death.

For instance, you could look for a "flatline" on the cardiac monitor, which indicated asystole, complete lack of cardiac activity. Or you could put your fingers over the carotid artery, on the side of the neck, to feel for a pulse. But never use your thumb to check for a pulse, he warned, because there's a small artery that runs through the pad of your thumb, which means that if you check for a pulse with your thumb, the pulsation you feel may be your own.

Another way to declare someone is to check a pupillary light reflex. If the pupils were fully dilated and didn't shrink when you shined a light in them, then the pupils were "blown," indicating that the person was brain-dead.

Lastly, he said, you can check for a corneal reflex, which is the last reflex to go before death. To check a corneal reflex, you open the eyelid and touch the eyeball, usually with a cotton-tipped swab. If the eyelid tries to close, the patient still has a corneal reflex. If the eye doesn't react at all, they have lost their corneal reflex—another sign of brain death.

"Here, why don't you give it a try," he said, taking a cotton-tipped swab from the breast pocket of his white coat.

Thankfully, the funeral home workers arrived just then. We stepped back from the bed, and I watched as two men in their twenties, both wearing dark suits, rolled the woman into a black bag and zipped it up. Then they lifted the black bag onto a gurney, rolled it down the hall, and took the elevator to the basement, where the funeral parlor van was waiting to transport the corpse.

A few days later, I was working in the ER when paramedics wheeled in a body that was covered in a white sheet. Blood was seeping through the sheet at the head of the gurney. The paramedics had radioed in a few minutes before that they were bringing in a body that was DOA, dead on arrival.

"Follow me," the attending said, and we followed the paramedics down the hall into a small exam room. Once the door was closed, the paramedics told us that the man was a high school history teacher who had retired early because of progressive multiple sclerosis. Since retiring the year before, he had become more and more depressed. His wife had come home from the grocery store that morning to find the man on the floor of their garage, where he'd put a shotgun in his mouth and pulled the trigger.

The paramedics shook their heads and walked away.

The attending told me to put on gloves and practice checking for a pupillary light reflex and a corneal reflex.

I didn't want to touch a dead body, or turn a tragic situation into a trite learning opportunity. But being a student on clinical rotations is like being a cadet in boot camp; unless you want to get punished or expelled, you always say yes when your supervisor tells you to do something.

I put gloves on and pulled back the sheet to find that the lower half of this man's face was destroyed beyond recognition. Blood from the exit wound in the back of his skull had soaked the top half of the gurney.

The man's eyes were open in a vacant stare. I didn't need a penlight to examine them because the man's right pupil was very obviously blown. At the attending's prompting, I retrieved a cotton-tipped swab from a glass canister on the counter and touched it to the man's cornea. Of course, nothing happened. He was very, very dead.

We covered him up with the sheet, turned off the light, and closed the door behind us. A few minutes later, men from the funeral parlor came to take the body away. I watched as they left a short while later, wheeling the occupied black body bag on a gurney toward the staff-only elevators that led to the basement, a dimly lit, dungeon-looking labyrinth where patients were forbidden to go.

At one hospital I worked at, every time a baby was born, the hospital played fifteen seconds of a lullaby over the loudspeakers throughout the entire hospital. I used to love to hear those notes breaking through the chaos and exhaustion that characterized the rest of my day. The hospital recognized that new life fills us with hope and joy and promise, and they shared the news with every staff member, patient, and visitor.

But when it came to death, no music ever played and no announcement was ever made. Instead, men in black suits quietly took dead bodies through back hallways, restricted elevators, dark corridors, and secret doors, drawing as little attention as possible.

Lives ended very differently than they began.

Not with fanfare, but with secrecy.

Not with public announcements, but with fiercely guarded privacy.

Not with a bang but a whimper.

O N MY FIRST Monday morning in Togo, I woke up at six thirty and looked out the front window of my room at the guesthouse to see Matt and a medical assistant walking through a long line of people waiting in triage—many of whom had spent the night there because they were so desperate to be seen. The line started at the hospital gate and stretched at least a quarter mile.

The hundred people who were ill enough, or fortunate enough, to get appointments that day made their way from triage to registration, where they were assigned a number and given a small green booklet called a carnet (pronounced *car-nay*), which clinicians used to write down the date the person was seen, the diagnosis, and any prescriptions the patient needed. Instead of storing the carnets at the clinic, as is done at US doctors' offices, the patients held on to their carnets and brought them to each appointment.

Some patients had gone so long without any medical care, their carnet was almost full after just one visit. Their diagnoses spanned multiple pages, and their list of prescriptions often included medications for scabies, gonorrhea, pinworms, malaria, pneumonia, diabetes, high blood pressure, and arthritis.

After receiving their carnet, the patients went to the cashier's office to pay for their appointment. It cost fifteen hundred CFAs—the equivalent of three dollars US—for an appointment, and they had to pay before they could be seen.

Once they paid, they were told which of five exam rooms they'd been assigned to. They would go sit outside that exam room and wait for their name to be called.

Patients were seen in the order they arrived. The clinic opened at 8 a.m. and closed at 5 p.m.—which meant that some people waited on those benches for up to nine hours in hundred-degree heat before their name was called.

At seven thirty that Monday morning, I met Matt at registration and he told me I would be working out of Exam Room 3 that day. Then he introduced me to my translator, who would be working with me every day I was in clinic.

My translator's name was Omari. He was a handsome, thin, six-foot-tall twenty-six-year-old who had attended university in Kara, the town where Massiko and I had stopped for peas. Omari told me he had majored in English, and besides French and English, he spoke four indigenous languages.

"You speak six languages?" I asked Omari.

He nodded and flashed a shy smile.

Matt led us to the exam room and unlocked the door. There were already dozens of patients sitting on the wooden benches outside, waiting to be seen.

The room had an exam table, a computer, a sink, and three chairs. There was a ceiling fan, but no air-conditioning. It was 8 a.m. and already it was hot and humid inside the room.

Omari went to registration and retrieved the stack of charts for the patients who had been assigned to our room.

He handed me the stack and then said, "Are you ready, Sarah?"

I wanted to say no. *No, I'm not ready. I've never seen a case of malaria or typhoid, never practiced medicine outside the United States, never treated a Togolese patient.*

No, I did not feel ready.

But I nodded anyway.

MY FIRST PATIENT was a sixty-five-year-old man who was wheezing. He had never smoked, but the dust he had inhaled from a lifetime of working in the fields had caused chronic irritation in his lungs.

As I motioned for him to sit on the exam table, I asked him, "*Ça va?*" (*sah-vah*), which means, "How's it going?"

The man shook his head as he struggled to breathe. "*Ça ne va pas,*" he said. It doesn't go.

I put an oxygen saturation monitor on his index finger. It read 84 percent. He was right. It wasn't going at all.

I asked Omari to get a wheelchair so we could transport the patient to one of the ER beds in the hospital, where the on-call doctor would take care of him.

Once Omari returned, I wheeled the patient down the sidewalk to the hospital's front entrance as fast as the wheelchair's rusty wheels would go.

Omari and I helped the man into one of the ER beds, and I handed his chart to Laura, who was the on-call doctor that day. "We'll take good care of him," she said as she smiled and patted the man's knee. That was one of my favorite things about Laura—when she smiled, her whole face lit up and her green eyes sparkled. In my opinion, she had the best bedside manner of any of the clinicians at the hospital. I was looking forward to working with her, and learning from her example.

Laura quickly wrote some orders in the man's chart and handed it to Kojo, a forty-five-year-old Togolese male nurse with a short stature, a round face, and a ready smile. He had graduated from the nursing program and moved to Togo six months before, when the hospital opened. Even though he'd been on the job for less than half a year, he had quickly proven his proficiency, and had been promoted to head nurse. Within minutes of receiving Laura's orders, Kojo had hooked the patient up to the monitor, started an IV, given him a dose of steroids, and started a nebulizer treatment.

Omari and I returned to the clinic. In the course of the morning, I diagnosed people with hepatitis B, malaria, eye infections, osteomyelitis, scabies, and uterine fibroids. I had a copy of the hospital treatment manual on the desk next to the computer, so if there was a condition I wasn't familiar with, I looked it up and followed the recommendations.

Just before noon, I saw a sixty-year-old woman who came to clinic with her son because she'd had constipation for the past week. Her belly was also getting more and more distended.

I examined her. Her blood pressure was low, and her heart rate and respirations were fast. Her belly was taut and a little tender.

I sent her for an upright abdominal X-ray. It should've come back showing a snaking pattern of intestines with some stool and maybe some gas. Instead, the X-ray was solid gray.

I admitted her to the hospital and asked the surgical team to consult, thinking that maybe she had a bowel obstruction and needed surgery. If that was the case, she might be home in three or four days.

After she was admitted, I asked Omari if he was ready to take a lunch break—the clinic closed from noon to 2 p.m. every day to give staff time to eat and take a siesta.

"You can take your lunch whenever you are ready," he said. "I myself am fasting." I had forgotten that Omari was Muslim and it was Ramadan; he and other Muslims would be fasting from sunrise to sunset for forty days.

I agreed to meet him back at the clinic at 2 p.m. I walked to the dining hall to eat, and he walked to the male staff lounge—which had a bathroom, lockers, a shower, and five cots—to sleep.

IN THE AFTERNOON, the surgical team did an ultrasound on my sixty-year-old patient and found that the woman had metastatic cervical cancer. She had metastases in her liver, and her whole belly was filled with cancer and fluid, which is why her X-ray had looked so abnormal.

They prescribed her diuretics to remove some of the fluid from her belly, as well as morphine and anti-nausea meds. Todd called the chaplains to come and together, they told the family that the woman was beyond surgical help. There was nothing to do but keep her comfortable for the next few days or weeks, until she passed away.

I was in clinic for the rest of the afternoon. My last patient of the day was an eighteen-year-old girl who'd had pelvic pain for the past twenty-four hours. Her urine pregnancy test was positive. I sent her for an ultrasound, which confirmed what I had suspected—that she had an ectopic pregnancy.

In ectopic pregnancies, instead of the fertilized egg implanting in the uterus, it implants in one of the fallopian tubes. The only treatment is surgery. If the fallopian tube is not removed, the fertilized egg continues to grow until the tube ruptures, which can cause a woman to die of massive internal bleeding.

I paged Paul, and we discussed the case by phone. A few minutes later, he came to the exam room with a wheelchair to transport her to the OR.

"Do you want to assist?" he asked me.

I was finished with patients for the day, and my evening was free. So even though I hadn't scrubbed in for a surgery since my surgical rotation in grad school, I said, "Sure."

I said good-bye to Omari, and went to the women's locker room and changed into a pair of scrubs. Then I met Paul at the deep stainless-steel sinks outside the OR. We put on hats and masks, and then used iodine soap to scrub from our fingernails to our elbows.

Next to the sink was a whiteboard. When I was in the OR two days before, saying good-bye to the baby who had died, the board had been blank. But today, someone had written,

Pensée du jour
"I can accept failure, but I can't accept not trying."

—Michael Jordan

Even though it was the "thought of the day," the quote stayed there the whole three months I was in Togo.

I walked past that whiteboard several times a day during my time at the hospital, so I was reminded of the quote frequently. I thought about the words over and over and over again as I worked twenty-eight-hour shifts, went days without sleep, and lost more patients than I could count.

I agreed with the latter statement. Because I was both compassionate and competitive, I could never accept not trying.

But what did the former statement mean, I wondered again and again.

What did it mean to be able to accept failure?

I GRADUATED FROM PA school in 2004, which meant that by the time I arrived in Togo in 2015, I had more than a decade of experience in emergency and urgent care medicine.

When people asked me what it was like to practice medicine, I told them it was like being a Catcher in the Rye—a reference from one of my favorite books, written by J. D. Salinger in 1951.

The book gets its name from the Robert Burns poem "Comin' Thro' the Rye." In the book, Holden Caulfield, a freethinking kid, runs away from boarding school and sneaks into his little sister's room one night to tell her he's alive and okay. As they talk in the darkness, he whispers that he thinks Burns's poem is the key to his life's calling.

The poem actually says, "Gin a body meet a body comin' thro' the rye," but Holden translates the poem, "If a body catch a body comin' thro' the rye."

In his mind, there are lots of kids playing in a rye field beside a cliff. And he's standing on the edge so that if the kids get too close to the edge, he can catch them before they fall off.

My career in medicine felt like I was standing on the edge of the cliff between life and death, catching sick patients before they toppled off the edge and died.

And I was good at it. I had gotten an excellent education at Yale, and I also had keen clinical judgment, which came from experience, pattern recognition, intuition, and attention to tiny details.

One of the first patients I saw after I graduated from PA school was a young woman who came in with "migraines," for which she had seen several other doctors who had all prescribed her Imitrex, a common migraine medicine, and Vicodin, a potent narcotic for pain. But as I was asking about her symptoms, she said several things that sent up red flags in my mind, because they weren't typical of migraines. The headaches always happened first thing in morning—she would wake up in incredible pain and stumble to the bathroom to vomit before she was even fully awake. Instead of refilling the medicines she'd been prescribed in the past, I sent her for a CT scan that showed a brain tumor. The neurosurgeons removed it a few weeks later, and declared her cancer-free.

Another time, I was working in the ER on a summer evening when a mom brought her five-year-old daughter in with a head injury. The girl had been running across the lawn, caught her foot on the edge of the swing set, tripped, and fallen forward, hitting her head on the ground. She had a small "goose egg" the size of a quarter on her forehead.

I asked the mom screening questions that separate dangerous head injuries from non-concerning ones. The mom said the girl had not lost consciousness, had not vomited, and was acting normally.

"Great," I said. "Put ice on the swelling and come back if she develops any new symptoms."

"There is one thing," the mom said as I was getting up to leave the exam room. "When she fell, she got a rash."

I raised my eyebrows. "Is she allergic to grass?" I asked, because the only explanation I could think of for why a fall would cause a rash is if she was allergic to what she fell into.

The mom shook her head.

"Was there poison ivy by the swing set?"

Again, the mom shook her head.

I was getting frustrated, because what the mom was saying was illogical and impossible. Falls don't cause rashes.

"Okay, so show me what you're talking about," I said, my tight voice betraying the impatience I was trying to hide.

She lifted up the girl's T-shirt, and I saw hundreds of tiny dots that were purplish red, like pinpricks, on her chest and abdomen and back. I pressed one with my finger, and it stayed a deep, angry purple color. It was non-blanching, which meant that it was not a superficial skin problem; it was a petechial rash, coming from the blood vessels underneath the skin.

Suddenly, she had my full attention. I ordered a CBC, a complete blood count, that came back a few minutes later showing that the girl's platelet count, which should have been over 150,000, was 2,000. Instantly, I knew what had happened. Since she had so few platelets, her blood lacked the ability to clot normally. When she fell, the force caused her capillaries, microscopic blood vessels, to rupture and bleed.

Patients with platelet counts less than 5,000 are at risk for spontaneous bleeds—which means they can suddenly start gushing blood from their head or their GI tract without any trauma. Since this girl had fallen, she was at an even higher risk for a brain bleed. I ordered a STAT CT scan that ended up being normal.

Then I had her transferred to a children's specialty hospital, where she spent several days receiving IV medication to bring her platelet count back up. She ended up making a full recovery—but if I had blown off her mom's seemingly illogical story, the girl could've gone home and bled to death that night in her sleep.

In addition to the dramatic stories I amassed from catching patients *comin' thro' the rye*, there were lots of ordinary successes as well. Patients with high blood pressure, diabetes, strep throat, pneumonia, ear infections, and pre-cancerous moles that I was able to appropriately treat and cure. I lanced boils, sutured lacerations, removed splinters, and set broken bones. I alleviated pain, I fixed problems, I healed wounds.

Working in medicine came with plenty of challenges, like insurance paperwork, obstinate patients, and crowded waiting rooms. But despite the challenges, and despite the fact that I felt hungry and exhausted and depleted at the end of every shift, I couldn't think of a more rewarding profession than practicing medicine, than catching body after body *comin' thro' the rye*.

A ND THEN THERE were the patients my colleagues and I didn't catch—
not because of an oversight, but because we simply couldn't catch them.
They were too old or too sick or they got to us too late.

The first patient I lost in my clinical practice was a little boy.

A few weeks into my first job in the ER, paramedics came running through
the door "coding" a two-year-old boy—meaning they had intubated him and
were squeezing a large rubber Ambu bag to ventilate his lungs, and they were
doing chest compressions. They had radioed us a few minutes before to tell us
they were en route with a pediatric code 3—a child who was in cardiac and
respiratory arrest.

A doctor, three nurses, and I ran to our main resuscitation room to get
ready. The room had large, round overhead lights, a cardiac monitor, intubation supplies, IV medications, and a defibrillator that shocked patients'
hearts back to life.

As we transferred the boy's limp body from the paramedic's stretcher to
the bed, the medics filled us in on the story. The boy's father had been watching the boy while the mother was at work. When it was bath time, the father
put the boy in the bathtub and began running the water. Then the phone
rang and the father went to answer it. He was only gone for a matter of minutes, but by time he came back to the bathroom, the boy was facedown in a
tub full of water.

The paramedics knew when they arrived on the scene that there was very
little chance of the boy surviving. He had no pulse, and it had been ten minutes since the father had found him. The father had attempted CPR, but
when the medics arrived, the boy was unconscious and had no pulse.

But the medics attempted full resuscitation efforts anyway—just in case
there was any chance they could bring him back, and so the parents knew
that everything had been done to try to save their son.

We coded the boy for half an hour. I did chest compressions on him, the heel of my hand pushing down on his sternum one hundred times a minute. And a nurse stood at his head and squeezed the Ambu bag to deliver oxygen to the boy's lungs four times a minute. Even on a child, CPR is tiring. So every three cycles of chest compressions, I switched places with the nurse, and I bagged him while she did the compressions.

One of the other nurses stood nearby as the "scribe," writing down each medication and the time it was given. The doctor called out orders and watched the cardiac monitor on the wall to see if the IV epinephrine and the CPR had any effect.

We never got a pulse back, and the boy never took a spontaneous breath.

Half an hour after the boy had arrived in the ER, the doctor checked the boy's pupils, and they were blown—the boy was brain-dead. There was no chance of bringing him back.

The doctor called the code, and in a second the room went from a frenzy of activity and noise to quiet resignation. Two of the nurses left the room to care for other patients. The other nurse and I stayed behind to remove the IV and breathing tube and wipe off the blood trickling from the boy's mouth.

In the meantime, the doctor walked down the hall to a private waiting room—a small room with couches, dim lighting, and tissue boxes where the families of the sickest patients waited to get word of their loved ones.

A minute later, a guttural scream came from behind the private waiting room's closed door as the father learned that his son had died. Everyone froze in their tracks at the echoing, heartbreaking sound.

"Noooooooaaaaaaaahhhhh!"

At first I thought the father had yelled the word *no*. But then I looked down at the paperwork on the counter and I realized that the father had just yelled his son's name.

In a tragic and surreal irony, the boy who had drowned in the bathtub was named Noah.

I LOVED THE ER, but the overnight shifts and the frenzied pace were exhausting, so I left that job and began working in an urgent care clinic. The last patient I took care of before leaving for Togo was a sixty-five-year-old man who had written "difficulty breathing, cough, coughing up blood for a year" as the Reason for Visit when he signed in at the clinic's front desk.

The nurse took him back to an exam room. A few minutes later, she came out of the room, more hurried than she had been before.

"I can't get it to read above 91 percent," she said of the pulse ox device she was holding—a clip that fits onto a fingertip and uses a small laser to measure the amount of oxygen in the small blood vessels there. When little kids were afraid of it, I told them not to worry, the red laser light would make their fingertip glow just like ET's, and it was kind of true.

The nurse handed me his chart and the pulse ox, and, with my stethoscope around my neck, I headed to the room.

The second I stepped in, my heart skipped a beat. Ninety-one percent was not a mistake. The man sitting on the edge of the exam table was lanky and emaciated and his skin was ashen, somewhere between a pale gray and a faint green. Wispy strands of white hair covered the sides of his face. His sunken cheekbones seemed to pull on his lower eyelids, which made it look like his eyes were wider open than they should've been.

Or maybe it's not an illusion, I thought as I listened to him gasp for each breath. *Maybe he's panicked because he truly cannot breathe.*

I took a quick history, asking him about his past medical problems, prescription medications, and allergies. I asked him if he smoked, and he told me he smoked a pack a day for forty years, but quit two years ago. I asked him if he'd ever been diagnosed with asthma or emphysema and he shook his head, but he also hadn't been to a doctor in more than a decade.

As he was answering my questions, I made a note that he was "speaking in 3–4 word sentences." It was a quick way of assessing how short of breath a person is. If they can't get a full sentence out with one breath, it means their breathing is shallow. And the fewer words they can string together, the more serious the situation is.

When he told me, "I used to—" (gasp) "smoke a lot but—" (gasp) "I quit," I knew his lungs were dangerously low on oxygen.

I talked to him for less than two minutes, then begin to examine him.

Touching patients' bodies, lifting up their clothes, and sometimes examining private places can feel intrusive. I never wanted my patients to feel like I was a stranger invading their privacy; I wanted them to feel like I was a trusted professional who cared not only about their body, but also about their dignity.

But when a patient like this man was very sick, I cut the formalities and began examining them immediately, trying to find clues as fast as I could, clues that would help me discern what was making the patient ill so I could intervene before it was too late, before they fell off the edge of the cliff.

For critically ill patients, it doesn't matter to me or to them that I've never met them before, that I'm adjusting or removing their clothes, putting my hands on the bare skin of their neck and back and chest and belly. After all, do you need to know your lifeguard's name before you let him wrap his arm around your chest and carry you to shore?

I reattached the pulse ox to the man's finger. While I was waiting for it to register his current oxygen saturation and heart rate, I did a cursory exam. I lifted the otoscope, the metal-handled light, from its cradle on the wall and shined it into his mouth. His throat was clear; his tongue wasn't swollen. He had no signs of an upper airway obstruction.

Then I put my stethoscope on and held the flat circle, called the diaphragm, against his chest, just to the left of his sternum. I heard a steady, loud rhythm.

thump THUMP. thump THUMP. thump THUMP.

His heart was beating 112 times a minute, in a normal rhythm. I lifted the back of his white T-shirt up and put the diaphragm against the right side of his mid-back.

"Take a big breath in and out with your mouth open."

After being a physician assistant and saying that phrase so many times, it felt like a mantra. *Take a big breath in and out with your mouth open.* Or, for my Spanish-speaking patients, *Abre la boca y respire profundamente.*

The man opened his mouth and inhaled deeply, and I heard loud wheezes—a whistling sound air makes when it is forced through narrowed passages.

I listened to his left and right lower lung fields, then to his left and right upper lung fields.

Diffuse wheezing. All his airways were constricted. He likely had COPD, chronic obstructive pulmonary disease, from decades of cigarette smoking. And because he hadn't gone to the doctor for so long, the disease had gone undiagnosed and untreated.

I told him my working diagnosis and treatment plan as I reached for the nebulizer machine under the sink.

"You probably have COPD from smoking so long," I said. "You need nebulizer treatments and steroids to improve your breathing. If the treatment works, I'll give you prescriptions and a referral to a pulmonologist, a lung specialist. If the treatment doesn't work, you'll have to go to the hospital. Does that sound okay?"

He quickly nodded.

I opened a small plastic pouch that contained clear tubing that connected the machine to a small well. I twisted open a small plastic vial of albuterol, a medicine that would open his airways, and poured it into the well. Then I screwed on the top and attached a four-inch-long tube with a mouthpiece on it.

"I'm going to give you medicine to help you breathe better," I said as I put the breathing tube in his mouth and turned the machine on.

A loud whirring noise filled the room and a fine vapor began flowing from the breathing tube.

"Just keep the mouthpiece in your mouth and breathe normally," I said. "The treatment takes ten or fifteen minutes. I'll be back to check on you then. Are you okay?"

He nodded. His eyes looked a little less wide, a little less panicked, than they were when I first walked into the room.

Or maybe it was just my imagination.

FIVE MINUTES LATER I was sitting at my desk writing on another patient's chart when I suddenly snapped my head up, listening intently. I could've sworn I heard something.

A few seconds later, I heard it again. A barely audible, "Help."

I walked to the patient's room and as I opened the door I saw him slouched in the chair, his head leaning against the wall, his body sliding out of the chair. His face had gone from pale to stark white. His lips were blue. Sweat was pouring down his face. His eyelids were fluttering. He looked at me and pleaded weakly, "H—h—h—elp."

My emergency medicine training kicked in and adrenaline surged through my body like an electric jolt. I remember learning in my EMT course that the first step you take for someone who's dying is not first aid or CPR; it's calling 911 to get the patient transported to the ER as fast as possible.

I leaned my head out the door and yelled to the receptionist. "I need an ambulance *now*. Call 911."

"Okay!" she called back.

I stood in front of the patient with my left knee in between his, my hands on his shoulders pressing him against the back of the chair, trying to use my body to prevent his from crashing to the floor.

I yelled for my nurse Sandy, a twenty-five-year-old woman from India, who was down the hall in the break room. She arrived a second later and helped me lower the man to the floor. I needed him flat on the floor for two reasons. First, his brain would get more blood because it wouldn't have to fight gravity. Second, if he coded, I'd be able to start CPR.

"Get oxygen," I barked at Sandy. No time for please or thank you or a pleasant tone. All of a sudden, seconds mattered.

The man was gasping for air. It was hard for him to breathe when he was completely lying flat, so I knelt on the floor and put his head in my lap. I put my left hand on his chest so I would know if his heart stopped beating. He grabbed my right hand with his.

"W—wh—what's h—h—h——happening?" he gasped.

"I've got you," I said. Not, "You're in respiratory distress, on your way to respiratory and cardiac arrest, and possibly death if I can't bring you back." No fear or panic or medical explanations. Just, "I've got you."

He repeated his question two more times. And twice more I told him, "I've got you. It's okay. I'm here and I've got you."

He squeezed my hand tightly, then lifted his head to get as close to my face as possible.

"D——d——don't——let——me——go." His chest was heaving as he forced the words out.

My pulse quickened because in medicine there's a phenomenon called "sudden sense of dread." If an ill patient suddenly feels panic and dread, it usually means they're about to die. It's as if their mind and spirit know before their body does what's about to happen.

My patient has a sudden sense of dread, I thought as I knelt there on the floor. *My patient is dying on me.*

Sandy returned with a green metal oxygen tank.

The patient's breathing slowed and nearly stopped. The pulse ox was still attached to his finger and was now reading 82 percent. I used a piece of clear plastic tubing to attach the Ambu bag to the oxygen tank. With my left hand, I held the mask over his nose and mouth. With my right hand I began squeezing the Ambu bag at regular intervals, forcing air into his lungs.

A minute later, his eyes opened and he startled as if he'd nodded off to sleep and was suddenly waking up. He was breathing on his own again, so I stopped bagging him.

He flapped his right arm around, trying to find my hand. He grabbed onto it and pleaded again, "Please. Don't—let—me——go."

Oh my God. He's dying, I thought again. *This man is dying on me.*

He was gripping my hand with all his might—as if my arm were a lifeline that kept him tethered to this world and he was literally holding on for dear life.

Sirens grew louder and louder, and then paramedics ran into the room and descended on my patient. His head was in my lap, so I couldn't get out of the way. I sat there on the floor, holding his hand, as the paramedics started an IV, cut off his shirt, put EKG patches on his chest, and hooked him up to their portable oxygen tank. On the count of three, they lifted his weak body onto the gurney and rushed out the door. With lights flashing and sirens blaring, they raced toward the closest emergency department.

My patient coded when they hit the sliding glass doors of the ER, and the doctors tried and tried, but they couldn't get him back.

The man who pleaded "Please—don't—let—me—go—" was gone.

When I got the phone call from the hospital, I sank down at my desk and put my head in my hands. The image of Bernie, my anatomy lab cadaver, flashed through my mind. And suddenly I wondered if his right arm had been bent at a ninety-degree angle because of muscle contractures from his stroke or if his arm was bent and his fingers were clenched because, as he was dying, he was clutching someone's hand, begging "Please don't let me go."

NOW HERE I was, on my first day of work at the Hospital of Hope, standing at the sink next to Paul, contemplating the *pensée du jour*.

I can accept failure,
but I can't accept not trying.

I had spent the past ten years of my career trying to save patients' lives and, mostly, succeeding. There were a handful of "failures," of patients I couldn't catch before they plunged off the edge of the cliff in the rye field. I remembered each one of them, mostly because losing patients was such a rare occurrence. But for each loss, there were a thousand successes.

Now I wondered what it would mean to try—and accept failure—here in Togo.

When we had finished scrubbing our hands and forearms, Paul and I entered the OR where a surgical tech helped us put on sterile gowns and gloves.

The young woman with the ectopic pregnancy was lying naked on the table. The anesthesiologist had already sedated her, and then he had inserted a Foley catheter into her bladder—because she was unconscious with no bladder control, but also because a full, distended bladder is more likely to get accidentally nicked during surgery than one that is empty and flat.

The woman's arms were stretched out and strapped down to arm supports that ran perpendicular to the table. An IV dripped saline into her left arm to keep her hydrated, and to keep the vein open in case we needed to deliver IV medication or a blood transfusion in an emergency.

The surgical tech had a sponge saturated in iodine, which he used to wash her lower abdomen and suprapubic area, starting in the center and moving outward in larger and larger circles.

Then Paul and I stepped up to the table, standing across from each other.

The surgical tech stood next to Paul with a tray of surgical instruments and a suctioning unit.

The surgery began when Paul held out his right hand. "Scalpel," he said, and the surgical tech placed one firmly in Paul's flat palm.

"The ultrasound showed the ectopic was in the right fallopian, right?" Paul asked me. I nodded. I had checked, double-checked, and triple-checked the ultrasound to make sure we operated on the correct side. If we got it wrong and removed the normal fallopian tube, and then had to go back and remove the tube with the ectopic pregnancy, the woman would be infertile for the rest of her life.

Paul steadied his hand by resting its heel on the woman's right iliac crest, the place where the pelvic bone rises just below the abdomen. And then he slowly made a three-inch diagonal incision. The first cut was shallow, just breaking the skin. Then he made the same motion several more times, with an increasing amount of pressure, cutting through one layer at a time. The epidermis, the dermis, the subdermis, the cutaneous fat, the fascia (the glossy, thin white filament that covers the muscle), and then the muscle itself.

Once he got into the muscle, blood began seeping out of the incision.

"Suction." Paul said, and in a second the surgical tech inserted the hard, clear plastic tip into the wound and the blood was suctioned through several feet of tubing, ending up in a clear cylinder attached to the wall. The cylinder had black horizontal notches that indicated 100, 250, 500, and 1,000 milliliters so surgical staff could measure exactly how much blood a patient had lost.

"Protractors."

The surgical tech handed him two straight pieces of thin metal, each about nine inches long, that were curved at the end. Paul put a curve under each edge of the incision and then put the handles in my hands. "Hold these," he said, and I pulled the edges wider apart so Paul could see underneath.

He used his fingers to widen the incision he'd made in the muscle. Using fingers or round tools to expand an incision is called blunt dissection, and it's safer than using sharp instruments that might accidentally puncture or cut vital structures underneath—like the bladder or ureters or major blood vessels.

Once he'd separated the muscle tissue wide enough, he moved the protractors down until I was holding open not only the skin, but also the muscle.

He dug deeper with his fingers until he pulled out a translucent tube that was as thin as a coffee stirrer and less than two inches long. One side was attached to an ovary, the size of an almond, and the other was attached to the uterus, the size of a small pear.

He deftly worked to cut the fallopian tube at the place where it attached to the uterus. After the surgical tech suctioned the blood away, he sutured the vessels and ligaments and watched it for a few minutes to confirm that all the bleeding had stopped before he closed the main incision.

When I was doing my surgical rotations in grad school, there was almost always music playing in the OR. The surgeon got to play DJ, deciding what the OR staff would listen to that day.

But there wasn't any music in the OR in Togo. The room was completely silent except for the soft, regular beep of the monitor that indicated the rate and rhythm of the woman's heartbeat, and the occasional slurping sound of the suction machine.

Especially because I had been working in medicine for more than a decade, it was easy to forget what a mystery the human body was, what a wonder modern pharmacology and technology are, and what an honor it is to be able to bring healing to people's inmost places. But every now and then, like in the OR that day in Togo, I got a fresh reminder of what a privilege it was to care for someone's body.

If, as the Bible says, the body is a temple, Paul and I had entered the Holy of Holies, the most inward, private place of a woman's body where new life miraculously, mysteriously begins. And to see her reproductive organs from the inside was a view that even the patient herself would never glimpse. We literally knew her body better than she did.

In addition to being a Catcher in the Rye, practicing medicine was sometimes like being a priest, administering sacraments of antibiotics and pain medicine, performing rituals like surgery and suturing, touching brokenness and making it whole.

After Paul cut the right fallopian tube off, he laid it on the tray along with the surgical instruments. The right ovary, something between the size of an almond and a grape, was still attached to the tube. Once he had made sure all the internal bleeding had stopped, he sutured the muscle, then the fascia, then the skin.

In the United States, anything removed during surgery gets sent to pathology and examined under a microscope to confirm the diagnosis (in this case, that we had, in fact, removed an ectopic pregnancy) and to make sure we weren't missing another diagnosis (like ovarian cancer).

But there was no pathology department in Togo. In fact, when the surgeons here did need to have a tumor's origin identified, they had to preserve the sample; when visiting surgeons returned to the United States, they put the sample in their carry-on luggage and, once they arrived, mailed it to the pathology lab where Todd had made an agreement.

The process of obtaining a sample, preserving it, sending it back with a surgeon, and then waiting for the final report often took months. So most of the time, the doctors in Togo made their best guess and treated the patient accordingly.

Since there was no place to send this fallopian tube for further analysis, I asked Paul if I could dissect it.

"Sure," he said.

After the patient had been transferred to a gurney and wheeled to one of the beds in the ER where a nurse would watch her until she woke up, I took a scalpel and made an incision down the length of the tube, and then opened it. Inside, there was a hard, brown circle, not much bigger than a grain of sand, with a small clear sac around it.

It was amazing that something so small you almost couldn't see it with the naked eye could be potentially life threatening.

When we'd finished the dissection, Paul and I removed our masks, hats, gowns, and gloves, and scrubbed our hands and arms in the stainless-steel sink.

"It's kind of crazy when you think about it," I said, musing out loud.

"What is?" he asked.

"The human body," I said. "It can survive rollover car accidents and major surgeries and five-story falls and massive infections. And yet, in other cases, it succumbs to something that's literally microscopic."

Paul nodded in agreement, and then we stood there at the sink, washing our hands in silence, confounded by the paradox that the human body can be so resilient and so fragile at the same time.

PAUL LEFT TO check on patients he'd operated on earlier that day, and I walked to the dining hall, where the cook had left a plate in the fridge for me with a tuna salad sandwich, potato salad, and chips.

Lana, a thirty-year-old American hospital chaplain with blond hair and an athletic build, was sitting at the table with Tanya, talking about a patient who wasn't expected to live through the night.

As I sat down next to her with my plate, Lana turned to me. "I think you admitted her," she said.

It was my lady with cervical cancer. She'd taken a turn for the worse and had begun vomiting blood late in the afternoon. Her vital signs worsened, and now she was barely conscious.

I left my half-eaten sandwich on the table, grabbed my flashlight, and ran to the hospital to see her.

How was it possible that a woman who had been walking and talking this morning was dying tonight?

I found her lying in a bed in ISO 1, where the nurses had moved her so she and her family could have some privacy. The woman was half conscious and clammy. There was dried blood around her mouth. Her son and daughter were in the room with her.

A Foley catheter drained urine from her bladder, and an IV in her left arm delivered fluids and pain medication. Three patches on her chest and a pulse ox on her finger were attached to the monitor above her bed, which displayed her vital signs.

For a patient who was dying, she was receiving very few interventions. No oxygen mask, no blood pressure cuff, no blood transfusion, no monitor bells going off. There was nothing more to do, except keep her comfortable as she faded away. At this point, her care was more like hospice than an ICU.

Her heart rate was in the 140s. Her oxygen went down to 82 percent when she drifted off to sleep.

Her daughter kept trying to wake her mom up, calling her name, shaking her shoulders, dripping cold water into her mouth. Like me, the daughter couldn't understand, let alone accept, that her mom had been walking and talking this morning, but tonight she was nearly gone.

Her daughter looked like she was maybe twenty years old, which made me think my patient was younger than sixty, but there was no way to know for sure, since most people in Togo don't have birth certificates.

Lakshmi, a female Togolese chaplain, told me that the patient and her son and daughter lived in a village in Burkina Faso that was about three hours north of Mango.

They spoke a Burkina Faso dialect that no one in the hospital understood. So Lakshmi had called Atsu, a male Togolese chaplain and the only person in the hospital who spoke that dialect. Atsu walked thirty minutes from his home to the hospital, in the dark without a flashlight, so he could translate for the patient and her family.

The son and daughter were understandably distraught. They'd had no idea when they brought her to the clinic that morning that by nightfall, she would be actively dying. I wanted to tell them that I was as surprised as they were, but instead I stood at the woman's bedside silently while the son and daughter deliberated about what they should do.

Atsu explained that we were glad to admit the patient and continue giving her IV medications to keep her comfortable until she passed away—which would cost five thousand CFAs per day.

Or if the family didn't want, or couldn't afford, that option, they could take her home.

After discussing it for a few minutes, they said they wanted to take the woman home.

My heart sank.

Because here she was, lying in a bed in between clean, crisp white sheets with promethazine to keep her from vomiting and morphine to ease her pain. And I felt like maybe that was the only thing I had accomplished for her all day—to make her comfortable.

Our pharmacy didn't have any oral narcotic pain medication, so if her children took her home, we couldn't prescribe medicine strong enough to treat her pain. We could send her home with promethazine pills for nausea, but if she started vomiting again, she wouldn't be able to keep the medicine down.

I was also afraid that maybe her children thought we were killing her. Maybe they believed their mom came in not-too-sick and somehow, while she was at our hospital, we had caused her to start dying.

Atsu talked with the son and daughter in their language, and then translated their words to Lakshmi and me. He said that her children were not mad at us; they were very appreciative of our care. They wanted to take her home so their friends and family could say good-bye to the woman while she was still alive, while she could still hear their words of love and praise.

They also wanted to take her home because they had spent almost all their money on one day of care, and the three-hour taxi ride would be cheaper if she was still alive.

When she saw the puzzled look on my face, Lakshmi explained that taxis in Togo are legally allowed to transport dead bodies, but they charge up to ten times more because afterward, they have to take their taxi to a marabout and an imam to have the evil spirits of death removed.

The chaplains offered to help the woman's children find transportation. As the four of them were leaving, the daughter motioned for me to stay behind with her mom.

The woman's nurse, Cecily, an American woman in her mid-twenties who was here for a one-year term, came in to remove the woman's Foley catheter and IV so the woman would be ready to leave whenever the taxi showed up.

Cecily lifted up the patient's gown to pull the catheter out, and we saw that she was hemorrhaging blood from her rectum.

Cecily left for a minute, then returned with a basin of warm soapy water. Together we washed the woman's body, changed the soiled sheets, and put a new gown on her. Then Cecily left, and I was alone with the woman.

Her oxygen was dropping. Flies crawled over her face and between her lips. I swatted them away.

As I stood there next to her bed, I suddenly realized how tired I was. I had started seeing patients in clinic fourteen hours ago, then gone to the OR to assist Paul with the ectopic surgery, and now I was completely exhausted.

I pulled up a chair next to the woman's bed and sat down. She got restless and threw the sheet off, her right hand thrashing around. I gave her my right hand, and as soon as she grabbed on to it, she settled down. I thought of the last patient I had lost before I left for Togo, and of Bernie, whose arms had been bent the same way this woman's was now.

Please don't let me go.

I placed my left hand on the woman's clammy forehead and silently prayed for her. I prayed for the woman to experience joy and life and light on the other side of eternity. And as I prayed, I felt an overwhelming spiritual peace and light in the room—like a hole was opening up in the veil that separated heaven and earth, and Divine Love was pouring through.

Sounds faded away and time stood still.

My spirit felt weightless.

Without any effort on my part, all negative thoughts and memories and emotions simply ceased to be.

Centuries ago, the Celtic Christians called this the Thin Space, the place where the division between earth and heaven, between the visible world and the invisible world, becomes almost nonexistent. The Thin Space is the place where we get a taste—an infinitesimal taste—of what awaits our souls on the other side of eternity.

I had heard about the Thin Space before, but sitting in that hospital room in Togo on that muggy Monday night, I experienced it for the very first time in my life. Instead of being repulsed by the presence of death, which was rapidly consuming the body of this woman who was dying before my eyes, I found myself being drawn closer in. I was drawn to this place, drawn to this woman's bedside, longing to go deeper into this miracle, wanting to steep my soul in the depths of this mystery.

Please don't let me go. The words echoed in my head.

I remembered letting go of the man's hand as the paramedics rushed him into the ambulance. I remembered getting the phone call from the hospital that he was gone. In the end, I couldn't hold on to him. It was a failure I still struggled to accept—especially because I knew how desperate he was to stay.

But with this woman, it was so different. It didn't feel so much like a failure to let her go as it felt like an honor.

Her inevitable death did not seem horrific to me. Instead, it was infused with hope, because sitting at her bedside I experienced the other side of the

Thin Space, and I knew that for the rest of eternity, she would be held in hands that were much stronger and gentler and more loving and knowing than mine could ever be.

I looked at the monitor above her bed. Her heart rate was now in the 180s because she was rapidly losing blood from hemorrhaging tumors in her abdomen. Her oxygen saturation dropped to 75 percent.

She was fading fast. It was time to say good-bye.

I didn't know if she could hear me or not, but with my left hand on her forehead, I whispered, "Mama," with the accent on the second syllable. *maMA*. Omari had told me it was a term of endearment for older Togolese women.

"Mama, you were born into Love, you will die into Love, and you will be held in Love every second in between."

I blinked away tears as I traced the sign of the cross on her clammy forehead with my thumb.

"Whenever you're ready, you can go to God," I said. "You can go home to God."

Her eyelids fluttered, but she didn't open them. Her heart rate accelerated and her oxygen saturation dropped even lower. I wondered how long her poor body could keep going before it finally gave out.

I sat there holding her hand in the still, sacred, peaceful Presence until her son rushed into the room. He and the chaplains had flagged down the cab, and it was waiting at the hospital's front gate.

Cecily offered him a wheelchair to transport his mother to the car, but he shook his head. Instead, he scooped up his mother's nearly lifeless body in his arms. I gently kissed her forehead, and then stood there with tears in my eyes as I watched him carry her away.

The son called Atsu the following morning to inform him that the woman had died in the backseat of the taxi, when they were halfway home.

AFTER I WATCHED the young man carry his unconscious mother to the taxi, I helped Cecily clean the room and change the sheets to get it ready for the next patient.

It was nearly midnight, but I was too full of thoughts and emotions to sleep.

In PA school, I sometimes had to do overnight rotations, where I slept in a room at the hospital and responded to emergencies if my pager went off. If there weren't any patients to care for, or if I had trouble sleeping, I used to go to the pediatrics ward to hold the babies.

Some parents slept in a recliner by their child's bedside at night. Other parents went home, leaving their child alone for the night. And other hospitalized children were wards of the state, removed from their parents' custody because the doctors suspected that the children had been abused.

When I did my surgical rotations, I was on call every third night for a month. During that time, there was a two-year-old baby girl admitted with burns on her lower legs and a broken right arm. Her parents were arrested and charged with child abuse. When I walked through pediatrics one night, I found her awake in her crib, whimpering.

I asked her nurse if I could hold the girl, and she nodded, relieved to have one less crying child to have to deal with that night.

I picked the girl up from her crib, moving her gently so I wouldn't disturb the cast on her right arm and cause her further pain. There was a rocking chair in the corner of her room, so I sat down and cradled her in my lap, and softly hummed the notes of Brahms's lullaby until she fell asleep.

Even though the girl's injuries healed well enough for her to be discharged after a few days, she had to stay in the hospital because the social workers couldn't find a foster home to take her. She was in the hospital for the entire month I was on surgical rotations. So every three nights, if we didn't have any surgical cases, I would walk over to the pediatrics ward and rock the girl to sleep.

My senior resident, who either slept or watched movies or played Ping-Pong in the residents' lounge on the nights we were on call together, found out what I was doing and told me I was crazy for taking care of a patient who wasn't my responsibility.

"What are you, a saint or something?" he asked.

I took his words more literally than he'd intended.

"Only Catholics can be saints," I said.

"So?" he said.

"So I'm not Catholic. I grew up Baptist. I don't think Baptists have saints."

He laughed at me and walked away, but I meant what I had said.

My impression growing up was that while Catholics could aspire to the elevated distinction of sainthood, the best a Baptist could do was to become a humble, repentant sinner. "Good" Baptists were not elevated in status; "good" Baptists underwent a self-imposed sinking down to the floor, face-down, nose in the dirt, groveling at God's feet and begging him for mercy.

AFTER MAMA'S SON carried her to the taxi, I wandered into the pediatrics ward to see if there were any children to hold, but they were all asleep. So I walked down the hall to the maternity ward. There I found a Togolese woman asleep in bed with her newborn son lying next to her. The baby's eyes were open and he was actively kicking his arms and legs. I gently picked him up and held him, swaying back and forth to see if I could get him back to sleep.

As I was holding him, I heard Grace, a twenty-seven-year-old midwife from America, on the other side of the curtain. She was coaching a Togolese woman through delivery.

"With your next contraction, put your chin to your chest, hold your breath, and push!" Grace said in French.

And with a loud moan, the woman did. Twenty seconds later, she gasped for breath as the contraction dissipated. With the next contraction, she pushed again, and her gasping was followed by the warbling cry of a baby.

"It's a girl!" Grace called out. As Grace waited to deliver the placenta, the nurses scurried to clean the baby, put antibiotic ointment in her eyes, put a cap on her head, and wrap her in a clean blanket.

Grace delivered the placenta and placed it in a small plastic ice bucket. In Togolese culture, all women bring a bucket with them to the hospital when they come to deliver a baby, because it's considered good luck to take the placenta home and bury it in the yard.

After the woman's perineum was washed and she was covered with a clean sheet, the nurses placed her baby girl on her chest, and I heard the sweet, soft sound of a baby suckling her mother's breast for the first time.

A short while later, the baby boy I was holding fell asleep. I laid him in the bassinet next to his mom's bed and left the maternity ward.

As I walked away, I thought about the babies who had just arrived in this world, and the sixty-year-old woman who was leaving it.

In birth, we receive souls into the world from God, and in death we send them back to God, for eternal keeping and care.

Especially in Togo, birth and death—and the life in between—were often filled with pain and struggle and fear. But underneath it all, holding both the patients whose lives we were able to save, as well as the souls of those who escaped our grasp and died, were the arms of Divine Love.

We are born into Love, we die into Love, and we are held in Love every second of the life we live in between.

I FELL INTO A rhythm in Togo, working half of my shifts in the outpatient clinic and half of my shifts at the hospital.

The clinic closed at 5 p.m. and dinner was served at 6 p.m. In the hour in between, I usually went for a walk to unwind my mind, decompress from the stress of the day, and explore Mango further.

Todd had worked at a hospital five hours south of Mango for several years when he and other missionaries began to pray that God would provide them with the financing and the land to build a hospital farther north, where people were dying at alarming rates because they didn't have rapid access to quality medical care. There were several government-operated clinics, but they were often understaffed, undersupplied, lacking basic lifesaving supplies such as oxygen, blood transfusions, and nebulizers.

Patients were often misdiagnosed and treated with whatever medication the hospital had on hand, whether it was the appropriate treatment or not. During my time at the Hospital of Hope, I saw patients who came to us after being unsuccessfully treated at the nearby government hospital. Some had viral infections that were treated with five antibiotics instead of appropriate anti-virals. Some had surgical issues that were treated with Tylenol instead of a surgical consult. Several children with malaria had life-threatening anemia, and were given vitamins for days instead of being sent to us for a STAT blood transfusion.

Todd and Matt spent a long time exploring northern Togo and working with government officials to find available land. When they were given the opportunity to purchase acres of land a mile outside of Mango, they bought the property immediately. The fact that hundreds of patients showed up every morning in the triage line, and the list for patients awaiting surgical procedures was growing longer and longer, was confirmation that the Hospital of Hope was needed—and necessary—in this part of Togo.

THE DOWNSIDE OF Mango was that it was far away from the airport, grocery stores, ice cubes, cell service, libraries, reliable Internet, movie theaters, landscaped gardens, coffee shops, and lots of other conveniences.

But the advantage of Mango was that it was unpolluted and its natural beauty was undisturbed. Sunrises and sunsets were spectacular because there were no skyscrapers to obscure the expansive sky. In the rainy season, you could walk in any direction and see miles upon miles of vibrant green fields. Mango overlooked the Oti River and on the outskirts of town, cliffs above the river offered sweeping views of the valley below. At night, the stars were spectacular, because there was no light pollution to dull the sky.

During my evening walks, I either explored one of the many narrow red dirt paths that cut through the cornfields surrounding the hospital, or I took the main road to the market, about a mile away from the hospital.

On a Wednesday evening, I finished a long day in clinic and decided to walk to town to get a cold drink. Halfway between the hospital and the town, I noticed three boys squatting around a small fire they'd built under a tree by the side of the road.

I waved as I crossed the road toward them, and they waved back.

"Are you cold?" I asked the boys in French, pointing to their fire.

The oldest boy, who looked about twelve, shook his head. The sun was low in the sky, but it was still nearly ninety degrees outside.

"Are you bored?" I asked.

The middle boy, who looked about eight, nodded.

"You don't have anything to do?" I asked.

All three of them shook their heads, and I remembered that school was out for the summer, and wouldn't resume for two months.

"What do you like to do?" I asked them.

The littlest boy, about five years old, jumped up and started running around, kicking an imaginary ball. "Futbol! Futbol! Futbol!" he yelled.

"You want to play futbol with us?" the oldest boy asked.

"Sure," I said, imagining how embarrassed my three athletic brothers in the United States would be if they knew their unathletic sister was about to play sports in public in Togo. "Where's your ball?"

"We don't have one," the eight-year-old said.

I laughed. They were not only inviting me to play with them, they were also "inviting" me to provide them with a soccer ball.

The sun started to set, and I knew I needed to head back to the compound because dinner would be served soon.

"I don't have time today," I said. "But can I come back on Saturday?"

They nodded.

Two other little boys swung down from a large branch overhead. "Saturday?" they asked in unison.

"Yes," I said. "I'll come back on Saturday at eight in the morning."

"Eight," the oldest boy confirmed.

I nodded.

He took a stick, traced the number 8 in the sand, pointed to it, and said again, "Eight."

"Yes," I said. "I promise I will come back on Saturday at eight."

THE DAY AFTER I met the boys, I worked an on-call shift with Laura. Around noon, the security guard wheeled a fifty-five-year-old man to the nurses' station. The man was clearly in distress, leaning forward, clutching his knees, trying to suck air into his lungs. In medicine, the posture is called tripoding, and it indicates that someone is in severe respiratory distress. He was wearing a stained white collared shirt with the top five buttons undone. I wondered if he had been in too much of a hurry to fasten all the buttons, or if he thought that loosening his shirt would somehow help him breathe.

His wife was a willowy woman with callused hands who wore a threadbare ankle-length dress of faded red-and-green-striped fabric, and a matching headscarf. Her face was impassive, but I saw fear flash in her deep-brown eyes as she watched her husband struggle to breathe.

Raima, a petite twenty-five-year-old Togolese nurse who wore hijabs to work in keeping with her Muslim faith, was assigned to the ER area that day. She quickly rolled the wheelchair to the ER bay and helped the man into an empty bed. Laura and I rushed over. Laura did a quick assessment, listening to his heart and lungs, feeling his abdomen, and checking peripheral pulses in his wrists and feet while asking the man and his wife rapid-fire questions in French. I grabbed the IV-starting kit from the nurses' station, put a tourniquet on the man's left arm, and started looking for a vein. Kojo ran to the supply closet to get an oxygen mask while Raima took the patient's vital signs.

The man's blood pressure was elevated. His heart rate was a rapid 120 beats per minute. And most concerning of all, his oxygen was dangerously low, hovering around 75 percent.

Kojo turned the oxygen up as high as it would go. Laura ordered labs to check the man's red and white blood cell counts, his electrolytes, and his liver and kidney function. Unfortunately, we didn't have the capability in our lab to check other relevant tests—like a D-dimer to rule out a pulmonary embolism (a blood clot in his lung) or cardiac enzymes to rule out a heart attack.

We gave him aspirin, blood pressure medicine, and morphine for pain and anxiety. Despite the medicines and the oxygen, he failed to improve. He continued to lean forward in bed, holding his knees and gasping for air.

Half an hour after he arrived, we switched him from a face mask to a BiPAP device, which applied a high pressure when he inhaled and lower pressure when he exhaled.

When that didn't help, Raima went to the storage closet to retrieve the CPAP device, the strongest respiratory equipment we had. It applied high, continuous pressure to force as much oxygen as possible into a patient's lungs.

The hospital couldn't afford ventilator machines that automatically breathed for patients for long periods of time. There were only two ventilators in the hospital, and they were reserved for intubated surgical patients, who were extubated as soon as they began to wake up from anesthesia. Even if we could afford ventilators to keep patients alive for days, we would also need a blood gas machine in the lab to monitor the levels of oxygen and carbon dioxide in patients' blood, and a team of respiratory therapists who knew how to adjust the ventilators accordingly.

The other problem was that most medical equipment was not designed or manufactured for rural West Africa. The sand, dust, heat, and humidity quickly took their toll on fragile, precisely calibrated equipment—and the closest trained repairmen were thousands of miles away.

When the hospital first opened, a company from the United States donated a portable X-ray machine. It broke after two days because a windstorm blew sand and dirt into the hospital through the open windows and screen doors, and lodged in the machine. When I left the hospital in October, it was still sitting in a closet, unused and unusable. Todd decided it wasn't worth bringing in a repairman from Europe because, even if they were able to repair it this time, the next time there was a heat wave or a windstorm, the machine would just break down again.

I KNEW THAT IF the CPAP machine didn't help my tripoding patient, we were going to lose him.

As we were waiting for Raima to return with the CPAP device, I pulled a chair over and invited his wife to sit down. I stood at the man's side with my hand on his shoulder. As I watched his chest heaving with each breath, all I could think was that he was working *so incredibly hard* to breathe, and we had no way of knowing exactly what was wrong with him. His blood work had come back, and it was normal. The labs we really needed—the ones that would check for a blood clot or a heart attack—were labs we didn't have.

However, even if we were able to accurately diagnose his problem, there was nothing we could do that we hadn't already done. Even if we knew he was having a heart attack, we didn't have a cath lab to unblock clogged arteries. Even if we knew he had a blood clot in his lung, we didn't have thrombolytics—the class of medication known as clot-busting drugs—to dissolve it.

I silently prayed for him to make a miraculous recovery because at this point, that's what it would take to save him: a miracle.

The man looked up at me with desperation. "Madam," he said as his chest was heaving, as he was using every muscle in his body to move air in and out.

How is it possible that he's in such distress and yet he's so maddeningly polite? I wondered.

"Madam—I—can't—breathe," he heaved. His eyes locked with mine. I wanted to look away, but instead I held his gaze.

"I know. We're coming," I said, because it's all I knew how to say in French, and all he needed to know.

We're coming. We're trying.

A few minutes later, Raima returned, and we switched the patient from BiPAP to CPAP. We gave him more aspirin and more morphine. We did everything we could do for him, and he hung on, using every fiber of every muscle in his body to pull in oxygen for hours and hours.

And then, just before midnight, about twelve hours after he arrived at the hospital, he gasped for the last time.

And then he died.

EARLY ON SATURDAY morning, I went to the market to buy soccer balls. The only balls I could find were twelve-inch rubber balls with soccer ball markings printed on them.

At 8 a.m., true to their word, ten boys were waiting for me under the tree where they'd been making the fire the day I met them. When they saw me coming down the road toward them, they began waving their arms and calling, "Sarah! Sarah!" As if I could miss them.

They took the balls and led me to a rectangular dirt soccer field with one lone goal made of large tree branches. There was a cement school building on one of the long sides of the rectangle, and a cornfield on the opposite side. There were small clusters of thatched mud houses behind both of the goal lines.

The boys divided themselves into two groups. The older boys took one of the balls and played at the half of the soccer field that had the goalpost. The younger boys took the other ball and played at the other end of the field.

I noticed a four-year-old boy sitting on the sidelines, holding the third ball, too intimidated to play with the other kids.

I sat down next to him and put my right arm around his shoulder. He scooted a few inches closer to me. We sat there together, watching the boys running around, kicking the balls, yelling with joy, doing cartwheels and backflips, occasionally stopping to wave at me.

With my left thumb, I brushed away tears as I let the weight of the past week sink in, and allowed the frustration and grief of losing patients to wash over me. I acknowledged that death and grief and pain are inevitable parts of life—especially life here in rural Africa, where diseases were rampant and resources were limited.

And then I took a deep breath and smiled as I let the simple joy of these boys well up inside of me. I realized that joy does not arise in the *absence* of sadness. Joy arises in the *midst* of it.

In the midst of death, here was life.

In the midst of despair, here was hope.

In the midst of the world's least happy country, here were ten little boys running, jumping, giggling, and yelling, "Futbol, futbol, futbol!"

I WOKE UP SUNDAY morning to the sound of rain pattering on the tin roof. I was relieved. Rain would give us a reprieve from the heat and humidity, and it would help the farmers' crops flourish.

Rain in northern Togo was, for the most part, a welcomed occurrence. Rain meant that the melons, corn, onions, tomatoes, okra, cucumbers, and peppers that were currently planted in the fields around Mango would thrive. Rain meant that the Oti River would continue to flow and provide the village with a consistent supply of water. Rain meant that there would be more yams, rice, beans, and cornmeal that families could stockpile and ration out during the dry season, which lasted nine months or more.

The downside of rain was that it created pools of standing water, which became breeding grounds for mosquitoes. Whenever it rained, we could count on seeing a surge of malaria cases at the hospital in the weeks to come. According to the World Health Organization (WHO), sub-Saharan Africa has a disproportionate amount of malaria, accounting for 88 percent of the world's malaria cases and 90 percent of the world's malaria deaths. Children are particularly susceptible to this parasitic infection. More than two-thirds of patients who die of malaria are children under age five.

That Sunday when I woke up to rain, I spent most of the day in my room at the guesthouse, drinking coffee and journaling the events of the past week to the soothing sound of raindrops pattering on the tin roof and splashing in expanding puddles outside my door. I tried to be grateful for the ways in which the community would benefit from the rain instead of fearing for the lives of young children who were at an increased risk of contracting malaria during this season.

The Internet worked for a few hours in the afternoon, so I was able to post some stories on my blog and email my parents to tell them I was alive and well.

In the evening, as they did every Sunday, the Americans gathered for church in the dining hall. The large room was filled with sixty metal folding chairs. One of the chaplains played a few hymns from YouTube and we all stood and sang along.

A lot of the lifer missionaries were there with a mission called ABWE, which stands for Association of Baptists for World Evangelism. Their theology was very conservative, and some took pride in being considered fundamentalists.

"After all, it means we've mastered the fundamentals," Brett, one of the American chaplains, told me.

The hymns we sang during the three months I was there included words like *slave*, *sinner*, *wretch*, and *worm*. We sang about the debt we owed to God, the debt we could never repay. We sang about being saved from the eternal fires of hell.

I loved the music, but the lyrics made me feel demoralized and discouraged. I thought about the resident asking me if I was a saint. No, the lyrics reinforced. Baptists do not aspire to be elevated as saints. We aspire to be worms, wretches, slaves, and sinners, snatched from eternal flames, lying face-down at the feet of God, mourning a debt we can never repay.

The first week I was at the hospital, the chaplain in charge of organizing the Sunday-evening church services that month asked me if I would speak. So that first Sunday in Togo, after the singing was finished, I gave the talk I'd given at dozens of universities and churches since *The Invisible Girls* book came out. I told the story of the Invisible Girls, and how it reminded me of the story of Hagar in Genesis 16.

Hagar is a pregnant, enslaved girl running away from an abusive mistress when God appears to her and cares for her. She becomes the only person in the Bible to give God a name. She calls him El Roi, "the God Who Sees."

"I have now seen the One who sees me," Hagar said.

I spoke about how God has seen each of us in love, and out of that experience we see the Invisible People in the world—in this case, northern Togo—who for so long had gone overlooked, unseen, and unloved. To use Massiko's words, Love looks around and sees us, and Love asks us to look around as well, to see the people around us through the compassionate eyes of God.

It wasn't until months later, after I'd left Togo, that I got an email from one of the missionary women that was half criticism and half apology. She said that many of the missionaries took the apostle Paul's words, "Women are to be silent in church," literally, and were offended when I "preached" to them that night because I'm a woman. She acknowledged that she had been rude to me for the next three months because of that first Sunday.

I had felt her cold shoulder, and I had noticed the way that some of the other missionaries kept their distance from me, but I never understood why. Regardless, it made the experience of Togo exceptionally lonely because I never felt fully accepted by the team. I never felt I was "one of them." In fact, I felt more camaraderie with Omari and other Togolese Muslim staff members than I did with the American Christians. The Muslim staff members didn't judge me based on minor theological differences, and they didn't split doctrinal hairs. Instead, we worked together as a team to accomplish a shared goal: to provide the highest level of care to our patients.

My heart sank when I learned that Sunday-evening services were attended only by the sixty white missionaries who worked at the hospital. The Togolese staff members were not invited. Even though I disagreed with this practice, which seemed like blatant segregation, I showed up every Sunday evening to participate because I was trying to be a good teammate.

Each week I sang songs I didn't quite believe, songs with severe theology and archaic vocabulary. After the opening songs, we watched a DVD sermon series. The preacher was always a white man whose explanation of the gospel, the "good news," was little more than a diatribe about hell, judgment, and damnation.

I kept asking myself the same questions: If it weren't for the fear of hell, would these missionaries still have uprooted their lives in the United States to come to Togo, or would love have been enough bring them here? Would the suffering of patients on this side of eternity have been compelling enough to bring medical missionaries here, or were we only concerned about eternal destinies?

Was it just as high a calling to care for people's bodies as it was to care for their souls?

It was hard for me to reconcile fear-based theology with 1 John 4, which says "there is no fear in love." Plus, the most commonly repeated command in the Bible, mentioned 365 times, is "Do not be afraid." So why would we make fear such a central tenet of the gospel?

Why would we rather smash people's heads against commandments set in stone than offer them the balm in Gilead?

Every Sunday evening, after the sermon finished, we stood to sing a closing hymn. Decades after Annie Dillard published it, I felt I was living her "Singing with the Fundamentalists" essay.

After every Sunday service, I returned to my room with a heavy heart.

My heart sank even further when I learned that, despite my efforts to integrate into the missionaries' community, I had been judged for telling a twenty-minute story about the amazing grace of the God Who Sees.

For the love of everything holy.

WHEN I WAS in college, my roommate and I often had conversations about gender and women's rights. Before I got to college, my understanding of what a woman could and couldn't do in the world was dictated by the Bible and by church-imposed rules. I assumed that women outside of strict faith communities had just as many opportunities, and just as much freedom, as men did.

But in college, I was exposed to a broader culture. I encountered Virginia Woolf's writing, and was especially intrigued by her quote, "For most of history, Anonymous was a woman." I realized that even non-Christian colleges had courses on women's literature and women's history because for so long, women in nearly every country, every time period, every academic discipline, and every career field had been overlooked, underrepresented, and underpaid.

I took an informal poll of the eighty girls in my dorm, asking each girl the same question: If you could choose your gender, which gender would you be?

Many of the girls were confused by the question because it had never occurred to them that they could've had a different experience of the world. Others thought the question wasn't worth contemplating, let alone answering, because it was rhetorical. And others looked at me with worried glances, concerned that I was struggling with gender identity issues.

Since then, I have read thousands upon thousands of pages about what women around the world have endured because of their gender.

Baby girls in China have been left on trash heaps or strung up in trees, left to die from exposure and starvation.

Girls in Africa have been subjected to female genital mutilation to prevent them from being able to experience sexual pleasure so they would presumably be less likely to cheat on their husbands.

Girls in Afghanistan have been shot in the head and had acid poured on them for having the audacity to go to school.

Women across the world have been kidnapped and sold into sexual slavery.

A few years before I went to Togo, I was researching the Chinese practice of foot-binding as part of a writing project. I read in great detail about girls having the bones in their feet broken, contorted, and bound to make their feet look like delicate lotus flowers. The practice was often performed in winter so the girls could plunge their shattered feet into the snow to dull the excruciating pain. One of my housemates came home from work to find me sobbing on the couch that afternoon. When she asked me what was wrong, I was crying so hard, it was difficult to speak. "Their feet—these little girls—they hold them down and they crush their feet."

In religious communities, women are often forbidden to become pastors or elders. In extreme cases, they're forbidden to speak in church. Women's clothing choices and appearances are more regulated in religious communities, and more scrutinized in the secular world.

Knowing what I know now about the mistreatment women around the world have endured, what I think I was really asking back in college—when I polled women with that question, *If you could choose your gender, which gender would you be?*—was that if being female is a liability that leaves you vulnerable to abuse, discrimination, and torture, why would you choose that gender? What, if any, assets were there to being female?

I spent years searching for an answer to these questions: Is there value in being a woman? If so, what is it?

For a long time, the only answer I could come up with was that it's valuable to be a woman because you can experience the miracle of conception, gestation, and childbirth.

But while giving birth is a beautiful thing—and every time I've witnessed a birth in my medical career, I've cried tears of wonder and joy—even that experience is fraught with complications, risks, and mortality, not to mention agonizing pain.

When the chemotherapy I had in my late twenties left me permanently unable to have children of my own, the question became even more poignant and personal for me. Since childbirth, the singularly unique female experience, was off the table, what, if any, advantage was there to being female?

In Togo, gender was even more apparent to me than it had been in the United States. Being female felt like a liability among the American Christians, as evidenced by the way some of them treated me after that

Sunday-evening talk. And being female was a liability in the culture, where women's clothing was strictly scrutinized and regulated by men in the conservative Muslim community. I resented the fact that the men who were dependent on me for medical care somehow felt entitled to regulate what I wore while I was healing them and, in some cases, literally saving their lives. It seemed like covering my ankle bones and kneecaps was more important to them than my clinical competency.

As an independent woman, adamant about women receiving the same respect, dignity, opportunities, and compensation as men, the fact that I was forced to comply with rules that men made but didn't have to follow themselves was maddening to me.

And yet, in the midst of the frustration of being a woman in the conservative Muslim and fundamentalist Christian cultures I encountered in northern Togo, an answer to my question began to appear. What, if any, value was there in being a woman instead of a man?

The value was that millions of women in Togo and around the world were suffering—and I was in a unique place to help them.

Because I was one of them.

I HAD BEEN WORKING at the Hospital of Hope for a few weeks when one morning, as I arrived at clinic, a Togolese medical assistant named Tahib approached me. He was a lanky, quiet young man in his early twenties who had a gentle manner with patients, and always had a willing attitude no matter how tired or busy he was. Sometimes, after we'd seen the last patient of the day, Tahib would come sit in the exam room with Omari and me and tell us stories about growing up in Mango, and about his dream to go to medical school one day.

"*Excusez-moi*, Sarah," he said that morning, tapping me on the shoulder. "Do you mind seeing the ninjas?" he asked in French.

I racked my brain for a few minutes, trying to figure out what he meant, trying to remember a French word that sounded like ninja.

Finally, I gave up and I asked Omari to help me understand what Tahib was asking.

"He's asking if you will see the ninjas," Omari said.

"What ninjas?" I asked, exasperated.

"You know," Omari said, pointing in the distance to a woman in a burka walking toward the hospital. "The ninjas."

Tahib explained that the other PA who was working that day was François, a Togolese man who was unsettled by women whose faces he couldn't see. Plus, François didn't like seeing female patients in general because every time he needed to do a breast or pelvic exam, he had to find a female nurse's aide to chaperone the exam.

"Will you see them?" Tahib asked again.

I nodded. Yes, I said. I would see all the Ninjas.

During my time in the clinic, I saw lots of women in burkas, who usually came from a few hours north of Mango, near the border of Burkina Faso, where there was an even larger conservative Muslim population than we had in Mango.

These women were always accompanied by their husband or a male relative. Some of them wore hijabs, which covered their head and chest but not their face, and others wore burkas, which obscured their head, their face, and their eyes.

I often needed to ask the women to undress in the exam room so I could do a thorough examination. They always looked at the male relative for permission before removing any clothing. Some men gave women permission to remove everything, down to their undergarments. Others gave them permission to only remove their veil.

Also, the male relative often did all the talking on behalf of the female patient.

I wondered how these women felt about living their lives unseen and unheard by everyone except their husbands.

For the first few days that I saw all the Ninjas, I let the male relatives speak for the patients, and I let the male relatives dictate how much clothing a woman could or could not remove. But I quickly realized that I was participating in an unfair—and sometimes medically unsafe—misogynistic culture. And so I became more assertive. Each time I brought a Ninja and her male relative in the room, I explained that I would only see her on two conditions.

First, the woman had to be allowed to speak for herself. And second, she had to remove any clothing I needed her to remove in order to do an appropriately thorough exam.

"If I can't see her, I can't help her," I said to male relatives who were reticent to let a female patient remove her veil and robes for an exam. I must've said that line at least a thousand times. "If I can't see her, I can't help her."

To their credit, all the men acquiesced except for one.

A young man had brought his seventeen-year-old wife to the clinic because she'd had several months of nausea and upper abdominal pain. She was wearing a burka, covered in black fabric from head to toe. And she was wearing black gloves and black socks. Every millimeter of her skin was covered.

I was able to put my stethoscope on top of her robes to try to listen to her heart, lungs, and abdomen, but she was wearing so many layers, it was very hard to hear anything. And I was able to palpate her abdomen over her robes, but again, the exam was limited by the fact that she was wearing so many layers.

There was a blood test we could do to look for a bacteria called H. pylori, which causes the majority of stomach ulcers and is ubiquitous in many African countries. I wanted to test her for it before committing her to the treatment regimen, which included two antibiotics and two other medicines that reduced the production of stomach acid, all of which she would need to take for several weeks.

But the husband wouldn't let her remove any of her clothing—which meant we couldn't even roll up her sleeve to draw blood. So I prescribed her the four medications to treat H. pylori and told her to come back if she didn't improve. While I was explaining the treatment plan to the patient and her husband, with Omari translating, I sat on a stool next to the woman, and I rested my hand on her knee, hoping that our fifteen-minute encounter had, in some small way, helped to affirm her dignity and value.

I came to enjoy taking care of the Ninjas, insisting that they speak for themselves, insisting that I be allowed to give them thorough care, showing them—and the men who accompanied them—that these women were precious and that they were worthy of compassionate, excellent care.

The Ninjas were Togo's ultimate Invisible Girls, and I was honored to see them.

THE OTHER PLACE gender was very apparent in Togo was in the pediatrics ward.

During one of my on-call shifts, two baby boys died in maternity, and another boy died in pediatrics. I noticed that often, the maternity ward and pediatrics ward were full of baby girls.

"It seems like just the boys are dying," I mentioned to Tanya. "Has anyone ever studied survival rates based on gender?"

"Oh yes," she said. She told me that gender and race had been extensively studied in Neonatal Intensive Care Units (NICUs) in the United States. The studies showed that black baby girls did the best, followed by black baby boys, followed by Caucasian baby girls. Caucasian baby boys did the worst.

Tanya said the research was so compelling, when she was working in the NICU in the States, she gave the male preemies female nicknames and referred to them as "she" instead of "he," thinking maybe if these patients thought they were girls, they'd fight like girls and be more likely to survive.

So what I noticed in the pediatrics ward in Togo, that baby girls were surviving at higher rates than baby boys, was not a coincidence, and the phenomenon was not all in my imagination. From birth, these little Togolese girls truly were ninjas, born with an extra amount of fight in them that no one could explain.

Dear Ninjas, I whispered over the cribs of little girls who were fighting malaria and typhoid and meningitis. *Dear Ninjas, keep fighting.*

WITH THE NUMBER of pelvic exams I did on the Ninjas and other female Togolese patients, it was inevitable that I would encounter women who had undergone female genital mutilation (FGM).

And I did.

Before I went to Togo, I prepared myself by reading more about the practice. I learned that FGM has been practiced by communities in twenty-nine out of fifty-four African countries, as well as parts of Yemen, Iraq, Malaysia, and Indonesia, from as far back as 25 BC.

The World Health Organization (WHO) has classified FGM into four types, ranging from having only the clitoris removed, all the way to having the entire vulva excised, the gaping perineum sewn together with only a small hole left for passing urine and menstrual blood.

FGM is nearly always performed on minors, most of them girls under five. It is often performed without anesthetic, with sharp, non-sterile objects like broken glass, tin can lids, or razor blades. It causes excruciating pain, infections, and childbirth complications. Several organizations are working to end FGM, though an estimated three million girls in Africa still undergo it each year. Western countries didn't begin to ban FGM until the 1980s. The United States finally banned it in 1997.

Before it was called female genital mutilation, it was called female circumcision. But Marion Stevenson, a missionary nurse from Scotland who spent twenty-two years working in Kenya, thought that circumcision was too gentle a description of the procedure because it compared FGM with male circumcision, which was not nearly as dangerous or traumatic.

Plus, while male circumcision can prevent HPV (the virus that causes cervical cancer and genital warts) and HIV, female genital mutilation doesn't prevent health problems; it creates them. Following Stevenson's lead, the Kenya Missionary Council began using the term mutilation instead of circumcision in 1929.

I did a lot of pelvic exams in Togo, not only because I saw a large percentage of female patients, but also because many of the women were in polygamous marriages and were exposed to a lot of sexually transmitted diseases. By law, men could have up to four wives. In addition, many Togolese men traveled to neighboring countries like Nigeria and Ghana for work, because the Togolese economy was poor and there were few jobs. While they were away from their wives, men often had sexual encounters with other women.

I saw an inordinate number of women who came in with pelvic pain and vaginal discharge. When I asked one of the Ninjas to describe her symptoms to me, she said, "My uterus won't stop crying."

Whenever I did a pelvic exam, Omari and the man accompanying the Ninja would stand at the head of the bed to offer the woman at least a little dignity and privacy. Omari needed to stay because I needed him to translate for me. And the men who brought the Ninjas to the clinic refused to leave them unattended.

One afternoon, an eighteen-year-old Ninja came in with her brother. She had been married to her husband, who had two other wives, for one year. She had never been pregnant. For the past six months, she'd had vaginal discharge and intermittent fevers.

When it came time to examine her, I asked her to remove her underwear and lie down on the table with her feet in the stirrups. While she did this, I had my back turned to her because I was putting on gloves and lubricating the end of the speculum with petroleum jelly. I turned around, sat down on the stool, and suddenly I was facing her perineum, which was so scarred, it was barely recognizable. There was no clitoris and no labia. It was just one flat, thick scar with a dime-size hole in the center.

I'm usually good at being stoic when I see unexpected things during an exam, but I was so stunned and horrified by the appearance of her perineum, I couldn't finish the exam.

"Could you tell her to sit up?" I asked Omari.

She sat up, and I covered her waist with a sheet.

"Can you ask her how old she was when she was cut?" I asked.

Omari asked her, but she said she didn't know.

"Can you ask her if intercourse is painful?" I asked.

Omari asked her the question, and her eyes brimmed with tears as she nodded.

"Yes, very," Omari translated.

In that moment, I didn't feel like an objective clinician. I felt like an outraged big sister, intensely protective of this girl—and other Ninjas like her—who suffered simply because they'd been born female.

I wanted to hunt down the people who had mutilated this woman. I wanted to shake her brother and ask him how he could've let this happen to his little sister. I wanted to smack around her husband, who experienced sexual pleasure during intercourse while this woman only felt excruciating pain.

"Tell her I'll be right back," I said to Omari. I left the exam room and walked to the bathroom, where I splashed cool water on my face and took a moment to let my emotions abate. Then I went to the supply closet and got a pediatric speculum, half the diameter of a normal speculum, to make the exam more comfortable for her.

I went back into the room, performed a pelvic exam as gently as possible, diagnosed her with chlamydia and gonorrhea, and prescribed antibiotics for her, her husband, and the other wives.

After they left, Omari looked at me and said, "Are you okay?"

"No," I said, trying to swallow the anger and outrage I felt at the trauma some women undergo simply because they are born female. "No, I'm not okay. But let's keep going anyway."

As I washed my hands, he called the next patient's name.

The most unsettling experience of my first year of PA school was dissecting our cadaver, Bernie. The most unsettling experience of my second year of PA school was learning how to do male and female genital exams.

For the male genitourinary (GU) exam, our class carpooled from Yale to the University of Connecticut medical campus, about forty-five minutes north of New Haven. The coordinator split us into groups of five, and my classmates and I, wearing our short white student lab coats, paraded into exam rooms where our professional patients were waiting.

My group entered our assigned exam room to find a sixty-something-year-old man with white receding hair and a short cropped white beard standing in front of the exam table in a button-down long-sleeved shirt and cowboy boots—and nothing else. He was naked from his waist to just below his knees, where the boots began.

He greeted us warmly, and invited us all to gather around as he held his genitals in his hand and pointed out anatomical landmarks and told us what these various topographies were called.

He gave us a play-by-play guide to the male exam, beginning with squeezing on the head of the penis to see if you could express any discharge to the hernia exam, which involved jamming a finger through the scrotum into each inguinal area and asking the patient to turn his head and cough.

"Do you know why you ask a man to turn his head when he coughs?" he asked.

We shook our heads.

"It's simple, really," he said, leaning back against the table comfortably, as if he were a tenured professor explaining English literature. As if he were not standing in an exam room naked from the waist down, with five grad students staring at his genitals. "If he didn't turn his head, he'd cough right in your face!"

It was a joke. A male GU exam joke. He grinned, pleased with himself, and the smile lasted for half an hour as each of us awkwardly attempted to perform a genitourinary exam on him. After I'd taken my turn, squeezing the head of his penis, palpating his testicles, and asking him to turn his head and cough while I checked for an inguinal hernia, I peeled off my gloves and breathed a sigh of relief. I couldn't wait to get out of that exam room, get away from this man and his exhibitionism, and drive home.

But just as we were ready to leave, he turned toward the table, lowered his elbows onto it, and put all of his weight on his arms, arching his wrinkled buttocks toward us.

"And now for my favorite part—the prostate exam!" he said with a wink.

To LEARN THE female genital exam, our class of thirty-five students walked two blocks down to the Yale School of Nursing building, where nurse practitioner students volunteered to teach medical students the female pelvic exam.

The men in our class were nervous, but doing a female pelvic exam wasn't intimidating to me, for the obvious reason that I was a female. I knew what the parts looked like and what they were called, and I'd had a pelvic exam, just one, a month before I started grad school. But still. It was more than I could say for the prostate exam.

I'd run into some of the nurse midwifery students in the medical school library during my first year of classes. I knew them to be earthy, strong, liberal women who advocated home births and rhythm method birth control and sexual freedom. Earth was their Mother, and from this Earth they had sprung as fellow goddesses—or so the bumper stickers on their dilapidated Volvo station wagons proclaimed.

My classmates and I took our seats in a classroom where one of the nurse practitioner students showed us graphic charts of female anatomy. She then brought out a tray of instruments: a speculum, forceps, a vaginal ultrasound probe, and a cervical brush—a miniature plastic-bristled broom used to collect cervical cell samples for Pap smears.

She explained the logistics of a pelvic exam, and then we were divided into groups of three and taken into the next room, where there were a dozen pelvic exam tables and two NP students at each table. One NP student was lying on her back with her feet in stirrups, naked from the waist down. The other NP student was standing next to the table, fully clothed. We learned that they were "pelvic teams," and they alternated between examiner and examinee every time they taught this class.

Our NP instructor wanted to talk to our group before we began practicing the exam, which made me uncomfortable because all I could think was that this other poor NP student was lying on her back, half naked, and I would be much, much more comfortable if she could put her clothes back on. Or if we could at least put a sheet over her wide-open legs.

But the examinee seemed content to lie there indefinitely while the instructor talked to us, and she even occasionally raised her head up from the table and contributed to the conversation.

Our instructor began her talk by forming a V with her index and middle fingers. "V is for Vagina," she said in a whisper, as if there really were a goddess lurking somewhere nearby and we were approaching her throne. Or in this case, her pelvis.

"V is for Vulva," she said next. I wondered if this was going to turn into some kind of crazy alliteration exercise. V is for Vagina. V is for Vulva. V is for Vasectomy. V is for Very, Very uncomfortable right now.

Then she stopped and looked at her fingers and said, "Do you know what else this stands for?" I shook my head.

"This is the symbol for peace," she said. "Let this be a reminder to you that when you come to the vagina, you come in peace."

She turned to the genitalia of the NP patient and put her ungloved, V-shaped fingers against the other woman's labia. "Peace to your perineum," she said. She turned back to us. "Say it with me," she whispered. "Peace to your perineum. Peace to your perineum."

That afternoon in Togo, as I waited for Omari to bring the next patient in, I couldn't get the image of that Ninja's mutilated, scarred perineum out of my mind. The disparity between how we had been trained to approach women's perinea and how this woman—and millions of others—had been mutilated was sickening.

Respectful clinicians and sexual partners do come to the perineum in peace. But there are so many evil people who do not come to the female perineum in peace, who do not approach it with respect, who do not affirm its dignity but yank it away.

Sometimes V is for Vulva and V is for Vagina. But sometimes, as in the case of female genital mutilation and rape, V is for unspeakable Violence.

I FOUND OUT WHERE babies come from when I was eight years old. Sort of. I wouldn't know until age thirteen, when I read the "Reproduction" chapter of the R encyclopedia, how babies were conceived. But when I was eight, I found out how babies made their entrance into the world.

My mom was pregnant with my little sister, and a few months before the due date, my three brothers and I spent a Saturday morning at the hospital participating at a Big Brother/Big Sister certification course with other children while our parents were down the hall taking a childbirth class.

Our instructor was a tall, stout woman in her late forties with frizzy permed hair, large glasses, and a piercing voice. First she pointed to a chart on the wall that had illustrated pictures of what a fetus looked like at each week of gestation.

I remember thinking how odd it was that the sizes were all compared to food. First, the embryo was the size of a pea, then a peanut, then a lima bean, then a grape. She continued the list of produce—clementine, mango, eggplant—and all I could imagine was going to the grocery store and seeing fetuses where the bins of fruits and vegetables used to be.

And then, she said, when the baby was the size of a large butternut squash, it was time to be born. The uterus muscles contracted to squeeze the baby down and out and then—

—and then, to the surprise and mortification of every child in the room, this large woman proceeded to climb onto the table in the front of the room and balance on her tailbone while stretching her open legs into the air. She held a baby doll against the crotch of her elastic-waisted tan pants and mimicked a woman in labor. Her large glasses slipped down her nose and her face reddened as she tried to writhe, keep her balance, suspend her open legs in the air, and hold the baby doll against her crotch, all at the same time. I cringed as she writhed and screamed for an inordinate amount of time.

Finally, mercifully, her "labor" ended and the baby was delivered.

A long piece of red licorice doubled as the umbilical cord. The instructor, now standing in front of the table, took two shoestrings and tied them around the licorice about three inches apart from each other. She took some scissors and cut between the strings, severing the cord into two even halves.

Then she passed around a white plastic bowl that contained a cow's liver to show us what a placenta looked like.

After the embarrassing "labor" ended, my brothers lost interest in the rest of the demonstration and began to thumb-wrestle each other. But I absorbed everything with an intense concentration because, unlike my brothers, this was something that could actually happen to me someday.

Childbirth was something—perhaps the only thing—that made it interesting, even important, to be a girl.

WHEN I WAS in high school, I decided to get my emergency medical technician (EMT) certification so I could make sure I was truly interested in medicine before I invested time and money in a four-year pre-med degree, and so I could have a job during summer breaks to save up money for college and grad school.

The class had about twenty people, equal numbers of men and women.

Every Saturday for four months we sat in a cold, empty ambulance bay at a fire station, learning how to handle any emergency medical situation—including heart attacks, strokes, burns, electrical shocks, car accidents, falls, poisonings, stab wounds, and hypothermia. Also, we learned how to deliver a baby in the back of an ambulance.

For this lesson, the teacher set up a table at the front of the room with white bath towels, a basin of water, shoestrings, and scissors. I remembered seeing this collection of supplies a decade earlier, when I was earning my Big Sister certification from the loud woman in elastic-waisted pants. But next to all the supplies I'd come to expect, the instructor set down a Pringles can. I had no idea how a cylinder of chips could possibly be related to delivering a baby.

The instructor taught us about childbirth by explaining a series of charts. The first chart was female anatomy. The ovary is connected to the fallopian tube. The fallopian tube is connected to the uterus. The uterus is shaped like an upside-down pear, and the narrow part of the pear is called the cervix. It has a rubbery consistency and it's about two inches long. It leads into the vaginal canal (also called the birth canal), which leads through the vaginal opening (the introitus).

The next chart depicted the size of a fetus in each month of gestation—again, compared to produce. A grape, a kiwi, a mango, a small watermelon.

The third chart depicted the stages of labor. The uterus began to contract, which pushed the baby's head against the cervix. This pressure flattened the cervix, which went from being a two-inch rubber plug with a pinpoint hole in the center to being a thin rubber ring with a large open center.

And this is where the Pringles can came in.

The instructor held up the tube so the lid was facing us. "Anyone know what Pringles have to do with childbirth?"

We were mystified.

He took the lid off and held it up. "The diameter of a Pringles lid is ten centimeters," he said. "The same diameter of a cervix when it is fully dilated."

Now not only produce but also Pringles was on the list of foods that would forever remind me of gestation and childbirth. And then the instructor added cucumbers to the list of birth-related foods by telling us that a baby passing through a woman's vaginal canal is the same ratio as a cucumber passing through a man's urethra.

All the men in the room cringed and crossed their legs.

The instructor explained "crowning," when the baby's head first becomes visible at the introitus. Then the delivery, then the cutting of the umbilical cord, followed by delivery of the placenta.

We had a short lunch break, and then we came back to practice our delivery skills.

The instructor produced a life-size model. To learn CPR, we'd used Resusci Annies, life-size mannequins of a woman from her chest to her head. This model looked like Resusci Annie's missing bottom half. It was a female mannequin that started at the belly button and ended at the knees, with a small hole where the vagina should be. With the instructor standing behind the mannequin, pushing the baby through the hole, I successfully completed my first "delivery."

I completed my first real delivery when I was on my OB/GYN rotation in PA school. I was so nervous, I forgot everything I'd learned about Pringles cans and shoestrings and placentas. The attending physician put his hands on top of mine and helped me guide the baby out of the birth canal. The mother had an epidural, so it was much quieter than the childbirth demonstration I'd seen when I was eight.

The delivery went smoothly and quickly and suddenly, I was holding a new baby in my arms. It was a miracle to watch new life enter the world, and it was a privilege to be the one to announce, "Congratulations! It's a girl!" and watch the parents' eyes fill with tears as they held their daughter for the first time.

THE DAY AFTER I saw my first case of female genital mutilation, I reported to the hospital at 7 a.m. for my next on-call shift. Tanya had been on call the day before. She and Laura and I sat at the nurses' station while Tanya gave us sign-out, explaining the diagnosis and treatment for every patient admitted to the hospital.

When she had finished, Tanya went home for a much-deserved shower and nap. Laura and I split up the list of patients and rounded on them, performing an exam, ordering tests and medications, and writing a chart note for each one.

Laura looked a little pale that morning, and in the early afternoon she looked even more pale and tired. And then she suddenly ran to the bathroom and vomited. When she came back, she sat down at the nurses' station next to me and rested her head on her arms.

"I think I have malaria," she said.

I logged into the computer and ordered a malaria blood test for her. It was called a Goutte Epaisse (GE), French for "thick drop," because the test was performed by thickly smearing a patient's blood onto a glass slide and examining it under the microscope to look for the malaria parasite.

Her GE came back positive. She told me it was the third time she'd had malaria in the past year. I was amazed by her tenacity. Despite malaria, she stayed in Togo, worked twenty-eight-hour shifts in hundred-degree weather, and raised four small children. And despite how she felt this morning, she had still shown up, prepared to work a full shift.

I wrote her a prescription for Coartem for the malaria and Zofran for the nausea, and offered to take overnight call so she could go home and sleep.

She readily agreed, and told me to call her if I encountered any questions or problems.

Around 10 p.m., the hospital was quiet, so I went to the doctors' lounge and lay down on the futon, hoping to get a few hours of sleep. Just as I lay down, the phone rang, and the lead nurse told me that a man had walked into the hospital with a snakebite on his wrist.

I jumped up, grabbed my stethoscope, and ran down the hall to find a man sitting on the edge of a stretcher in the ER bay, his arm wrapped in a stained white T-shirt. He was a farmer and it was rainy season, which meant he was working eighteen- to twenty-hour days in the fields to care for his crops so he could have a good harvest. He had been weeding his fields in the dark because he didn't have money for a lamp or a flashlight. While he was reaching down to pull weeds, an echis—a thin, beige, poisonous snake—had bitten his wrist.

He had whipped out his machete from his belt, chopped the snake in half, and brought it with him, wrapped in a corn husk.

I ordered a bleeding time lab test for him and, while we waited for the result, I washed the bite site with sterile water, then covered it with antibiotic ointment and a bandage.

I knew from reading the Hospital of Hope treatment manual that half of poisonous snake bites in Togo respond to antivenin, and half don't. The snakebites that do respond are the ones that affect the blood's clotting mechanism—the hemorrhagic snakebites.

Because the antivenin was incredibly expensive, we had to determine which patients would and would not respond to it by ordering a blood test called a bleeding time. The patients who had prolonged bleeding times were likely to respond to treatment, so they were prescribed antivenin. If patients had a normal bleeding time, they would not respond to antivenin, and they were sent home—most of them, to die.

Thankfully, this man's bleeding time came back abnormally high, so I ordered two vials of antivenin to be given through his IV. I also wrote him for SAT/VAT to protect him from tetanus, and I wrote him for four milligrams of IV morphine because he was in a lot of pain.

We would continue to give him antivenin every few hours until his bleeding time came back to normal. Which meant that I was going to be up all night.

While I waited for the antivenin to take effect, I walked to pediatrics to see if there were any cute babies to hold, but they were all asleep. So I wandered into the maternity ward.

Only one of the four beds was occupied—a woman was nine centimeters dilated, and was expected to deliver within the hour.

An American family practice doctor in his fifties named Nelson, who had left his practice in Michigan to volunteer in Togo for six weeks, was on call that night. Todd had convinced Nelson to come to Togo to give Grace a break. The hospital used to have two full-time American midwives, but the other had gone back to the United States to get married, so Grace had been here by herself, doing 24/7 call, for six weeks straight.

"Do you want to do the delivery?" Nelson asked me.

"Sure," I said.

I went with him to check on the woman. She was now ten centimeters dilated, but the head hadn't descended far enough for her to start pushing yet. She was laboring like most women in Togo do—without any IV medications, and without an epidural.

After a few more contractions, we had her try pushing, but she didn't make any progress. So we used gravity to help things along. The nurses had her walk around in between contractions. When that got to be too uncomfortable, we had her labor while she was sitting on the birthing stool, which looked exactly like the ones used thousands of years ago—a short wooden stool with a hole in the middle for the baby to drop through.

A few contractions later, the baby had moved farther down. The woman got back in bed, and with the next contraction we had her push again.

"Close your mouth, drop your chin to your chest, and push," I told her in French.

She pushed for half a contraction, and then with a cry of anguish lay back and refused to push anymore.

"Push!" I encouraged her.

She shook her head at me. "No, no, no," she insisted.

"Did she really just tell me no?" I asked the nurse incredulously. I was used to the caricature of American women in labor, desperate to get the delivery over with, yelling, "Get this baby out of me!"

The nurse smiled and said, "This is nothing. We had a woman in labor a few months ago who literally crossed her legs because she didn't want to push the baby out."

Oh boy, I thought as I shook my head.

I looked at the woman again and said, "Push! It's time to push!"

She shook her head again and insisted, *"No. No pushing."*

"Why?" I asked her. "You're so close!"

She shook her head. "It feels bad," she said.

I almost laughed out loud.

"It feels bad," says a woman in unmedicated labor who's ten centimeters dilated. That's got to be the biggest understatement of all time.

But instead of laughing, I took her sweaty hand, looked deep into her eyes, and said, "I know. I know it feels bad, but I need you to do it anyway."

She agreed to try again and a few minutes later, with a final cry of agony, she pushed a beautiful, healthy eight-pound baby girl into the world.

I cut the cord and dried her off, then wrapped her in a blanket and handed her to her mom, whose tired face relaxed into a smile as she held her baby for the first time.

As I left the maternity ward to check on my snakebite patient, the word *anyway* echoed in my head.

I know it hurts, but I need you to do it anyway. I wondered how many times I was going to say that to women here.

And I wondered if maybe that's what God was saying to me, too, as I struggled to adapt to life in Togo—to the hot climate and the austere living conditions and the high mortality rate, as well as the theology of the fundamentalists.

Maybe there was no way around how hard this experience was going to be for me. Maybe I needed to have the courage to push through the long shifts, the heat, the uncomfortable interpersonal dynamics, and all the other annoyances.

As the poet Christian Wiman said, "In a grain of grammar, a world of hope." Maybe the key to new life, depth, growth, and endurance lay in the power of one word.

Anyway.

As THE SUN was rising the following morning, my snakebite patient's latest bleeding time result came back, and it was normal, which meant that, with several rounds of antivenin, we had completely reversed the toxic effects of the snakebite, and he could go home.

After sign-outs, I was supposed to have the rest of the day off. But Laura was still very ill and the clinic was short-staffed, so Tanya asked if I would go to clinic and see some patients before returning to my room.

I had been awake for going on thirty hours and all I really wanted to do was go to bed. But I knew the numbers. If we had four providers in clinic, we could see a hundred people. Which meant that when a clinician was missing, there were twenty-five to thirty patients that Matt would have to turn away at the gate. So despite my fatigue, I agreed to go work in the clinic for the afternoon anyway.

I went to the bathroom and splashed cool water on my face to wake up, got a lukewarm cup of coffee from the dining hall, and walked over to the clinic, where Omari was waiting for me with a large stack of charts. Half of them listed "*Tout les corps fait mal*" as the Reason for Visit. The phrase meant "whole-body pain" or, literally, "all the body feels bad."

I'd heard that phrase over and over again. It was one of the most common reasons patients came to the clinic. "*Tout les corps fait mal.*"

And it was no wonder that their whole bodies hurt, because most of them had spent their entire lives doing manual labor. The women carried heavy buckets of water and bundles of firewood on their head. They went through as many as a dozen pregnancies in their lifetime. Then, after the baby was born, they carried it on their back for two years.

The men hoed large fields with small, handheld tools that required them to be stooped over all day. They chopped firewood, mixed cement, and carried heavy loads of building materials.

The Togolese people who weren't lucky enough to have a bicycle or a moped walked everywhere they needed to go. At night, they slept on the ground without a mattress or a pillow. They got malaria over and over and over again.

It would be a miracle if their bodies didn't hurt after all that.

"Tout les corps fait mal" was a common complaint but a discouraging one, because the best I could do was to write them a prescription for ibuprofen for the pain and ask them to rest as much as they could. I couldn't undo the effects of living in a developing country their whole lives. Eventually, the prescription would run out and those who lived far from the hospital would have to find a way to make the journey back to get a refill, or simply do without.

Omari called the first patient's name. She was so stiff, she shuffled when she walked, and her upper body was tipped forward about twenty degrees. She was only thirty-five, but she walked with the gait and posture of an eighty-year-old woman.

When I examined her, I realized that she wasn't actually talking about whole-body pain; the pain was really just in her low back and hips. She told me her back had gotten progressively stiff over the past two years, and now her pain was debilitating.

I examined her and isolated the problem. Her sacroiliac joint (SI joint), the place where your back meets your hips, was nearly frozen.

I had a lot of other patients waiting. I had been up all night and I was beyond exhausted. The quick solution would've been to write her for pain meds and send her out, but that wouldn't solve the problem, and this woman would be suffering for many years. Or I could take an extra fifteen minutes with her to explain the problem and show her some stretching exercises that would help more than meds.

I decided to take an extra fifteen minutes with her so she could (hopefully) spend the next few decades of her life without this pain.

With Omari translating, I explained her problem, and then I told her I could show her exercises to do. I warned her that the exercises would be painful at first, but they would help.

"Is that okay?" I asked her.

She nodded eagerly.

First, I had her lie on her back and hug her knees to her chest. As she drew her knees in, she felt sharp pain, and sucked her breath in quickly. Then she started to hyperventilate.

"No, like this," I said as I pointed to my face and took a deep, slow breath in through my nose and then gently, slowly blew it out through my mouth. "Breathe like this until the pain goes away."

And to her credit, she did. She lay there breathing slowly and calmly, letting the pain and stiffness leave her back. Finally, her face relaxed. The pain had passed.

Next I had her rock her knees side to side, then hold her knees to her chest one at a time. The last exercise was to lie on her stomach with her hands palms-down next to her shoulders. I showed her how to straighten her elbows until her upper torso was off the floor (in yoga, it's called the Dolphin Pose). As she held the pose, tears sprang to her eyes as her back extended farther and her hips stretched more than they had in two years.

"Keep breathing," I said. "Keep breathing, and the pain will pass."

She kept breathing until, a few minutes later, her face relaxed into a smile. "It's better! It's better! It's better!" she said, and looked at me with surprise, as if I'd just worked a miracle.

But all the credit went to her, because she had endured longer than the stiffness, longer than the pain, and that's what healed her. Because, like the woman I had delivered the night before, she persisted anyway.

A T 5 P.M. I finished seeing my last patient, said good-bye to Omari, and walked back to my room. I didn't go for my usual evening walk, and I skipped dinner, opting to take a shower and go to bed instead. Sleep was infinitely more appealing than food at that point.

As I lay in bed, I thought about the woman in maternity who told me "It feels bad" but pushed through the pain anyway. I thought about the woman with SI joint pain whose eyes had brimmed with tears as she endured the pain of the deep stretch, but had persisted in it anyway, until the tight muscles relented and her joints were free.

Anyway.

A single, simple, powerful word.

Anyway.

Togo was more physically demanding and emotionally challenging than I had expected. I already felt depleted and ready to leave. I had no idea how I was going to endure the rest of my three-month commitment.

I had never been homesick before in my life, but now I felt something akin to homesickness—an unsettling, sinking, despondent feeling that dampened my appetite and, sometimes, literally made my chest ache. I was withdrawing more and eating less. Being alone felt like the next best thing to going home.

I thought about the woman at the airport who had asked me, "Sista, are you sure you're strong enough for Africa?"

Since day one, I had questioned whether I had what it took to survive in Togo. Now I was even more unsure.

For several mornings now, I had flipped through my Bible, looking for something—anything—to help me stay. Something to help me keep going *anyway*. Something to give me hope in the midst of an intolerable situation.

The closest I came to finding comfort was Deuteronomy 31:6, "for the

LORD your God goes with you; he will never leave you nor forsake you." The promise is repeated again in Hebrews.

The verse was comforting the first time I read it, but the more I thought about the word *forsake*, the more I wondered, *If Togo is a God-forsaken place, does that mean that God has forsaken me here, too?*

SINCE I HAD skipped my walk the evening before, I woke up at dawn the following morning and went for a walk along a narrow dirt path that wound through fields of waist-high cornstalks and knee-high tomato plants.

As I walked, I silently talked with God. The two main questions I asked were, "Why did you bring me here?" and "How can I stay?"

The path I took ended at a grove of trees at the edge of the cliff overlooking the Oti River. I sat beneath the trees, faced east, and watched the sun come up.

I witnessed the sky transitioning from lavender to periwinkle to light blue, the homes and crops and trees and roads of Mango glistening in the early-morning sun. Mango was beautiful. Heartbreaking and beautiful.

In truth, I didn't want to leave Mango. I just didn't know how to stay. I wasn't homesick, I was *heresick*, suffering not because I was absent from home, but because I was present in a difficult situation.

As I watched the beautiful sunrise unfold, I thought of something Massiko had told me on our drive from Lomé to Mango. We were talking about seasons in Togo, and Massiko said that because the dry season in northern Togo is so long, when farmers plant new trees, they purposefully give them less water than they need so the roots will learn to grow deep and tap into a more constant water source.

Now, as I sat beneath the trees at the cliff, it occurred to me that maybe if I accepted my heresickness and rested in it instead of fighting it, I would tap into a deeper source of wisdom and endurance than I'd known before. Maybe, as in the case of my patient with SI joint pain, if I breathed into this stretching experience long enough, the pain would go away and I would be healed. Maybe if I had the courage to stay in this difficult place instead of looking for ways to avoid or escape it, I would not only grow but actually flourish in this experience.

Henri Nouwen once wrote, "Let's be patient and trust that the treasure we look for is hidden in the ground on which we stand."

Maybe we don't only find treasure when we persist in our efforts to improve the developing world. Maybe we also find it when we patiently stand on the ground of relationship conflicts, monotonous jobs, family misunderstandings, arduous writing projects, disciplined eating plans, ascetic living conditions, demanding fitness regimens, discouraging ministries, and myriad other situations that don't feel good—but *are* good—for our souls.

And maybe, I thought as I brushed the dirt off my long gray skirt and began to walk back to the hospital to start my next shift, *maybe waiting for treasure "hidden in the ground on which we stand" was what heresickness was all about.*

I FELT LIKE I'D gotten off on the wrong foot with the missionaries and with the country of Togo. When I'd first arrived, despite feeling like I didn't quite fit in, I had tried to start conversations, participate in group activities, attend weekly church services, and eat meals with different teammates. But despite my best efforts over the first few weeks I was there, the experience got harder, and I liked it less and less.

I had expected to love Togo immediately because I love adventures, I've traveled a lot, and I've never been to a new country I didn't like.

I had expected to fall in love with the Togolese people immediately, the way I had fallen in love with the Somali girls.

I had expected to love practicing medicine overseas, because it's what I had wanted to do since I was a teenager, sitting in church listening to talks by missionary nurses and doctors our missions committee supported.

I had expected to love living in West Africa, because I'd been looking forward to living here since I was in high school. I had taken French as my language elective because it was the official language of most of the countries here. I had romanticized the experience of living overseas ever since I saw a low-budget film called *First Fruits* in which two (very handsome and single) missionary guys get malaria while they're ministering to enslaved people in the West Indies.

Now here I was, twenty years later, working at a hospital in Togo, "living my dream"—and it ended up giving me scarring nightmares.

I had truly expected this experience to be an emotional high. I thought I would fall in love with everything about Togo. I knew it would be physically and emotionally draining, but I thought any downside would pale in comparison with the rewarding experiences.

And then.

A few days after I arrived at the hospital, Paul took a woman to the OR who had a massive infection because she'd gotten into a fight with her husband's other wife, who bit her arm. The bite got infected, the woman had a fever of 103, and as Paul was wheeling her to the OR, he said to me, "Pray I don't have to amputate the whole arm." Thankfully, he didn't.

I arrived at the hospital the following morning to begin a twenty-eight-hour on-call shift. Paul asked if I would change the woman's dressing. I was standing at her bedside, tending to her wound, when her husband came to visit her. She stared daggers at him. He stood above her, barking words at her in a language I couldn't understand. It wasn't quite the picturesque mopping-sweat-off-a-patient's-brow experience I'd been expecting.

Then there was a woman who came in with a huge cut on her arm. Her husband had tried to decapitate her with a machete. When he swung the blade at her head, she flinched and the blade hit her upper arm instead. When Paul got an X-ray, he saw that the knife had not only cut her skin but also severed the bone in her arm.

During my first on-call shift, we had a patient who was coding, and while I was bagging her, another patient tapped me on the shoulder. He wanted to know his test results. He could see that there was a patient actively dying, and yet he thought this was a good time to interrupt CPR so he could find out if his diarrhea was caused by an amoeba or not.

Seriously? I thought as I shooed him away.

At the outpatient clinic, security guards had to escort patients into the triage area one at a time. Otherwise, brawls broke out over who got to be seen first. When I was seeing patients in the exam room, other patients often barged in without knocking, demanding their test results. I asked Omari to start locking the door.

A few days after I walked to the cliffs to talk to God about heresickness, I woke up at 6 a.m. to journal and spend more time in prayer.

I was dreading working another shift in clinic, dealing with the same behaviors I'd already gotten sick of. Finally, in exasperation, I said, "God, I love these people but some days I really don't *like* some of them!"

I felt like a terrible person for saying that. But there was so much relief in finally being honest with myself.

The more I thought about it, the more I realized that God probably feels this way even more than I do.

John 3:16 says that "God so *loved* the world," not that God so *liked* it.

God got exasperated with, and even angry at, some people he loved. Jesus got angry at hypocritical religious leaders, and cried over others who were too dense to hear, let alone accept, the good news he was trying to tell them.

I'm sure there are many times when God stands in heaven watching the selfish, insane, hypocritical, mean, dumb things we do and shakes his head. "I so love these people," I'm sure he says to Jesus. "But I don't so like them."

And yet—God keeps loving the world anyway.

Not the "love" that entails a dopamine surge or a wave of pleasant emotion, but the love that is generous to people who have not earned it and don't deserve it.

As I cared for Togolese patients in clinic, I developed a new appreciation for the God who continued to so love the world.

For the God who—was it too much to hope?—maybe so loved me.

D URING MY NEXT shift at the hospital, there was a lull in the afternoon, and I asked Raima, the Togolese nurse I was working with that day, about things to do in Mango.

She said that every weekday there was a market in the center of the village, where merchants sold produce, freshly baked bread, fabric, rice, herbs, toiletries, and "medicine" of questionable quality. But on Sundays there was a bigger market that happened at a different location that offered a lot more variety, plus live music and food carts.

I asked her for directions, and she told me that to get to the Sunday market, you start walking toward the center of the village, but at the fork, instead of going left, you go right, and it's about two miles down that road.

The following Sunday, I decided to walk to the market. There were always men with mopeds at the front entrance of the hospital who offered taxi services, but I didn't use them. I was convinced they would overcharge me because I was white—and besides, I wanted the exercise. So on Sunday morning, I set off toward the market. I walked the long dirt path from the guesthouse to the front entrance of the hospital and, remembering Raima's directions, instead of going left toward town, I went right.

I followed an eight-foot-wide red dirt road that led north. Every few hundred yards, there were narrow dirt paths that split off from the main road and led toward clusters of thatched-roof, one-room homes.

I had been walking for about thirty minutes when I came across a group of six women who were walking the opposite direction, toward town, with stacks of branches on their heads that they used for their cooking fires. There was a twelve-year-old girl with them, carrying the same amount of weight as the adult women.

"Where are you going?" she asked in French.

"I'm going to the market," I said in French.

She translated what I'd said into Tchakosi (*chuh-KOE-see*), and the women giggled and kept walking. I didn't understand why walking to the market was funny. I waved to them and kept walking.

A while later, I came across two gray-haired men who were sitting in the shade of a broad tree, drinking water from a shared tin canteen.

They waved at me, and one of them asked where I was going.

"To the market," I said in French.

One of the men shook his head. "There is no market," he said, pointing north on the road I was walking on.

"Yes," I insisted. "On Sundays, there is a special market, and it's this way."

The men said nothing more. They waved good-bye, and I kept walking.

A mile later, I came across a teenager who was on the side of the road with his bike. He'd tied a twenty-five-pound bag of rice to a metal rack on the back of his bike, but the front tire was flat, so he couldn't ride it.

As I walked by, he beckoned me over.

I crossed the road to where he was standing.

He pointed to the flat front tire and explained that he earned an income by making deliveries with his bicycle. He had run over a sharp stone that had punctured his tire. There was a mechanic in his village who could fix it, but he couldn't afford the mechanic's fee.

"How much to fix it?" I asked.

"It would cost a thousand CFAs," he said.

I opened my wallet and gave him fifteen hundred CFAs. *"Merci, merci, merci,"* he said, thanking me profusely as he kissed my hand.

"Are you going this way?" I asked, pointing north in the direction I was walking.

He nodded.

"Can I walk with you?" I asked.

He nodded again, and we began to walk together as he pushed his bike beside him. As we walked, he explained in French that he was sixteen years old, and he was an orphan. His mother and father had died of AIDS when he was nine. He'd been sent to a village outside Mango to live with extended family, but when he arrived, they refused to take him in because they didn't even have enough resources to care for their own children, let alone an orphaned relative.

He'd started to make his own living by working as a bicycle messenger and delivery boy. He earned enough money to buy food, but not enough to pay for lodging. So he carried a blanket with him wherever he went, and he often slept on the ground at night, risking malaria and poisonous snakebites as he slept outdoors.

We walked together for a mile and a half, until we reached the small dirt road that split off from the main road and led to his village. He said good-bye and, again, kissed my hand. I waved good-bye to him and kept walking.

I had left the hospital compound at 1 p.m. At 4 p.m., I was still walking on the road that led north, and I hadn't seen any markets or any signs that led to a market. Just small dirt paths that led to clusters of homes in the middle of thousands of acres of fields.

Church was starting at 6 p.m. and I realized that if I had any chance of making it back on time, I needed to turn around.

So I admitted defeat, turned around, and walked back to the hospital.

I made it back to the compound in time for church, red-faced and sweaty and overheated.

"What have you been up to?" Todd asked me.

I explained that I'd tried to walk to the Sunday market and had either misunderstood the directions or taken a wrong turn somewhere, and had ended up walking three hours north without finding anything.

Todd threw his head back and laughed out loud for a long time.

"What?" I asked him. "What's so funny?"

"Sarah, you almost walked to Burkina!" he said, laughing so hard, his eyes welled with tears.

"So?" I asked.

He was laughing so hard, he couldn't speak. That's when his wife, Beth, said gently that I had walked the opposite direction of the market and had, indeed, been close to walking into the neighboring country of Burkina Faso.

She went on to explain that to reach the Sunday market, you went left out of the hospital gate, not right. It was only when you were in the center of Mango that you took the right side of the fork and walked two miles to the Sunday market.

I nodded and took note of the directions I had misunderstood. But it was too late to save my reputation. Word got around, and to the missionaries, for the rest of the time I was in Togo, I was known as Sarah, the girl who walked to Burkina.

THE FOLLOWING MORNING, I had a rare day off. I was still in bed when I heard Todd's voice outside my room.

"Is Sarah around, or did she walk back to Burkina?" he asked Hazel, who laughed and said she didn't know.

He knocked on my door. I quickly put a long skirt and a sweatshirt over my pajamas and opened the door.

He had pulled two plastic chairs near the door.

"Can we chat?" he asked.

"Sure," I said.

We sat down, and he handed me a mug of hot black coffee he'd gotten from the dining hall.

"I have a favor to ask of you," he said.

"Okay, I'm listening," I said as I took my first sip of coffee, squinting in the warm morning sunshine.

Todd began to explain that one of the most common problems they encountered at the hospital was infertility. In the few months the hospital had been open, hundreds and hundreds of women had come seeking help because they couldn't get pregnant. It was a common problem in Togo, and it was especially problematic because a woman's value was often defined by how many children she was able to bear for her husband. If a woman was not able to get pregnant, her husband often divorced her, leaving her with nothing.

Divorcing an infertile woman was such a common practice that, before Todd performed a hysterectomy, he sat down with the woman's husband, explained that once he removed the uterus, the woman would not be able to have any more children, and made the husband promise not to abandon his wife after the surgery.

The infertility workup included a pelvic exam, STD testing, and an ultrasound for the woman, and a semen analysis for the man, which meant it was not a short visit or a quick problem to solve. The other clinicians didn't like seeing infertility patients because none of them were trained in OB/GYN and they preferred to see patients in their specialty—Tanya and Betsy saw the majority of the pediatrics patients, and Emilie and Laura saw the majority of internal medicine patients.

"So," Todd said, "we were wondering if we could send all the infertility patients to you on the days you're in clinic."

I took another sip of coffee and studied the pack of sheep and goats that were eating grass nearby. Marc let them out of the Farm each morning, and they wandered around the compound together, eating grass as they went. It was good not only because it gave the animals nutrients and prevented the need for a lawn mower, but also because it was easier to see snakes in short grass.

"I don't know, Todd," I said.

I didn't mind seeing more women, or doing more pelvic exams. I was already seeing all the Ninjas anyway.

"Why would we encourage fertility when pregnancy and childbirth put women at an increased risk for health problems and death?" I asked. "If I'm going to do women's health, I'd rather do Pap smears to detect cervical cancer before they come in metastatic."

Not only had my sixty-year-old patient died of cervical cancer, but in the past week we'd had two women in their early thirties who were diagnosed with metastatic cervical cancer as well. In the United States, it is detected by a Pap smear and, when caught early, is entirely curable. But with no screening available, women in Togo weren't diagnosed with cervical cancer until it was too late.

"In order to do Pap smears, we'd need a full-time pathologist," he said. "Do you know a pathologist that wants to come live in Togo?"

I shook my head. I didn't personally know any pathologists who wanted to live in the developing world. And sending Pap smears to the United States was impractical, not only because it would take months to get the results back, but also because the sheer volume of slides would be more than anyone could carry to the States in a suitcase. And even if we could get the slides to a US lab, how could a woman in Togo afford to pay a lab bill that would comprise around 20 percent of her annual income?

The deck is stacked against these women in so many ways, I thought as Todd sat next to me in silence, waiting for my answer.

Who is stacking the deck? I wondered as I watched the herd of sheep and goats meander toward a new patch of grass. In Vegas, they say "The house always wins." In this case, who was the house? Who, exactly, was winning when young women couldn't get screened for curable cancer?

Asking questions led to more questions, and the search for impossible answers just made me mad.

More out of courtesy to my colleagues than out of concern for—or interest in—women with infertility, I agreed to see them.

"Fine, I'll do it," I told Todd.

He patted my shoulder as he stood up to leave. "Thanks," he said. "I'll let the staff know."

I watched the herd of sheep and goats meander toward their next feast, lapping out of puddles on the way.

I already resented having to do all the fertility workups because it didn't feel nearly as meaningful as detecting cancer and saving someone's life. If anything, it put women's health more at risk. Plus, after my cancer treatments, I was infertile, too. It seemed unfair that as a clinician, I had the ability to help women get pregnant while I was completely powerless to do anything to help myself.

Physician Assistant, heal thyself, I thought as I walked to the dining hall to get more coffee.

EVERY MORNING I was in clinic, Omari met with me with a tall stack of charts, and at least half of them were women with infertility.

I always asked them the same set of questions. When was your first period? At what age did you become sexually active? How long have you been with your current partner? Have you ever been pregnant? Has your partner ever fathered a child by another woman? When was your last period? How often do you have intercourse?

One of the first things I realized was that most of the women were, in some ways, incredibly attuned to their bodies. For instance, they knew exactly how many days it had been since their last period. When I asked that question in the United States, most of my patients pulled out their smartphones and looked it up on their period-tracking app, but the Togolese women kept track of the dates in their heads.

In other ways, though, Togolese women were completely ignorant of their bodies. Some of them told me they were married to husbands who lived in Nigeria because that was the only place the husband could find work. When I asked them how often they had intercourse, they said, "When he comes home."

When I asked how often that was, they said, "Every six months."

I literally had to ask Omari to translate, "You have to have intercourse in order to get pregnant," because the women didn't understand that the likelihood of getting pregnant was directly correlated with the number of times they had intercourse with their husbands.

Others had never been taught about ovulation, that they were most fertile in the middle of their cycle, in the two to three days that fell roughly two weeks after their last period, and two weeks before their next period.

Others hadn't realized that the fact that their husband was married to three other wives and none of the women had gotten pregnant indicated a problem with the man's fertility, not theirs.

All of the husbands who had accompanied their wives to the appointment were astonished when I told them that the infertility workup included an analysis of their semen, because the problem could be with them and not their wife.

There were a handful of men who brought in the Ninja they were married to and talked about her infertility as an accusation. When I told them that the infertility workup included not only tests for the women, but also a semen sample from the husband, many of the men argued with me, or came up with excuses why they couldn't, or wouldn't, undergo testing.

One afternoon, Omari explained to a man in Tchakosi that he needed to give a semen sample.

The man shook his head and said something, which Omari translated for me. "He says he cannot give a sample today because he has knee pain."

I burst out laughing and asked, "Omari, what kind of sample did you tell him we needed?"

In many cases, the cause of infertility was with the man's semen, not the woman's reproductive system. It was especially gratifying to be able to deliver this news to the men who had blamed their wives for the fact they couldn't have children.

I asked Omari to teach me how to say "Your sperm is weak" in French, Tchakosi, Moba, and Ewe, so I could deliver the news myself.

LAURA RECOVERED FROM malaria and came back to work the following week. At the end of her shift, Betsy and I sat with her at the nurses' station and she gave us sign-out before we began our day.

One of the patients Laura told us about was a five-month-old girl she'd admitted around midnight. The baby's fever, a positive malaria test, and seizures all pointed to what is, in Togo, a common diagnosis: cerebral malaria.

When I arrived in Togo, I'd known nothing about malaria, but now I knew a lot about the mosquito-borne parasite. And I had witnessed many cases of cerebral malaria, when the parasite traveled to a child's brain, causing seizures, comas, and sometimes death.

The little girl seemed to have a bad case of it. She seized all through the night, despite multiple doses of anti-seizure medication.

Laura added antibiotics to cover her for bacterial meningitis, which was, unfortunately, also a common diagnosis. Like malaria, meningitis could also explain the high fever and seizures.

As Laura was talking, a nurse started yelling in pediatrics. "Can I get a doctor over here!"

Laura, Betsy, and I ran over to find the little girl having such a violent seizure, her head arched all the way back, and the back of her head was nearly touching her upper back, between her shoulder blades.

The girl's oxygen saturation dropped to a dangerously low point, so I started bagging her while Laura ordered more anti-seizure medicine to be given in the girl's IV.

"I don't think that's cerebral malaria," Betsy said.

"What else could it be?" Laura asked. "We've covered her for everything…"

The little girl stopped seizing for a minute, and then she seized again, her tiny body contorting violently.

"Dear God…" Laura said in a stunned whisper as the only other possible diagnosis dawned on her.

Betsy finished the thought. "She has tetanus," she said.

A S I BAGGED the girl, Laura and Betsy went to look up the treatment for tetanus. We gave lots of SAT and VAT to prevent tetanus, but none of us had ever seen the actual disease before.

They read that they needed to give the girl a tetanus shot, as well as inject tetanus serum into the girl's spinal fluid.

In between seizures, Betsy performed a lumbar puncture and injected the medicine.

The seizures made the girl's epiglottis shut so tightly, she wasn't getting any oxygen. Laura paged the surgical team to take the girl to the OR to perform a tracheotomy. The plan was to create an artificial opening below the epiglottis and deliver oxygen that way until the tetanus infection started to resolve.

The baby's mother consented to the surgery. The surgical techs came to wheel the girl to the OR. The baby's mother rested her hand on the baby's leg as a final good-bye…and that simple, gentle touch irritated the girl's muscles and set off another round of seizures.

The girl's windpipe closed again. Her oxygen plummeted to 30 percent. I bagged her, but the muscles in her throat were so tight, I couldn't get oxygen in. The nurses gave her round after round of anti-seizure medicine in her IV, but nothing worked.

Then the baby's heart stopped. The medical assistant started chest compressions. The nurses gave her multiple doses of epinephrine. Nothing helped.

After thirty minutes of coding her, Laura checked the girl's pupils, and they were blown. She was brain-dead from the lack of oxygen.

With tears in her eyes, Laura shook her head. "Call it," she said.

One of the nurses looked at the clock on the wall. *"Heure de la mort: huit heure cinq."*

Time of death: 8:05 a.m.

The baby's mother was sitting in a chair around the corner, weeping, surrounded by the moms of other pediatric patients who were standing quietly by her side.

Laura went to tell her the news.

From around the corner, we heard a scream as the mother received the news that her baby was gone. It was as heart-wrenching as the father's "Noooooooaaaaaaahhhhh" I'd heard in the ER years before, but this time, it was in a woman's voice.

It made me realize that for all our differences, some things are universal. No matter their income, race, ethnicity, or language, parents love their children and experience unimaginable grief when they die.

Slowly, the crowd of nurses and surgical techs left the bedside until just one nurse and I stood there. We removed the IV and the Foley catheter and peeled the EKG patches off the baby's chest. I picked the baby up in my arms and held her while the nurse put a clean sheet on the bed. I noticed a yellow-and-white panya lying on the floor under the crib.

Fabric in Togo isn't sold by the foot or by the yard; it's sold by the panya, which is the length of fabric it takes to strap a baby to your back. The panya under the crib was the one the mother had used to carry her baby to the hospital on her back the night before.

That was the thing about panyas, I thought as I watched the nurse pick it up off the floor. They were intended to be used as baby carriers, but all too often they doubled as shrouds.

As I detached the baby from all the medical equipment, I looked over every inch of that girl's body to see how she'd contracted tetanus—which usually enters the body through an open wound, like a cut or a burn. The little girl had no signs of any open wounds, not even a scratch. Except—she had pierced ears.

Ear piercing was common in Togo, an easy way to differentiate girls from boys, and it was always done at home. There was no shopping mall with trained professionals whom you could pay to pierce your daughter's ears for you. There were no gloves, alcohol swabs, or clean needles for sale at the market, so mothers improvised with what they had at home.

As I cleaned the blood from the baby girl's IV site, a wave of anger washed over me. I was angry that our team hadn't been able to save her. Angry at

Togo for being so poor and so slow to develop that it didn't offer routine vaccines for kids. Angry at First World parents who have the luxury of choosing not to vaccinate their kids—parents who will probably never have to watch their kids die a grotesque death from a preventable disease. Angry at the way we spend money on stupid, unnecessary things while people with whom we share this planet are dying because they lack very simple, inexpensive medical interventions.

I was also angry that the mom had to live with the knowledge that she had accidentally caused her baby's death. She had pierced her baby's ears, thereby creating a wound for the tetanus to enter. And then, by innocently touching her daughter's leg to say good-bye when her daughter was on the way to the OR, she had triggered the already irritated muscles to contract again, which had closed off her baby's windpipe and killed the little girl.

The mother stumbled around the corner to see her baby girl. She was clutching the wall as she walked because it was everything she could do to stand. I pulled a chair up next to the crib and helped her sit down. She held her arms out, and I laid the baby's limp body in her mother's arms.

I wheeled a privacy screen in front of the chair so she could have a private moment with her daughter, without the pediatric patients and their parents looking on.

I stood next to the chair with my hand on the woman's shoulder. There was nothing I could do to bring her baby back, but at least I could let this woman know that she wasn't alone in her grief.

She gently stroked her daughter's tranquil face with her fingertips, as torrents of tears streamed down her face.

After a few minutes, she dried her tears with the yellow-and-white panya. Then she stood up, strapped her dead daughter to her back, bowed to me, and began the long walk home.

THE FOLLOWING FRIDAY morning, it was Laura's turn to lead staff devotions. She chose to talk about theodicy, the philosophy of God and suffering.

She read a devotional about four reasons why God allows suffering. The reasons made me cringe because they sounded like religious jargon, and because when I was going through cancer treatments, people gave me these same reasons and they weren't helpful at all.

The devotional said people suffer because we live in a fallen world where bad things randomly happen, because God's trying to sanctify us to be more like him, because God is trying to get our attention, or because God is punishing us for sin.

The doctors went around the circle and offered their own opinions and thoughts about the devotional. There was consensus that God is God, and therefore he is justified in doing whatever he does, even though we don't understand it.

"How about you, Sarah? What do you think?" Todd asked me.

I hadn't slept well for the past few nights, because every time I closed my eyes, I saw a weeping woman walking away from the hospital with a dead baby tied to her back.

I wasn't in the mood for a theological discussion, but a dozen people were waiting for me to answer Todd's question, so I forced myself to say something.

"Here's the bottom line," I said, feeling frustrated and annoyed and tired. "There's a lot I don't understand, and a lot of things I don't pretend to know. But I do know this: God is a loving parent whose heart breaks even more than ours do at the suffering people endure. What do I think? I think God's heartbroken."

Without even realizing what I was doing, I crashed my fist onto the table and said loudly, "I think God—is—devastated."

And then I excused myself from the table and ran to my room. Once the door was closed behind me, I sank down to the floor with my face in my hands, and I wept angry tears.

Why does God allow suffering? That's the question we like to ask. The question we use to get our brain tied up in theological knots. The question we argue about. The question everyone wants to know the answer to when suffering happens.

But I realized that morning that it's not the question I care about.

Because it's too easy to blame God for allowing suffering to happen, when it's really we who are allowing atrocities to happen to other human beings.

We—especially the people who live in the developed world—are the ones who find it so easy to use the money, access, and opportunities we have to make ourselves insulated, ignorant, numb, obese, isolated, and distracted while people in other parts of our town, or other parts of our country, or other parts of our world, are suffering.

We are the ones who buy in to the lie that there's nothing we can do to help people who are homeless or unable to pay their bills or unable to find clean water. We are the ones who are selfish and lazy, and we are the ones who allow suffering to continue.

According to the World Health Organization, 5.9 million children under the age of five died in 2015. Which means that one year, we lost almost as many children in the developing world as the number of Jews who lost their lives in the Holocaust. On average, we lose sixteen thousand children a day, most from preventable causes.

Jesus said, "Suffer the little children to come unto me." But instead, we let little children suffer while we spend money on tummy tucks and SUVs and laser tag and ten-thousand-square-foot houses and venti Frappuccinos and forty-dollar T-shirts and mani-pedis and Xbox games and cruises and martinis and all-you-can-eat buffets.

Why does God allow suffering to happen in this world?

I didn't know that morning. As I'm writing this months later, I still don't know. And maybe I never will. To be quite honest, I don't care all that much.

What I really wanted to know that morning in Togo, and what I still want to know today, is the answer to a different question. Not, *Why does God allow suffering?*

But, *Why do we?*

B Y THE TIME I had been in Togo for six weeks, my French had improved dramatically. Suddenly, the vocabulary words and verb conjugations I'd learned in two years of high school French and a semester in college came back to me. Plus, I began to learn medical terms and some local vernacular.

They called West African French "Black French" or "African French" because it differed from the French spoken in France—both in diction and in vocabulary.

I'd been to Paris several times before—including the weekend before I flew to Togo—and the syllables sounded like staccato notes, precise and delicate, landing in the front of the nose and on the tip of the tongue, delivered in rapid-fire succession. In Togo, the sounds were rounder and slower, centered in the middle of the mouth and the back of the nose, influenced by the accent of local dialects.

Also, the Togolese had invented phrases that, the American missionaries told me, horrified the French. One of the phrases the Togolese invented was *bon travaille* (*bon truh-VYE*), which literally means "good work."

Bon travaille could be used to wish someone a good day at work. I heard it often from the patients lined up on benches in front of the clinic who were waiting to be seen as I arrived to unlock the exam room in the morning and prepared to begin my shift.

It could also mean "Good job," which I heard from patients after I successfully sutured a laceration or lanced an abscess or splinted a fracture.

We also said it to women who had just delivered a baby, many of whom had labored for hours in ungodly heat without medication or an epidural.

"*Bon travaille, Mama,*" we said over and over to these women. "*Bon travaille.*"

Another phrase the Togolese invented was *du courage* (*do cur-AJH*)— literally, "of courage." They used it to mean "be of good courage," or "take heart" or "hang in there."

They also said, *"Bon arrivée"* (*bon ah-ree-VAY*), which literally means "good arrival." The patients lined up on the clinic benches said this to us, too, as we showed up for work.

The phrases they used made complete sense, but in "true" French, there was no such thing.

"Don't ever say that in Paris," Emilie warned me once after she overheard me say *"Bon travaille"* to a Togolese nurse who had successfully started a difficult IV. "If you say that in Paris, they will run you out of town."

IN ADDITION TO improving my French, I began to recognize indigenous languages, of which there were dozens.

Even though French was the official national language of Togo, many people knew only their local tongue, and spoke little to no French. So even the American missionaries who were fluent in French, and Emilie, whose native language was French, had to use a translator half the time.

At the nurses' station, there was a list of Togolese aides and nurses, and under each name the local languages that person spoke. Among all of the Togolese staff, twenty indigenous languages were represented, though it became difficult because some were only spoken by one or two staff members. If they were off that day, sometimes we'd call them at home and have a three-way conversation with the doctor, the Togolese staff member, and the patient. Other times, we had to use three translators to communicate with the patient, like a multilingual game of Whisper-Down-the-Lane.

French to Tchakosi, Tchakosi to Moba, Moba to Peuhl.

I came to recognize the sound of the most common languages spoken, though I could barely speak a word of them.

The chief language spoken in Mango is Tchakosi, named after the people group that lives there. Close to half of the patients who came to us were Tchakosi, so as I sat in clinic listening to the patients talk, and listening to Omari translate, I began to recognize the sound of the language and, in the case of Tchakosi, the distinctive click made at the back of the throat that indicated "I understand."

As Omari explained instructions to the patients, instead of nodding, they made repetitive clicking sounds as he went through the list with them.

I also learned the gestures that signified mutual respect. The cultures where people would stand at the end of the visit and bow, the people who would raise both hands with palms toward me in blessing, the groups who would prefer to shake hands, the ones who would prefer to hug—and, in the case of many

Muslim men from northern Togo and southern Burkina Faso, the ones who preferred minimal eye contact and no physical contact at all.

As I taught them about their bodies, their diagnoses, their medications, and preventive health measures, it occurred to me that I wasn't only teaching them; day in and day out, as I observed and remembered and replicated their customs, I was learning them, too.

THE FIRST TCHAKOSI word I learned was the word for "ow." In a haunting, existential irony, the Tchakosi word for "ow" sounds a lot like the English word *why*.

For the most part, women in labor endured the pain in silence. But toward the end of labor, when delivery was imminent and the pain was at its peak, they often began to wail.

Why, why, why, why, whyyyyyyyyy?

I ask the same question, sister, I wanted to tell them as I held their hands and coached them to breathe between contractions, and then push with all their might.

Why, why, why, why, whyyyyyyyyy?

I ask the same question, sister, I wanted to say as I wondered why the woman whose hand I was holding was born in what sometimes seemed like a literally God-forsaken place in rural sub-Saharan Africa where she married as a teenager, shared her husband with multiple other wives, watched many of her children die in infancy, and suffered the agony of unmedicated childbirth in hundred-plus-degree heat.

Why, why, why, why, whyyyyyyyyyyy? Sweat pouring down her face, a terrified look in her eyes, as she looked to me to make the pain stop.

Sister, I don't know, I kept wanting to say. *But keep pushing, keep going.*

For better or for worse, it will all be over soon.

THE HOSPITAL LOST one or two patients a day. On a very bad day, we lost three or four. Patients died of everything from meningitis to malaria to kidney failure to AIDS to sickle cell disease to pulmonary embolisms and strokes.

Since Togolese people didn't get immunized against hepatitis in childhood, a lot of them contracted hepatitis B and C, which increased their risk of liver cancer. So we had a lot of patients who died of terminal liver cancer, too.

In the midst of all the death, it was easy to lose sight of all the good the hospital was doing. Of all the people whose lives were saved because the Hospital of Hope was there. But there *were* glimpses of hope.

One night, Tanya was on call late when a nurse's aide came running in from the women's ward.

"A woman's intestines are under her bed!" he yelled.

A twenty-something-year-old woman had come in for emergency surgery on a large abdominal hernia. A few hours later, she had gotten out of bed, saying she had to go to the bathroom, squatted over a bedpan, and then climbed back into bed.

When the nurse's aide came by a few minutes later, he thought her intestines had fallen into the bedpan.

When Tanya ran over to see what had happened, she found that it was not the woman's intestines, but a twenty-seven-week-old fetus, still inside an intact amniotic sac with the placenta lying neatly beside it.

Tanya pulled the amniotic sac open with her bare hands and started yelling orders at the staff. She resuscitated the baby on the floor for half an hour and then they moved her to an incubator.

The staff was in awe.

It was a miracle. "Intestines under the bed" turned into a tiny life now living in an incubator in our pediatrics ward.

The staff was also relieved.

Because we had all seen so much death, finding unexpected (not to mention, totally adorable) life was like a cool breeze hitting your face on an arid day.

TWO DAYS AFTER Tanya found the baby under the bed, I showed up at the hospital at 7 a.m. to work my next on-call shift. As I was setting down my messenger bag and water bottle at the nurses' station, a nurse came around the corner from pediatrics. "The baby's crashing!" she said breathlessly.

I ran over to find Betsy and Tanya already at the bedside of the twenty-seven-week-old baby, with the side of the incubator flipped open. Humid, ninety-eight-degree air was spilling into the room. It was like standing in an oven.

The baby's heart rate and respirations had dropped, so Betsy was using the Ambu bag to give her oxygen while Tanya found the supplies to intubate her.

Betsy bagged her for a while, and then the baby's heart stopped.

I started giving her chest compressions. With adult chest compressions, you put one hand over the other and use the heel of your hand to compress the sternum, using your upper body as leverage. This baby was so tiny, I could do chest compressions with two fingers.

Blood started coming out of the baby's mouth, indicating a pulmonary hemorrhage. Tanya asked the nurse to bring over the portable ultrasound, and she put the probe on the baby's head. The ultrasound showed that the baby had an intracranial bleed, too. She was so premature, her blood vessels hadn't fully formed, and they were so fragile, they were rupturing in her lungs and in her brain. And there was nothing we could do to make it stop.

While the pediatricians intubated her and suctioned her, I kept doing compressions. It was already a hot day at the hospital, and standing by a hot isolette made it even hotter. As I stood there doing compressions, I kept using my other hand to wipe sweat out of my eyes.

Betsy used the Ambu bag to breathe for the baby. Tanya administered multiple doses of epinephrine to try to restart the baby's heart, but the monitor showed a bleak picture. When we stopped CPR for a few seconds, there was no heartbeat and the baby wasn't breathing on her own at all.

But we kept going. Despite all the evidence that the baby was gone and we had little to no chance of getting her back, we kept going because the parents needed us to try as hard as possible to save their child, and because we needed this. After long hours, little sleep, and countless patient deaths, we needed this baby-under-the-bed miracle to have a happy ending.

I had done a NICU rotation in grad school at Yale–New Haven Hospital, but even there I had never seen a baby coded as well—or for as long—as Betsy and Tanya coded that little girl.

And yet.

The baby didn't make it. We coded her for nearly two hours but we never got a heartbeat back.

It hit Tanya hard.

A sob escaped her lips as she tore off her gloves and mask, wiped sweat from her brow, and ran out of the hospital in tears.

The parents were sitting on a bench around the corner.

Betsy went to tell them the news, while I began to disconnect the baby from all the equipment so the parents could take her home. It was an all-too-familiar ritual. Removing the IV, pulling out the breathing tube, peeling the patches off her chest, washing the blood away from her mouth and nose with a cool washcloth.

Betsy asked the parents if they wanted to see the baby, and they said no. They just wanted to be able to take her home and bury her in the backyard. The mom handed Betsy the panya she'd brought to the hospital with her. The fabric was a vibrant yellow, green, and red zigzag pattern.

I wrapped her tiny body in the panya and walked over to the bench where the parents were sitting.

"*Je suis désolé*," I said. I'm sorry.

With tears in his eyes, the father nodded and held out his arms, and I handed him the body of his baby girl. Then I watched as he stood and slowly walked out of the hospital with his wife limping at his side.

THE WHOLE TIME I was doing chest compressions on that baby, I had been asking God why. Or maybe, if God is Togolese, I had been telling God, "Ow."

I had seen more children die in the past six weeks than I had ever wanted to see in my lifetime. Babies who died of respiratory arrest at birth, kids who died of cerebral malaria and intractable seizures. The five-month-old girl who had died of tetanus a few days before.

I had done chest compressions on these little ones, sometimes for hours, wondering why God allowed them to be in this world if he was just going to let them die so quickly after they arrived.

And I had asked God why I existed if there's nothing I can do to fix the horrendously high mortality rate for children under five—not only in Togo, but around the world. Why did God create me to be here in a world with problems I can't solve and issues I can't change?

As I was standing at the incubator helping to code the neonate, I thought back to the trip I'd taken to Israel in the spring.

At the Jordan River, where Jesus was baptized, there's a long wall that has the verse from Mark 1:11 printed in at least a hundred languages.

In English, the verse reads, "And a voice came from heaven: 'You are my Son, whom I love; with you I am well pleased.'"

But our tour guide took us to the Hebrew translation of the verse and told us that the verse literally translates, "You are my son. My soul wanted you."

My soul wanted you.

I might never be able to make sense of the kids in Togo who die so often, and so young.

And sometimes, I might not be able to make any sense of my own life—with all my imperfections and inadequacies, I have no idea why God put my soul into this body and let me live and breathe here in this world...and then, someday, pass on to the next.

No matter how hard I try, I don't think I will ever fully understand the reason for my existence—or anyone else's. And I will never understand why some souls are here for a century, and others come and go in a matter of hours.

Maybe the only answer we ever get for why God created our souls to exist on this side of eternity and the next is our Father's gentle hand resting on our shoulder like a dove, his deep voice whispering in our ear, "You are my child. My soul wanted you."

WHEN MY SHIFT ended at noon the following day, I went back to my room, took a long shower, put on cotton shorts and a T-shirt, and climbed into bed.

The Internet was working, so I checked my email and found a note from a friend who had emailed me every week I was in Togo with words of encouragement and hope.

"I don't know why, but this made me think of you," she wrote.

It was Ecclesiastes 3.

There is a time for everything,
and a season for every activity under the heavens:
a time to be born and a time to die,
a time to plant and a time to uproot,
a time to kill and a time to heal,
a time to tear down and a time to build,
a time to weep and a time to laugh,
a time to mourn and a time to dance,
a time to scatter stones and a time to gather them,
a time to embrace and a time to refrain from embracing,
a time to search and a time to give up,
a time to keep and a time to throw away,
a time to tear and a time to mend,
a time to be silent and a time to speak,
a time to love and a time to hate,
a time for war and a time for peace.

As I closed my eyes, which were bloodshot and burning from exhaustion, I thought about the familiar words,

To everything there is a season...
a time to weep and a time to laugh,
a time to mourn and a time to dance...

But this was Togo—*northern* Togo—where the dry season was three times as long as the rainy season. Where the season with no food was three times as long as the season where food sprang abundantly from the ground.

This was Togo, where I seemed to lose three patients for every one patient I was able to save.

To everything there is a season.

But some seasons are

just

so

long.

I WOKE UP FROM my nap a few hours later. I had three hours until dinner, so I changed out of my pajamas into a short-sleeved gray T-shirt and a long black skirt, and walked into town.

As usual, when the little children in Mango saw a white person walking through their streets, they stopped what they were doing, pointed at me, and chanted "*Bachuray*"—a Tchakosi word that literally means "The Peeled One"—because to the Togolese, white people look like we've had our skin peeled off.

"BaCHUray! BaCHUray!" the kids yelled as I walked through the village on my way to the market, past the one-room mud-and-cinder-block houses, through the dirt streets where guinea fowl, chickens, and goats roamed.

More children ran to join the crowd at the side of the road, staring at me. Together they chanted, "BaCHUray! BaCHUray!" as they giggled.

I stopped and waved to them, and they jumped up and down as they waved back. Two little boys, who looked like they were about four years old, ran up to me and gave me high-fives. Then they examined their palms to see if something miraculous, or disastrous, had happened to them when they touched my white skin.

I laughed at their puzzled faces, and resumed walking until I came to the soccer field.

Twelve little boys were there, running around, using a tin can as their soccer ball. When they saw me, one of them said, "Sarah! Sarah!" and they all ran up to me.

"What happened to the balls I bought you?" I asked in French.

"They broke," one boy said, practicing his English on me.

"The balls you bought us were no good," one of the boys said in French. "We need a FIFA ball."

He meant that they wanted a real, leather soccer ball like professional soccer players used in the Fédération Internationale de Football Association (FIFA), not the thin rubber balls I'd bought for them a few weeks before.

"Do they sell FIFA balls at the market?" I asked. I hadn't seen any when I'd gone to the market before.

"Yah, Sarah, yah!" One of the boys nodded emphatically.

The same four-year-old boy got excited and ran around in a circle yelling, "Futbol! Futbol! Futbol!"

"Okay," I said. "If you show me where they are, I'll buy you a FIFA ball."

The boy started giving me high-fives and hugging me. One of the older boys knelt down, took my hand, and kissed it.

I asked who wanted to walk to the market with me.

They all did.

To everything there is a season, I thought as we started walking, the boys dancing and skipping behind me as if I were the Pied Piper of futbol.

As we continued toward the market, my spirits began to lift, and I couldn't help but smile as I experienced anticipation and joy instead of the dread and suffering that had become all too familiar to me.

WALKING THROUGH THE village with my entourage of FIFA Boys created something of a spectacle. As we walked on the main path that led through Mango, I noticed that the motorcycle mechanics stopped changing tires, the welders stopped welding, the women who were cooking stopped stirring their pots of boiling rice. They all stopped what they were doing and looked up at the crowd of boys who were running and skipping and laughing, with me, a *Bachuray*, in the center of it all.

I was worried that we would draw negative attention, that people would resent the interruption. But instead, the people who looked up began laughing and waving. Other children ran out of their homes and joined the parade.

I was glad that some of the kids who joined us were girls—whom I rarely ever saw playing outside because once they were old enough to help with chores, they spent nearly every waking hour helping their mothers around the house, or selling their family's produce at the market. I was glad I had thought to bring the six-foot piece of rope from the welcome basket with me so I could teach the girls to jump rope if they didn't want to play soccer.

One of the older boys led us to the stand in the market that sold FIFA balls. I paid twelve hundred CFAs, the equivalent of six dollars US, for a red-and-white-stitched leather ball. The boys were so excited, they immediately dropped it to the ground and began running and kicking it back and forth to each other.

Unfortunately, as we were walking from the market back to the soccer field, the girls who had joined us left the parade to return to their chores.

When we got to the field, the boys divided into two teams, fighting over which team got to have the *Bachuray* on their side. Eventually, we agreed that I'd play with one team for the first half of the game, and with the other team for the second half.

For the rest of the afternoon, I ran around the field with them, playing, laughing, and giving high-fives.

Eventually, I got tired and sat on the sidelines for a while. I gulped cool water from my water bottle and splashed some of it on my flushed face and sweaty neck. The boys kept running over to where I was, doing cartwheels and somersaults and silly dances to entertain me.

To everything there is a season, I thought as the words of Ecclesiastes echoed in my head.

I was going to enjoy this "season" of generosity and joy, even if it was just for an afternoon.

These boys—whom I nicknamed my FIFA Boys—were good for my soul. I couldn't help but smile as I watched them skipping and laughing and running on the field, the littlest one who kept running circles around me, kicking a pretend ball, yelling, "Futbol! Futbol! Futbol!"

WHEN I FINISHED playing soccer with the boys, I walked back to the hospital, ate a dinner of spaghetti, salad, and garlic bread in the dining hall, and then returned to my room to write. I hadn't come to Togo to write, but the stories were so compelling, I couldn't help myself. Plus, since there was nothing to do in the evenings, writing became a fun way to pass the time.

That night, I wrote about the baby under the bed and the thought that each of us exists because God's soul wanted us. The Internet was working, so I posted the piece on my blog. By the following morning, it had been read eleven thousand times—my most-read blog post to date. And I began to wonder if my second book was supposed to be about Togo, if I was supposed to write the stories of people whose stories often went unnoticed and unheard because they happened in such a remote corner of the world.

When I first met my classmates in PA school, we had lots of conversations about how each of us had ended up pursuing a PA degree. I told them that in college, I was a pre-med major, but after frying my brain on science and math classes, I added a writing class for fun, to give myself a creative outlet and something to look forward to. I fell in love with writing and decided at that point that I'd go to PA school instead of medical school, and then I'd go to journalism school, and I'd be able to get degrees in both fields in the time it would've taken me just to do medical school.

When I was getting my PA degree, it seemed to my classmates—and even to me—that writing and medicine were separate, unrelated pursuits. But as I encountered more and more patients, my opinion on that began to change.

A few months into the program, we took a course on how to interview patients and write chart notes. A note is broken down into sections: Chief Complaint (what the current problem is), History (details about when the symptoms started and what the patient is, and isn't, experiencing), Medications, Allergies, Surgeries, Social History (tobacco, alcohol, and drug use, sexual orientation, occupation), Exam Findings, Test Results, Assessment and Plan.

Our instructor sent us across the street to Yale–New Haven Hospital once a week to interview and examine patients. We had to create a chart note and turn it in to be graded. I always scored the top in my class on the History part of the note.

When the instructor asked me to explain how I was able to write such clear, detailed, organized history, I shrugged and said, "I just listen to people tell me their story."

Without even realizing it, the writer in me was acting more like a journalist, asking clarifying questions, describing details, and organizing the story in a way that would make sense to an outsider.

Every symptom, injury, illness, and scar told a story, and it was up to me to discover what the story was and tell it well.

THERE WERE SOME stories that patients were eager to tell, and others that they wanted to keep a secret. But sometimes, their bodies betrayed them and told the story instead.

I was on my surgery rotation when my pager went off one afternoon, and I got a message to report to OR 7, one of the smaller operating rooms. I arrived to find my chief resident and our surgical attending standing over the body of a deceased elderly man with a balding head of white hair, scrawny arms and legs, and a slightly distended belly, lying on a steel table under the glare of operating room lights.

He had died that morning in the emergency room (I wasn't sure what the cause was). But he was a registered organ donor. So instead of having the funeral home come and wheel him away for burial, the staff had brought him up to the OR for inspection to find out what, if any, of his organs were usable.

Despite their age, elderly patients were often able to be eye and tissue donors. But first, the surgeons had to verify that the patient was free of contagious diseases.

I watched the chief resident examine the man's eyes, mouth, torso, groin, and extremities. Then the attending and I helped him flip the body over so he could inspect the underside. Even though the man's extremities looked scrawny, they were surprisingly heavy as deadweight.

The last thing the resident did was part the man's buttocks and closely examine the anus.

"You've got to be kidding me," he said.

The attending looked over the resident's shoulder. He stepped back, shaking his head.

"What?" I asked. "What are you looking at?"

I peered over the still-parted buttocks to see raised, gray protrusions scattered around the anus.

I knew what they were, but I had only seen them on young people's genitals.

"He has anal warts?" I asked incredulously.

"Yup," the chief resident said. "Automatically disqualifying. If he got warts, who knows what other sexually transmitted diseases he could've contracted."

As we left the room, the attending turned out the lights and we left the dead man lying naked and alone in the dark.

Next, we had to find the man's daughter and tell her the bad news.

The ER had called her hours before to let her know that her father was about to die. She arrived as quickly as she could, but it was too late. He was gone—and actually already in the OR being inspected by the surgical resident—before she arrived.

The ER staff had led her to the family waiting room, a small, quiet space with couches, coffee tables, and lamps that shed warm light.

The three of us walked to the family waiting room to find the daughter, an attractive, slightly overweight woman in her mid-forties who sat on the edge of the couch in designer jeans and a sweater, clutching a Kate Spade bag in her well-manicured hands. Her eyes were puffy and her tears had carved pale rivulets in the thick foundation that covered her cheeks.

The attending and chief resident sat down on the couch across from the woman. I stood by the door, not wanting to intrude in the situation, not wanting to spectate in what was about to be a very difficult conversation.

The attending spoke. "We're sorry to inform you that your father passed away this morning," he said.

The woman nodded. She retrieved a small Kleenex packet from her purse and dabbed her tears away.

Then the attending said, "As you know, your father chose to be an organ donor."

She nodded and a smile almost appeared on her face, as if this was the bright spot in her father's passing. That in his death, he would gift himself to others so they could live.

"Ma'am, unfortunately, upon examination of your father's body, we discovered that he, in fact, has—"

He had to breathe and swallow again before finishing. "He has anal warts. Which are sexually transmitted."

For a moment, the woman sat there paralyzed, eyes wide, speechless. After the stunned silence passed, she said, "I don't understand. How—why—how is that possible?"

"As far as you know, was your father gay?"

She shook her head fiercely. "No. No. He was married to my mother for forty-nine years."

The surgeon took another stab. "Was your father ever incarcerated?"

Slowly, she nodded, slack-jawed at the realization. "Yes. Yes, he was in prison for two years in the 1980s for embezzlement."

The attending nodded. "Well, unfortunately, because your father has evidence of a sexually transmitted disease, he is not a candidate for organ donation, and we'll be releasing his body back to your family."

The three of us stood and quietly slipped out of the room, leaving the daughter there to process the news she'd just received. I couldn't tell what she was reeling from more—the fact that her father had died, or that, at some point in his life, he'd been an anal-receptive sexual partner.

IF WE DON'T figure out what's wrong with her, we're going to lose her," the doctor said, shaking his head.

It was Sunday morning, the day after playing futbol with my FIFA Boys, and I was on call with Nelson, the family practice doctor who had let me deliver the eight-pound baby girl a few weeks before.

We'd finished rounding on our patients in pediatrics, maternity, and medicine. After putting on masks, gowns, and gloves, we'd entered the room of our last patient—a room the nurses referred to as ISO 3 because it was one of three rooms with a door where we could keep patients with contagious diseases in isolation, away from the other patients.

My heart skipped a beat when I saw her.

She was a five-foot-two-inch twenty-two-year-old woman who weighed eighty-three pounds. Her eyes were yellow with jaundice, and there was an oxygen mask on her face. She was sitting up in bed, breathing rapidly, her thin chest heaving with each breath, as if it took every muscle in her body to move air in and out.

We listened to her lungs, which sounded congested. She had tenderness in her right upper quadrant, where the liver is located. Her lips were pale. When we pressed on her nail beds, it took a few seconds for the color to return. If it takes more than two seconds for the color to return to the nail bed, it's called delayed capillary reflex. This patient was not getting enough oxygenated blood to adequately perfuse her body.

I studied the monitor above her bed. She was tachycardic, with a heart rate in the 140s. Her oxygen saturation was 90 percent—which was concerning, because she was already wearing a CPAP mask that was delivering the maximum amount of oxygen we could give her.

We finished our exam in a few minutes, left the room, removed our masks and gowns and gloves, and washed our hands thoroughly at the sink at the nurses' station.

"If we don't figure out what's wrong with her really fast, we're going to lose her," Nelson said again.

His words made me angry. I wanted him to stop saying, "We're going to lose her," and talk instead about how we were going to save her.

But to be honest, I was not mad at him for repeatedly talking about losing our patient. I was mad at myself for not being an infectious disease expert who could quickly pinpoint the diagnosis and choose an effective treatment.

I was mad at our lack of diagnostic equipment. I was mad that we didn't have a ventilator to breathe for this woman, buying us time to figure out how to heal her.

I was mad that this woman had waited so long to come to the hospital. I was mad that even though we were trying our best, treating this woman with several antibiotics, anti-virals, oxygen, nebulizer treatments, and anti-malaria medicine, she was getting worse instead of better.

And I was mad because I knew Nelson was right. If we didn't figure out what was wrong with her, we really were going to lose her, a young woman who was married with two children.

We sat down at the nurses' station and flipped through her chart. It was her fourth day in the hospital. She was admitted for pneumonia and respiratory distress.

We pulled her chest X-ray up on the computer—and there were large white patches in both of her lungs. Both lungs were filled with infection.

At first, the medical team thought she had leptospirosis, a disease that's transmitted by fresh water contaminated with rat urine. Before I got to Togo I had never heard of the disease. I'd read more about it in a tropical medicine textbook in the on-call room one night. As I researched the disease, I remembered it was rainy season in Togo. I thought of all the puddles I'd sloshed through on my walks to and from town, and I made a commitment to scrub my feet every night to get all the animal urine off.

This woman was on the right antibiotic for leptospirosis, but she was not getting better. The only other disease we could think of that affected both the lungs and the liver was tuberculosis. Emilie, the doctor who had admitted the patient, had ordered sputum samples, which had come back negative. Often, however, sputum samples don't provide enough organisms to show up on an analysis. In the United States, this patient would have a bronchoscopy, where a pulmonologist sedated her, inserted a scope directly into her lungs, and took sputum and lung tissue samples to be tested for TB or other pathogens. A bronchoscopy was considered the "gold standard," the highest and most accurate level of patient care. But we didn't have the capability to do bronchoscopies in Togo.

Levi, a forty-five-year-old general surgeon from Indiana who was volunteering at the hospital for three weeks, was on call that day. He lived in the United States but had been raised in South Africa, where his parents still served as missionaries.

Nelson asked Levi to come take a look at the X-ray.

As soon as Levi saw it, he said, "Oh yeah, that's TB for sure."

"How do you know?" I asked him.

"There's so much TB in South Africa, I've seen hundreds of chest X-rays like this," he said.

Then Levi asked me how much the patient weighed.

"Eighty-three pounds," I answered.

He nodded. "There's a reason they used to call this disease consumption. It eats up your whole body."

Now that we had a working diagnosis, we had to figure out the best treatment plan for her. There are five antibiotics used to treat tuberculosis. A patient has to be on at least three of them to effectively treat the disease. Our hospital only had two, and she was already on them.

There was a government hospital in town that treated tuberculosis, but the problem was, we didn't have portable oxygen tanks. We only had oxygen that was delivered through a wall-mounted unit. If we took this woman off the oxygen to transport her to the government hospital, she would die in a matter of minutes.

The more I thought about the case, the faster my pulse went.

This woman was going to die soon.

We knew what she had and what she needed.

We couldn't get her to the treatment center because we didn't have portable oxygen.

We could keep her here and give her oxygen, but only two of the three antibiotics she needed.

She was on all the oxygen we could give her, and she was still hypoxic.

Her body was wasting away.
Her lungs were giving out.
We were running out of time.
This woman was dying on us.
But there was nothing more we could do.

THAT AFTERNOON, A father rushed into the hospital carrying his unconscious two-year-old-girl in his arms. Kojo grabbed the girl, laid her on an empty ER bed, stripped her clothes off, and began taking her vital signs. I ran over, and just as I got to the bedside, the girl began seizing.

Her rectal temperature was 105.3 degrees. Her heart rate accelerated to two hundred beats per minute, and she stopped breathing. Her oxygen plummeted to 87 percent, then 85, then 80.

I yelled for an Ambu bag and began breathing for her while Kojo started an IV. I was sure she had cerebral malaria. I had seen it so many times, I knew the signs, workup, and treatment regimen by heart.

She needed STAT blood work—a GE to look for the malaria parasite, and a CBC to determine if she had anemia. In young children, malaria causes red blood cells to rupture, and children often came in dangerously anemic, needing several blood transfusions to bring their hematocrit back to normal.

Kojo pushed a dose of phenobarbital through the IV. Seconds later, the seizure stopped.

He handed me the girl's chart and I wrote orders for blood work, IV fluid for dehydration, rectal Tylenol for fever, phenobarbital for seizures, artesunate for malaria.

Her oxygen came back to normal and her heart rate went from 200 to 150 beats per minute. After I wrote orders, I did an exam. Her neck flexed easily—which meant she likely did not have meningitis. Her pupils were equal sizes and they constricted normally when I shined a penlight in her eyes. Her lungs were clear, her belly was soft, she had normal capillary refill, and she had no rashes. But she was still unconscious.

Her lab results came back a few minutes later, confirming that she did have malaria, and she was also significantly anemic. A normal pediatric hematocrit is between thirty-two and forty-two. Hers was eighteen.

I ordered a blood transfusion in addition to the other treatments, and admitted her to pediatrics.

I was touched by her father's devotion. He stood behind me, watching over my shoulder as Kojo and I cared for her.

When the little girl's vital signs had stabilized, her fever had improved, her seizures had stopped, and her blood transfusion had started running, the man crawled under her crib and went to sleep, refusing to leave his daughter's side.

NELSON LOOKED TIRED. He was on call that night for maternity. I told him that if he wanted, I would take call for the non-OB patients. He nodded gratefully. Since there was no one in labor at the moment, he went to his room at the guesthouse to get some sleep.

As he was leaving the hospital, I pulled him aside. "I just wanted to be sure—if the patient in ISO 3 codes tonight, there's nothing we can do?"

He shook his head sadly and left.

Just then Ibrahim, a lanky forty-year-old Togolese nurse who was caring for the patient in ISO 3, called me over to the woman's room. Her oxygen was down to 85 percent. She was working even harder to breathe. Her upper abdominal pain was getting worse. She had a panicked look in her eyes.

Her parents were standing at the foot of her bed. Her husband was sitting on the floor. They were watching this woman struggle, and watching me to see if—and how—I could help her.

"Get her four milligrams of morphine and two milligrams of Valium," I yelled to Ibrahim in French.

"*Tout suite!*" I added, the French equivalent of "STAT!"

In that moment, I knew I had just turned a corner with this patient.

Instead of working to save her life, my job was now to help her die with as little pain, anxiety, and suffering as possible.

Morphine and Valium are two of the most commonly used drugs for dying patients. Morphine for the pain in their bodies, Valium for the terror in their eyes. And both meds are sedating, reducing the consciousness of the suffering patient.

While we waited for Ibrahim to return with the meds, I put my hand on the woman's shoulder. "Can I pray for you?" I asked in French.

She nodded. Her husband and her parents nodded even more eagerly.

I prayed for her in English—because my vocabulary wasn't good enough to pray a full prayer in French.

"God, please be with my sister," I said. "I pray for a miracle, that you would heal her and bring her back to a full, healthy life with her family."

I paused and took a deep breath. Her monitor started dinging. I looked up and saw that her oxygen had dropped to 82 percent. I hit the silence button on the monitor.

"But if that's not what's going to happen, if it's time for this woman to go Home…" My voice cracked. I took another breath.

What would I want someone to pray for me if I was dying?

"Then I pray that you would be with her now, that you would comfort her, that you would help her not to be afraid, that you would help her not to suffer, that you would let your angels attend to her and carry her safely and gently to heaven, where there are no more tears, no more crying, no more death or disease."

Her husband and parents were standing at the foot of her bed together, eyes closed, heads bowed.

"Comfort her loved ones as well, and help them to feel your presence and your love tonight."

Ibrahim was back with the drugs.

"Amen," I said as I pushed morphine and Valium through her IV. A few minutes later, she was still in a good deal of pain, still panicked as she fought to breathe.

"I need more of both of these," I told Ibrahim, holding up the empty syringes. "*Tout suite!*"

I HAVE OFTEN HEARD people talk about doctors "playing God."
   I have never heard anyone use that phrase as a compliment.

"Playing God" is, without fail, used as an accusation implying that a medical professional has crossed an ethical line, has been off-puttingly arrogant, has exercised too much authority, or has made a unilateral decision that resulted in a patient's life being prolonged or ended.

But in reality, in its purest and most noble form, practicing medicine is playing God. It is imitating the Great Physician who is intensely committed to comforting, helping, and healing. It is following in the steps of Jesus, who healed the woman with twelve years of unstoppable menstrual bleeding, made blind people see, healed crippled people who couldn't walk, and raised the dead.

When we set broken bones and carve out cancers and suture wounds and alleviate pain, we are playing God in the best possible way. We are agreeing with God that while disease may be the present state in which we find the world, it is not the way it's supposed to be, and often it's not the way it has to be, and we do whatever we can to make it right.

Medical professionals spend tens or even hundreds of thousands of dollars to learn how to heal. We work eighty-, ninety-, hundred-hour workweeks, stay up all night, take call, staff ERs that are open 24/7. We are possibly the closest that humans can come to imitating the God who never slumbers or sleeps.

The parallels between medicine and theology are deeply meaningful to me, but at the same time they add to my frustration at the way women are discouraged, or disallowed, from being clergy in many denominations. Imitating God by bringing healing and consolation to people's bodies is a gender-neutral pursuit. Why should imitating God by bringing healing and consolation to people's souls be any different?

There are an undeniable number of ways in which medicine and religion are intertwined, and even allied.

When I worked in the ER and paramedics radioed to let us know they were en route with a Code 3, a patient who was unresponsive or in cardiac or respiratory arrest, the unit secretary announced "Code Blue, ETA two minutes" over the loudspeakers, and both doctors and chaplains ran to the resuscitation room.

Medicine and religion have similar ethical and legal regulations. What patients tell clinicians in exam rooms is, by law, as private as what parishioners tell priests in confession booths.

For many years, before couples were granted a marriage license, they had to go to a doctor for blood work to certify they didn't have syphilis, a sexually transmitted disease. In other words, they had to be evaluated by a medical professional before they could be married by a minister.

Both clergy and medical professionals are distinguished by white. For clergy, it's a white collar. For medical professionals, a white coat.

Whether it's sacraments or medication, both clergy and clinicians are administering tangible gifts as a means of compassion and grace.

All too often, as was the case with the woman dying of tuberculosis in Togo, not only chaplains but also clinicians administered last rites.

Morphine and Valium, the sacraments of the dying.

Tout suite, the benediction at the end.

AFTER I GAVE her the second round of morphine and Valium, I stood there with my hand on the emaciated woman's bony shoulder for a few minutes until her body relaxed, her eyelids grew heavy, and she laid her head back on her pillow and fell asleep.

Ibrahim spoke Tchakosi, so I asked him to stay and translate because, while the family understood a little French, Tchakosi was their first language, and I wanted to make sure they understood what I was about to say.

"We have done everything possible for her and, unfortunately, it's not working. She is very ill, and she will probably die in the next few hours."

I paused while I let the words sink in. The husband wiped a tear from his eyes. The father stared at the floor. The mother rubbed her daughter's foot and somberly nodded.

"The best I can do for her is to keep her comfortable," I said. "I'll do everything I can so she suffers as little as possible."

I asked if they had any questions, and they shook their heads.

"I'm here all night if you need me," I said as I left the room, quietly closing the door behind me.

THE HOSPITAL WAS quiet, and most of my patients were sleeping. I walked through pediatrics, where mothers slept under their children's cribs. The two-year-old patient with malaria was still unconscious but she hadn't seized since we admitted her, so that was a good sign. Her father was asleep on the floor under her crib.

All the lights in pediatrics were on, and the room was very bright. When I first started working at the hospital, I had turned off the lights in pediatrics every night, thinking the children and their parents could get more sleep that way. But the moms kept getting up and turning the lights back on. One of them explained to me that they thought that if the lights were off, we would forget about their children, or not recognize if there was a problem. Even though I explained to the women several times that their children were on monitors that would alarm if anything was wrong, they still preferred to sleep with the lights on.

Every night I was on call, I walked through pediatrics and prayed over each of the children. If one of them was awake or fussy, I'd hold them and sing them a lullaby until they fell asleep.

I walked from crib to crib, putting my hand on each child's forehead and softly whispering a blessing over them, praying for healing, praying for these little ones to grow up to be healthy, intelligent, empowered adults who would be able to lead their country out of poverty and suffering.

The last crib I stopped at was the two-year-old's. As I stood there with my hand on her forehead, praying that God would wake her from her coma, and prevent her from suffering any permanent brain damage in the meantime, the father woke up and slid out from under the bed, thinking something was wrong.

"It's okay, there's no problem," I whispered softly in French. "I'm just praying for your little girl."

I knelt down next to him and asked, "Is your wife coming? The little girl's mother?"

He shook his head and told me his wife had died giving birth to the girl, and now he was a widower, raising his daughter alone.

"I'm sorry to hear that," I said. "I promise I'll do everything I can to take good care of your daughter."

He smiled and gave me a thumbs-up before sliding back underneath the crib.

I left pediatrics and went to the doctors' lounge to get some sleep.

An hour later, the phone rang and the nurse said there was a patient who had just come in with difficulty breathing. As I put my shoes on and grabbed my stethoscope, I glanced at my watch. It was 11:45 p.m.

I arrived in the ER section of the hospital to find a thirty-year-old woman sitting on the edge of the bed leaning forward with her weight on her arms, which were outstretched in front of her, gripping the edge of the bed. Like the man who told me, "Madam—I—can't—breathe," this woman was tripoding, indicating she was in severe respiratory distress.

She had delivered a baby a few days before. During her pregnancy, she had been seen at our prenatal clinic several times for difficulty breathing and had been diagnosed with Peripartum Cardiomyopathy (PPCM). PPCM is a form of heart failure that otherwise healthy young women can develop during pregnancy or in the five months that follow. Though it is rare in the United States, we saw it often in Togo. The highest incidence of PPCM in the world was in nearby Nigeria.

This woman had had an echocardiogram, an ultrasound of her heart, a month before, which showed her heart was only one-third as effective as it should've been. Because her heart was not contracting very efficiently, fluid was backing up into her legs and into her lungs, and she was essentially drowning.

She had been prescribed medications, but she never took them, and she failed to show up at her scheduled follow-up appointment. Then, instead of coming to the hospital to deliver her baby, she'd delivered at home.

The nurses had already hooked her up to a monitor, and I saw that her heart rate was in the 150s, and her oxygen saturation was 85 percent. Her blood pressure was 200/106, dangerously high.

I ordered oxygen, an IV, two different blood pressure medicines, a diuretic to get the fluid off her lungs, and morphine for her chest pain.

Her oxygen saturation came up a little bit with the oxygen, but her blood pressure didn't budge, so I ordered two additional blood pressure medicines, and I pulled up a chair next to her bed. I ended up sitting there for more than an hour, slowly pushing medicine through the IV as I watched her vital signs on the monitor above her bed, trying to give her enough medicine to bring her pressure down without giving her too much.

It was a dangerously delicate balance. If her blood pressure stayed too high, it could cause a blood vessel in her brain to rupture, resulting in a hemor-rhagic stroke. But if we dropped her blood pressure too low, she could have an ischemic stroke from the lack of oxygen to her brain.

Finally, her blood pressure stabilized. The nurse had inserted a Foley cath-eter so we could accurately monitor the woman's fluid balance. After the diuretic, the bag filled with nearly a liter of urine as the woman's body began to unload the extra fluid it had been retaining. Her lung sounds cleared up, her blood pressure settled in a normal range, and we were able to switch her from fifteen liters of oxygen through a face mask down to two liters through a nasal cannula.

She relaxed and fell asleep. Before I left her bedside, I rested my hand on her forehead and whispered, "Thank you, Jesus."

I was relieved that her blood pressure had responded to the medications, relieved that she was comfortable enough to fall asleep, relieved that her baby wasn't going to lose his mom, relieved for a positive patient outcome, relieved that, if she stayed on medications for the next few months, she would likely make a full recovery.

I can accept failure, but I can't accept not trying.

It was incredibly gratifying to care for a patient and be rewarded with a successful outcome instead of having to grapple with yet another failure.

I returned to the doctors' lounge. It was after 1 a.m. when I kicked off my clogs and lay down to sleep.

FIVE MINUTES AFTER I lay down, the phone rang. The two-year-old girl in pediatrics with cerebral malaria was seizing again.

I quickly put on my shoes, grabbed my stethoscope, and ran to pediatrics. I arrived to find the little girl having a seizure, her small body contorting with muscle contractions, her eyes rolling back in her head. "Give her five milligrams per kilogram of phenobarb," I told the nurse. "And get me the Ambu bag."

I breathed for the little girl while Kojo pushed the medicine into her IV.

Minutes later, the seizure had stopped, and she was breathing on her own again. Her father had climbed out from underneath her crib, and he stood behind me the whole time, looking over my shoulder, watching us care for his daughter.

When the seizure stopped, he went back under the crib to sleep, and I went to the nurses' station to write in the girl's chart. A minute later, the monitor began to alarm. The girl's heart rate was dangerously high and she had stopped breathing. I ran to her crib to find her in the throes of another seizure.

I bagged her while Kojo pushed more phenobarbital into the IV. This time, the seizure didn't stop. We gave her a second dose of phenobarbital, then a third. I kept bagging her because she still wasn't breathing.

I ordered a second anti-seizure medicine called phenytoin.

I checked her pupils with a penlight and saw that the right one was larger than the left, and did not constrict when I shone the light in it. My heart sank. If the girl survived—which was a big if at this point—she was likely to have permanent brain damage.

The seizures eventually stopped.

"She's breathing again," I told her father in French. "But she's very sick. We're doing everything we can, but there is a chance your daughter will not survive."

He nodded.

Just as the nurse and I started to walk away, the monitor started alarming and we turned around to find that the girl was seizing again.

Again, I called for phenobarbital and an Ambu bag.

She seized again. And again. And again. Over and over, for the next two hours. We maxed out the dose of phenobarbital we could safely give her, so I ordered a third anti-seizure medicine.

It didn't matter. She seized anyway.

Then she started hemorrhaging blood from her lungs. It spilled out of her nose and mouth and pooled in the back of her throat. I suctioned it out and started bagging her again.

Finally, the bleeding and the seizures stopped, and the girl began breathing again.

I was exhausted, so I walked back to the doctors' lounge to get some rest. Even a few minutes of sleep would be a mercy, especially since I'd been awake for nineteen hours now.

On my way to the lounge, I checked on the woman in ISO 3. She was sleeping, which was good—at least she wasn't panicked or struggling—but her oxygen was down to 70 percent, which meant she wasn't long for this world.

Her husband had pulled up a chair next to her bed and was sleeping with his head resting on her stomach, his hand holding hers.

I fell into a deep sleep on the futon in the doctors' lounge. I was woken by the phone next to my head. I answered to hear Kojo's distant voice telling me that the girl in pediatrics was seizing again.

Kojo handed the phone to Ibrahim, who said in French, "ISO 3 is taking her last breaths."

I realized as I turned on the light that in my groggy state, I'd been holding the receiver upside down. No wonder his voice had sounded so far away.

Once again, I hurriedly put on my shoes, grabbed my stethoscope, and ran down the hall.

It was 4 a.m. and I was running through a hospital in rural West Africa, having to make a split-second decision about whether to rush to the bedside of a child dying of malaria or a woman dying of tuberculosis.

It felt surreal, like a dream.

No, like a nightmare.

I CHOSE THE CHILD—BECAUSE there was a chance she could survive, and there was still something I could do to help her. There was nothing I could do for the woman dying of tuberculosis except to give Ibrahim permission to give her liberal doses of morphine and Valium if she was suffering.

I spent the next hour at the bedside of the seizing child. Between seizures, I told her father again that his daughter did not have a good prognosis. She was getting worse instead of better, and if she kept bleeding into her lungs, she would go into pulmonary—and then cardiac—arrest, and there would be nothing further we could do to bring her back.

He nodded.

As I was using the Ambu bag on the girl for the tenth time that night, Ibrahim came over and whispered, "ISO 3 just died. Can you come declare her when you get a chance?"

I nodded. When we lost a patient, we had to fill out the death certificate and then the patient's family had to pay the medical bill in full—or make payment arrangements if they weren't able to pay it right then. Then they could take the body home for burial. In the Muslim culture, they were supposed to bury the body before sunset on the day the person died. If a patient died at or around sunset, the family had until the following sunset to bury the body.

I had to declare her dead and fill out the death certificate so her family could take her home and bury her.

By the time the child had stopped seizing long enough for me to leave her bedside, I went to ISO 3 to find that the woman's husband and parents were sitting on a bench outside the room.

I put on a gown and gloves and a mask, and walked into the room to see her tiny body wrapped in a large piece of fabric. Her mom had removed one of her long wrap skirts and used it as a shroud for her daughter.

I removed the fabric from the young woman's gaunt face, and found her vacant, still-jaundiced eyes looking blankly at the wall. Her mouth was slightly open. I tried to close it, but rigor mortis had already set in, and it wouldn't close. It made declaring her dead both simple—and macabre.

I covered her again, walked out of the room, and gently closed the door.

I put my hand on her mother's shoulder. She jumped off the bench and motioned for me to sit down.

"No, no, please," I said.

A mother who had just lost her daughter was offering me her seat because she thought I was tired and needed a place to sit.

She sat back down. I knelt in front of her and put my hand on her knee. Her husband and their son-in-law had gone to pay the hospital bill so they could take her body home.

"*Je suis désolé,*" I said. I'm sorry.

She clasped her hands in front of her and bowed forward in a gesture of goodwill and gratitude. I stood up and bowed to her, and then hurried away.

Because my little girl in pediatrics was seizing again.

I LOST COUNT OF how many times the little girl with cerebral malaria had seized, and how many doses of anti-seizure medicine the nurse had pushed into her IV.

She was getting worse. Now her right pupil was fixed and dilated, and her left pupil constricted sluggishly when I shined the light.

When she was first admitted, her oxygen saturation would go up to 100 percent between seizures. Now, no matter what I did, her O_2 saturation stayed at around 80 percent.

What with the internal bleeding, the malaria, and the lack of oxygen, her brain was dying.

And there was absolutely nothing more I could do.

Her father was still standing behind my left shoulder, watching us try to resuscitate his little girl. In the United States, we'd have intubated her and put her on a ventilator a long time ago, but we didn't have that equipment in Togo. We had to breathe for her by hand, squeezing the Ambu bag every few seconds to push oxygen into her lungs.

Between seizures, I put my hand on her forehead and silently prayed for her.

I wanted to yell, *Talitha koum!* (Little girl, get up)—like the Bible story. Or, Lazarus, come forth! like Jesus said when he raised Lazarus from the dead.

Little girl, wake up! I commanded her in my head. *In the name of Jesus, wake up!*

But instead, she kept seizing. And, each time a new seizure started, I kept saying, "No, no, NO!"

In my head, I knew this girl was dying. I knew she would continue to get worse until her breathing stopped. And soon after her breathing stopped, her heart would stop, too.

We could start chest compressions, but there was no hope of bringing her back.

My exhausted heart sank with the weight of this knowledge.

After spending most of the night trying to breathe for her, trying to keep this little girl from dying, I finally accepted the fact that the miracle wasn't coming. We were going to lose her.

I checked her pupils again.

Now her pupils were as large as they could be, and they were no longer responding to light. Her pupils were blown, which meant that this girl was brain-dead. She was gone.

I turned to her father, who was still watching over my shoulder. I looked into his haggard face and simply shook my head as I laid down the Ambu bag. Within minutes, her oxygen plummeted and her heart rate became erratic, swinging from the low 30s to the high 180s, and then it stopped.

I turned off the monitor and took a step back from her crib.

I looked at the clock on the wall. "Time of death, 6:02 a.m.," I whispered to Kojo.

Her father choked on a sob, and then he took off running.

I WENT AFTER THE father to see where he'd gone.

I ran outside to find that it was daybreak. The long night was finally over—but two of my patients hadn't survived it.

I walked around the compound, searching for the father.

As I came around a corner, I saw that the sun was just beginning to appear on the horizon and the father, who was Muslim, was kneeling down on a patch of dirt, bowing toward the sunrise—bowing toward Mecca—with his eyes closed, the sun glistening off the tears that were streaming down his face.

I turned away and left this man to his grief.

And to his God.

ICAME BACK INSIDE and returned to the little girl's crib to prepare her body so the father could take her home.

I pulled out her IV and removed the sticky EKG patches from her chest. I took the oxygen saturation monitor off her left big toe. I suctioned the blood out of her mouth and nose for the last time, and washed the crusted blood off her nose and lips.

As I washed her body, I whispered to her, "I'm sorry, baby. I'm so sorry I couldn't hold on to you. I'm so sorry I couldn't save you. I hope you are safe in the arms of Jesus, and I hope you can forgive me."

The father returned. One of the other moms in pediatrics handed him her panya to use for his baby. He nodded in thanks.

I helped him wrap his daughter in the fabric that had large orange and green swirls, and then I placed her limp frame in his arms.

I put my hand on his arm and said, *"Je suis désolé."* I'm sorry.

I wasn't sure what his response would be. I wouldn't have blamed him for being angry at me—for lashing out at me because he had lost his precious child, because he brought her to the Hospital of Hope and yet there was nothing we could do.

But instead the father bowed his head to me and said, "Thank you." He gently tucked the fabric under his daughter's chin. Other than her pale lips, she looked like she could've just been peacefully sleeping.

"Thank you," he said again in French. "There is love in your eyes. You looked at my little girl with love."

Yes! I wanted to yell as I watched the man walk away with his daughter's limp body swaying in his arms, knowing that in less than an hour, her body would be lying beneath the ground, in a hand-dug grave in her father's backyard.

Yes! I wanted to yell. I *did* love your little girl! But love wasn't enough!

FINALLY, MERCIFULLY, MY shift ended at noon. I had been awake for thirty hours.

As I walked back to my room to shower and to sleep, I thought about literary character Holden Caulfield's misinterpretation of the Robert Burns poem "Comin' Thro' the Rye."

If a body catch a body comin' thro' the rye...

In the United States, I lost very few patients. But here in Africa, I lost more than I could count. I tried so hard to save them, exhausting every medication and procedure and piece of equipment we had. And then, when all of that failed, I had to stand there helplessly and watch these people pass away.

If a body catch a body comin' thro' the rye...

For a brief second, I held on to these patients, but it seemed like a force beyond my control pulled them from my grip, and they fell over the cliff to their deaths.

If a body catch a body comin' thro' the rye...

I peeled off my clothes and stood in the shower, letting the cool water wash off the dirt, sweat, germs, blood, and tears of my last shift.

I tried as hard as possible to save my patients and yet they often died anyway.

I can accept failure, but I can't accept not trying.

No. I shook my head as the cool water cascaded down my weary shoulders. I still couldn't honestly say that. How can you accept something that's inherently unacceptable?

Accepting failure felt like resigning to injustice. Accepting failure felt like passively allowing an ungodly amount of suffering to continue in the developing world. Accepting failure felt like choosing to go with the current that carried an inordinate number of souls to their early deaths, instead of swimming upstream against it.

I could not accept that the Western world indulged in so many luxuries

while people in the developing world were dying from treatable and preventable diseases.

I could not accept that death rates in Togo were as lopsided as exchange
rates, and that the rampant death rate made it seem like lives in Togo were
cheap and dispensable, only worth a fraction of what US lives were worth.

If it took five hundred CFAs to equal one US dollar, did it take five hundred Togolese lives to equal the value of one American?

As I washed off the remains of the shift in which I had lost the young
woman to TB and the young girl to cerebral malaria, I remembered the
father's parting words.

"There is love in your eyes," he had said. "You looked at my little girl with
love."

And it was true. I had looked at the girl with love. I looked at all my
patients with love. And yet, despite loving them, despite vigilantly catching
bodies *comin' thro' the rye*, so many patients slipped through my fingers, and I
lost them anyway.

There is love in your eyes.

I changed into pajamas, turned on the fan, and crawled into bed. The last
thought I had before falling into a deep sleep was, *What if love isn't enough?*

THE FOLLOWING MORNING, Omari came into the exam room earlier than usual. He was smiling as he pulled a thermos and a small package wrapped in waxed paper from his backpack.

"Sarah," he said. "You know how you asked me about what Togolese people eat for breakfast?"

I nodded. Yes—I was very curious about authentic Togolese food and tried to sample it every chance I got. I was disappointed that the dining hall served American food all the time. I would rather have tried the local food than eat another meal of chicken potpie or lasagna or sloppy joes.

"Okay," Omari said as he placed the thermos and the package in front of me. "This is what we eat for breakfast."

He unscrewed the lid of the thermos, and I saw a warm, thick white liquid called bouille (pronounced *bwee*), made from crushed cornmeal, that the Togolese often drank with breakfast instead of coffee or tea.

Then he unwrapped the waxed paper and I saw four balls of fried dough, which were the Togolese equivalent of beignets.

He pulled a chair up to my desk, and we had breakfast together.

I took a bite of a beignet. The outside was slightly crunchy, and the inside was moist and warm and sweet.

"Omari, this is delicious!" I exclaimed.

His eyes lit up. "You like it?" he asked.

"Yes!" I said. "These probably have a million calories, but they're so good."

When he finished eating one of the beignets, he got up to wipe his hands on the towel by the sink. He sat back down again and said, "I have decided I want to be like you, Sarah."

"Oh yeah?" I laughed. "Why is that?"

"I want to see patients like you do. You are very smart and very fast."

"Thank you," I said as I bit into my second beignet.

"And something else," he said. He studied the floor for a moment, and then he said, "I want to see patients like you do."

"You said that already," I teased him.

"No, no, I mean, I want to look at people like you do."

"What do you mean? How do I look at people?"

"You look at people with love," Omari said.

I thought about Massiko's words, that love looks around.

And the father's words, "There is love in your eyes."

And now Omari's words, "You look at people with love."

Omari went to the registration office to get the charts of the patients who were assigned to our clinic room that day. While I waited for him to return, I thought about the patients who had died, the people I couldn't help, the lives I couldn't save, and once again I thought, *What if love isn't enough?*

OMARI RETURNED A few minutes later with a stack of forty charts, despite the fact that we tried to limit the number of patients a clinician saw to twenty-five a day.

It had been happening for a few weeks now. Because of my ER background, I was used to seeing patients quickly and efficiently, but still. Seeing an extra fifteen patients a day was exhausting.

The following week, Matt ended up investigating why staff continued to register more patients than we had available appointment slots. He discovered that there were taxi drivers who bribed registration staff to add patients' charts to the stack of people to be seen that day. The taxi drivers were telling people in the village that, if they paid for a taxi ride plus a little extra, the driver would guarantee them an appointment that day at Hospital of Hope. Lots and lots of people took advantage of this covert, convenient "service."

Once he found out what was happening, Matt put an end to it by chastising the taxi drivers and telling the registration staff that they'd lose their jobs if they accepted any more bribes. But in the meantime, the clinic was overwhelmed. We didn't have enough benches to seat everyone outside the exam rooms. People waited for hours at the lab to have blood drawn, and then they waited even longer at the pharmacy to get prescriptions filled. The hospital's security guards had to intervene often as more and more hot, thirsty, and tired patients got into fistfights over who was first in line.

After a breakfast of bouille and beignets with Omari, we started seeing patients. I had to deliver bad news to the first five of them.

A fifty-year-old man came in with three months of abdominal swelling and right upper quadrant pain. I sent him for an ultrasound. Todd was doing ultrasounds that day. He called me with the results. "He has stage 4 liver cancer," Todd said. "Crank up the diuretics and pain medicine and call the chaplains."

The chaplains were something of a cross between pastors and social workers. In addition to providing spiritual resources, they provided emotional support to patients and families and helped them figure out logistics like financial resources and transportation options.

I had mixed feelings about the chaplains. I appreciated that the team, as was the case with medical assistants and nurses, was a blend of Togolese and Americans, so it wasn't just white people offering help to black people. The chaplains also helped patients and their families with non-medical issues that the clinicians and nurses were simply too busy to handle.

However, the chaplains endorsed a very conservative theology that was more severe than what I felt comfortable with. When they had end-of-life conversations with terminal patients, they talked a lot about hell—to patients who were already the least happy people in the world. To people whose whole bodies ached and throbbed from a lifetime of manual labor. To people who'd lost their children to poisonous snakebites and malaria and starvation. To people who often didn't name their children until their second birthday because so many kids died before they had the chance to turn two; parents didn't want to get attached to a child who wasn't going to survive.

Emilie and Marc went to visit the parents of a young boy who had died despite Emilie's efforts to save him. The father wanted to show Emilie where the boy was buried, so he went into the backyard behind the house to dig up the grave. He accidentally unearthed the bones of the boy's older sister, who had died six months before.

If living with the bones of your deceased children in your yard isn't hell, I don't know what is.

The chaplains shared the gospel, which literally means "good news," with patients, but the chaplains' version of the good news was all about eternal hell and damnation.

They're already in hell, I wanted to insist. So please just skip to the good news part! Or, as I had thought before, They're already broken. So stop smashing their heads against commandments set in stone, and start soothing their wounds with the balm from Gilead.

Regardless of my personal opinions, I realized I was part of a team that was bigger than me, working for a hospital funded by a very conservative Baptist missionary organization, and so despite my reservations I did call the chaplains. Often.

I PAGED THE CHAPLAINS for my fifty-year-old patient with liver cancer. Brett and Atsu arrived a few minutes later and took the patient to an empty exam room next door. They made sure he understood his diagnosis and the fact that he would likely die in the next few days or weeks. They made sure he had family and friends to care for him, and asked if he had any further questions.

Then they explained hell to him, a place where people suffer eternal torment if they haven't asked Jesus to be their Savior. They asked him if he wanted to pray the Sinner's Prayer, repenting of a lifetime of sin, asking God for mercy and forgiveness.

The patient said he'd think about it. Then he slowly made his way to the pharmacy to fill his prescriptions for diuretics and pain medicine. Unfortunately, while we had IV narcotics to treat pain in hospitalized patients, the only pill form of pain medicine we had in our pharmacy, in addition to ibuprofen and Tylenol, was tramadol—a medicine similar to codeine that wasn't even considered a controlled substance in the United States until 2014. It wasn't nearly strong enough to treat the excruciating pain of metastatic cancer, but it was all we had.

If patients requested it, we would admit them for palliative, or hospice, care so they could get IV medicine for pain and anxiety. But it cost several thousand CFAs a day, which most patients couldn't afford. Instead of getting admitted to the hospital, most of our critically ill patients who were beyond help, like those who had major strokes or terminal cancer, ended up going home to die.

Later that morning, I saw a sixty-two-year-old woman who had been seen in the clinic for congestive heart failure several times. Her repeat echocardiogram that day showed that despite being on the highest doses of all the medicines we could give her, her heart function was rapidly deteriorating. "Crank up the diuretics and call the chaplains," Todd said again.

Then there was a seventeen-year-old boy whose X-ray showed a large tumor in his femur, or thighbone. He likely had an osteosarcoma, an aggressive bone tumor with a miserable survival rate.

A thirty-year-old was having a miscarriage, her third one so far this year.

Over and over and over again, I felt my heart sink as I looked at their ultra-sound reports and lab results and X-rays. Over and over again, with Omari translating, I had to deliver bad news.

Omari was very stoic, and very professional.

The next patient was a forty-five-year-old man whose lab results showed he had hepatitis B. I explained his diagnosis, and that people with hepatitis are at a higher risk for liver cancer and liver failure.

"Is there no medicine?" he asked.

I shook my head.

"Not even in America?" he asked.

His question caught me off guard. How could I tactfully answer it?

"Well, actually, yes, in America we do have medicine for hepatitis," I said.

"Okay!" He clapped his hands and leaned back in his chair. "Then please get me this medicine!"

I looked at Omari helplessly, searching for the words to explain reality.

"I can't," I told the patient. "I can't get you the medicine."

He looked confused. "But you said in America you have this medicine. And you are American, so you can please get it for me."

I explained that it didn't work like that. First of all, the amount it would cost for one month of medicine was more than this man, who worked in the fields and sold his produce at the market, would probably earn in his lifetime. And second, he would have to go to the United States to get the prescription for it.

I felt helpless as I watched the hope drain from his eyes.

I wondered what Omari thought of me, now that he had witnessed me tell one of his fellow countrymen that yes, there was a cure for his disease—but it was in America and no, he couldn't have it.

WE WERE SUPPOSED to have a lunch break from noon to 2 p.m., but we had so many patients to see, we continued working until 1 p.m. I ate lunch, lay down for a few moments under the fan in my room, then drank a large cup of coffee before returning to the clinic.

It was hot, I was tired from working a string of on-call shifts the week before, and I was tired of delivering bad news to patients. I was grateful for Omari, though. He translated efficiently, he helped control the stream of patient traffic, and he always had a good attitude.

I had discovered that he loved Coke, which was sometimes hard to find in the village. But there was a fridge in the dining hall for the Americans, where we could get a cold can of soda or juice for a dollar, so I returned from lunch with an ice-cold can of Coke for him.

His eyes lit up. He cracked it open and drank the entire can in seconds. Then he picked up a chart and called our next patient.

The afternoon was an improvement from the morning. The caffeine from the coffee I'd drunk after lunch kicked in and I had more energy, plus a cool wind began to blow across the fields, which was a welcome relief from the heat. And instead of having to deliver bad news, I was able to deliver good news to a string of patients instead.

The first patient of the afternoon was a woman I had seen weeks before for infertility. Her ultrasound was normal, she didn't have any sexually transmitted infections, and her husband's semen analysis had been normal. But as I had worked my way through the standard list of questions, I'd learned that they had only been having intercourse once or twice a month because the husband was a long-distance taxi driver whose trips often took him out of the country, to Burkina Faso or Ghana or Nigeria. I explained that they needed to have sex more frequently, and they especially needed to have sex when she was ovulating. I prescribed her Clomid, a medication that increases ovulation, as well and asked her to return in six months or when she missed her next period—whichever came first.

She was back because she had missed her period. I sent her to the lab for a urine pregnancy test, and the result came back positive.

"Congratulations, you're pregnant!" I said as I gave the woman a hug and shook the husband's hand. They were both beaming. I prescribed her prenatal vitamins and scheduled her an appointment in the prenatal clinic.

Then I had a follow-up appointment with a Peripartum Cardiomyopathy patient whose echocardiogram showed that her heart had regained its full function.

My last patient of the day was a three-year-old girl whom I'd cared for two weeks before in the hospital, where she had been admitted with cerebral malaria. Much like the two-year-old girl who'd died, this girl came in with a high fever, tachycardia, and seizures. I had admitted her and ordered exactly the same labs and the same treatment regimen for both girls. I had stayed up most of the night, bagging this girl whenever she had a seizure.

But then, just as the two-year-old girl had taken a turn for the worse in the middle of the night, this little girl had taken a turn for the better. By the following morning, we were able to stop the anti-seizure meds. After two blood transfusions, her hematocrit came back up to normal. Two days later, she was discharged from the hospital, and now she was back to follow up.

Her parents were Muslim, and they had dressed her in a long skirt and a matching headscarf. She sat on her father's knee on the bench outside while they waited for their turn. When Omari brought them into the exam room, the little girl ran to me with outstretched arms and climbed into my lap.

I was surprised, because a lot of children who have had IVs and other painful procedures are reticent to approach someone wearing a stethoscope. And also, moms in the village commonly threatened their children that if they didn't behave, a *Bachuray* would come and eat them. So when they saw a white person, children often ran away screaming.

But this girl was different. She sat in my lap and played with my stethoscope while I chatted with her parents. Then I gently laid her on the table and did a thorough exam, which was completely normal. She had made a full recovery. If I hadn't resuscitated her myself, I would've thought the girl in

front of me was a completely different child from the one who was unconscious and seizing two weeks ago.

I picked her up from the table and she wrapped her arms around my neck
and touched her forehead to mine. I smiled, thinking about how likely it was
that she would have died if the hospital hadn't been here.

Sometimes I tried and failed, but sometimes all the trying resulted in
unbelievably gratifying success. For a moment, as I held the little girl, the
world seemed right again as I basked in the reality that, in this case, my efforts
had paid off.

I hugged her so long, she started to wiggle to get free.

But I didn't want to let her go.

THE GOOD THING about Togo is..." Tanya began one morning as we were starting a shift together, sitting at the nurses' station, reviewing the list of patients we were caring for that day.

My ears perked up.

I had been here for two months now, and I'd never heard that phrase. "The good thing about Togo..."

She had my full attention.

"The good thing about Togo is that there aren't as many burn victims here as in East Africa." She went on to explain that in countries with mountainous regions, like Kenya, there are a lot more fires built because it gets so cold at the high altitudes. And because they build a lot of fires, there are a lot more kids who get burned.

For the three months I was in Togo, I only saw two burn victims. One was a ten-year-old boy who had fallen into a fire hands-first, and needed to have most of his fingers amputated. Every morning after his surgery, the nurse's aide changed his bandages, and the boy shrieked in pain. "Why, why, why, why, why?" he screamed in Tchakosi. His piercing screams echoed down the halls so loudly, they made everyone stop in their tracks.

I heard him screaming one morning as Tanya was giving sign-out to Emilie and me at the nurses' station at the start of our shift. The screaming continued for several minutes, and finally, I couldn't take it anymore. I slammed my hand down onto the countertop and yelled, "Can someone please get that kid to stop screaming?!"

I realized the second the words came out that they didn't convey what I meant to say. I didn't mean to imply that the child was doing something wrong, I meant that someone needed to order him enough pain medication to make him more comfortable during the bandage changes. I meant that it was our job to get him to stop screaming, not his.

I HAVE ALWAYS BEEN empathetic to pain control. After my mastectomy at age twenty-seven, I was in so much pain, I was shaking. Some of my friends from PA school were now working at the hospital. One of them came to visit me and saw how much pain I was in and wrote an anonymous order in my chart for the pain management team to come see me. By the time they figured out what medicine worked best for me, I had been in intractable pain for four days. Ninety-six hours of unforgettable torture.

But even before that experience, I used my vivid imagination to put myself in patients' shoes, which meant I often felt their pain.

When I was getting my EMT certification, one of our lecturers was a paramedic who used to enjoy telling us "war stories" from the field. Some of his favorites were about rollover car accidents that required the fire department to use the Jaws of Life, a large tool that could cut through a car's metal frame, to get the victim out. Inevitably, the person's body was mangled. Sometimes they were already dead, sometimes they were unconscious, sometimes they were screaming in pain.

The medic was telling me a story about a bad car accident one afternoon during a lunch break, and I cringed as he described the person's injuries.

"Sarah, you have to stop doing that," he said.

"Stop doing what?" I asked.

"Cringing," he said. "When I talk about accidents, I can tell that you're feeling the injuries I describe."

I nodded emphatically.

"Well, stop it," he said. "If you feel a person's pain, you cannot help them."

And to some extent, he was right. Sometimes my empathy was a liability. In some cases what a patient needed most was for me *not* to feel their pain so I could think clearly and act quickly.

But other times, empathy was an asset because it compelled me to keep the Golden Rule, to do unto others as I would have them do unto me.

WHEN I WAS in PA school, I was required to do an eight-week internal medicine clinical rotation, and I had to take overnight call every fourth night.

One morning, after I had been up all night, our team rounded on our patients with the attending physician. After rounds, those of us who had been on call the night before were allowed to go home.

The last patient we saw on rounds was an eighty-eight-year-old woman with congestive heart failure whose heart was functioning at 20 percent of normal capacity. A few days before, she'd come into the ER with a fever, abdominal pain, and vomiting. Her ultrasound and blood work showed that she had large gallstones, and her gallbladder was infected. If it had been any other patient, the surgeons would've taken her to the OR that night to do a cholecystectomy, or gallbladder removal.

However, the woman's heart was too weak for surgery. If they sedated her, it was very likely she would never wake up.

She was going to die either way—either from heart failure during surgery, or from a massive infection that would develop when the bacteria in her gallbladder spread to her bloodstream.

As our team stood over her bed, the woman moaned in pain. When the attending touched the woman's abdomen, she wailed.

The resident taking care of her said the woman was significantly dehydrated from the vomiting, so her veins were difficult to find, and the nurses hadn't been able to start an IV. They'd tried to give her Vicodin pills, but every time she swallowed them, she vomited them up again. They had tried rectal Tylenol, which diminished her fever, but it wasn't strong enough to touch her pain.

The resident said they could take her to interventional radiology to place an IV in a deeper blood vessel using ultrasound guidance.

"But…" The resident shrugged.

The attending physician nodded in agreement. "I wouldn't worry about it," she said. "It'll just be a few more days anyway."

And with that, we left the room. Rounds were finished, so the attending told me I could go home. But I couldn't go home and sleep when I knew there was someone suffering like this.

In the year between college and grad school, I'd worked as a phlebotomist to save up money for school. I went all over the hospital drawing blood from patients when the nurses couldn't find veins or didn't have time to try. I knew how to find veins no one else could, and I thought maybe, just maybe, I could find this woman's veins, too.

So instead of going home after rounds finished, I went to the nurses' station and retrieved the IV-starting kit, which had a blue rubber tourniquet, gloves, alcohol swabs, gauze pads, and IV catheters.

I quietly walked into the woman's room and sat on her bed. She moaned as I took her hand in mine.

"I'm going to try to start an IV on you, okay?" I asked her. She slowly nodded, without opening her eyes.

I put the tourniquet around her forearm and waited for a minute to let veins swell with blood and become more apparent. I remembered from my phlebotomy training that the best technique to find a vein is to go by what you feel, not by what you see. There are many superficial blood vessels you can see, but often they're not large enough to insert a needle into. The larger vessels are deeper—less visible, but more conducive to a blood draw.

I closed my eyes and rubbed my thumb across the back of her hand. I felt nothing except her fragile bones and tendons. I waited a minute and tried again. Nothing.

I moved my thumb to the side of her thumb. Then the back of her wrist. Then the front of her forearm. Then the back of her forearm. Nothing. Still nothing.

Finally, I felt a vein along the side of her forearm, a few inches below her elbow.

I wiped the site with alcohol, then uncapped a small IV needle.

"You might feel a poke," I warned her.

I inserted the needle beneath the skin and watched for blood to appear in the clear tube attached to the needle—an event that's called the flash. It lets you know that the needle has hit a blood vessel.

There was no flash. Without removing the needle from the skin, I pulled back a little bit and inserted it again at a slightly different angle.

Bingo.

There was a flash. I pulled the needle out, leaving the plastic IV catheter in place just beneath the skin. Blood started pouring out, and I realized the tourniquet was still on. I pulled it off, taped the catheter down, and attached a small syringe of saline to it. I pushed the plunger on the saline syringe, and it went through the IV easily. The IV was good.

A FTER SUCCESSFULLY STARTING the woman's IV, I went to the nurses' station, wrote orders in the woman's chart for IV fluids and morphine, and handed it to her nurse.

The nurse rolled her eyes at me. "Honey, are you blind? She doesn't have an IV."

"She does now," I said as I picked up my bag and walked away.

The following morning, we rounded on the woman again. This time, her adult daughter was sitting in a chair at the bedside, holding her mom's hand.

"The nurses said the student got the IV. Was that you?" the daughter asked me.

I nodded.

The woman gave me a big hug.

"Thank you, thank you, thank you," she said. "Mom is so much more comfortable now."

When I was in high school, I watched a movie where a new dad thanks the surgeon who did a crash C-section on his wife and saved her life along with that of the new baby. The surgeon simply said, "My pleasure."

I decided that if a patient ever said thank you to me, that would be the line I would use.

So after the woman hugged me, I nodded and said, "My pleasure."

In Togo that morning, as the boy getting his bandages changed was screaming, "*Why, why, why?*" I asked Tanya if I could write him an order for pain medicine.

"No," she said tersely. "He's a surgical patient. The surgeons don't like it when we write orders for their patients."

We went back to sign-outs, but it was hard to hear what Tanya and Emilie were saying because the boy's screams were so loud.

THE SECOND BURN patient came in a few days later. She was a two-year-old girl who had pulled a pot of boiling water on top of herself and sustained burns to more than 70 percent of her body. Her mom took her to a marabout and then an herbalist. She didn't come to the hospital until three days after the child was burned, and by then the girl was massively dehydrated from the fluid seeping out of the scalded skin. And the burns were infected.

Even in highly specialized burn units in the United States, the survival rate of patients with 70 percent burns is abysmal. Here in Togo, where we had no burn unit and the girl's burns were three days old and infected, she had almost no chance of making it out of the hospital alive.

But we tried. We admitted her to pediatrics and ordered antibiotics, IV fluids, and pain medication.

As she lay in her crib in pediatrics, barely conscious, she whimpered nonstop. If her mom touched her arm or leg, the little girl would start screaming.

One morning, I was doing rounds in pediatrics. After examining one child with malaria, I washed my hands at the sink, but there was no towel to dry them with. The next patient on my list to see was the little girl with burns. She was whimpering. I put my hand, which was still wet with cool water, on her forehead—and suddenly, she stopped whimpering.

That night, I walked through the pediatrics ward to pray over the kids, carefully stepping over the moms who were sleeping on mats next to their children's cribs.

The burn patient was whimpering. Her mom had gone home to get some food and a change of clothes, and would be returning in the morning.

I washed my hands with cold water and put my hand on the little girl's forehead, and she became quiet.

I wanted to sing her a lullaby, to send her off to sleep, to put her out of the pain that a simple, tragic accident was forcing her to undergo.

What do you sing to a child who is in such pain? What do you sing to a toddler who's dying?

In a hushed whisper, I began to sing,

Swing low, sweet chariot
Comin' for to carry me home
Swing low, sweet chariot
Comin' for to carry me home.

I sang the chorus a few times, and, when she seemed to have fallen asleep, I quietly stepped away from her crib.

Immediately, she began to whimper again.

So I returned, put my hand on her forehead, and for two more hours, I sang the simple lines over and over and over again.

Swing low, sweet chariot
Comin' for to carry me home.

A FEW DAYS LATER I was on call again, and there was a torrential rainstorm in the afternoon. In the middle of the storm, one of our security guards burst through the door yelling in French, "His intestines are leaving! His intestines are leaving!"

Behind him was a father carrying an eight-year-old boy in his arms. Several dirty towels and shirts were piled onto the boy's abdomen. As the father laid his son on a gurney, the security guard told me the boy had been kicked in the stomach by a cow.

And now his intestines were leaving.

I quickly worked to get the towels off the boy's stomach and then lifted his shirt to see that he had not been kicked, but gored by the horn of a steer. It had torn through the skin and muscle covering the boy's abdomen, and now his intestines were spilling through the tear, piled onto the outside of his stomach.

One of the nurses paged Todd, who was the on-call surgeon that day.

I put on gloves, then poured sterile water onto sterile gauze, and covered his abdomen with the wet gauze so the intestines didn't dry out. A nurse started two large-bore IVs with fluid. Another nurse cut off the boy's dirty, rain-drenched clothes.

As we worked quickly to care for him and get him prepped for surgery, the boy was eerily calm. Instead of screaming or crying, he lay on the gurney in wide-eyed shock, staring up at me.

The nurse gave him two shots, one in each thigh, for SAT and VAT. He didn't flinch or blink.

As we waited for Todd, I stood at the boy's side, holding his right hand with mine, putting my left hand on his forehead. He didn't speak English or French, so there was nothing I could say to comfort him. Instead, as he was studying my face, I gave him a smile, and his face relaxed a little bit.

Todd came running down the hall with two surgical techs, and they whisked the boy off to surgery. The operation took less than an hour. Thankfully, the steer's horn had only torn through the stomach wall, not through the intestines themselves. So Todd just had to push the intestines back in, and then sew the hole closed.

That night, when all the kids in pediatrics were asleep, I walked by their beds, putting my hand on each of their foreheads and praying a blessing over them.

I sang "Swing Low, Sweet Chariot" to the little girl with burns until she stopped whimpering and fell asleep.

I moved to the next crib and prayed for a five-year-old boy who was recovering from cerebral malaria. He slowly opened his eyes and looked at me. I smiled at him. He studied my face until his heavy eyelids slowly closed again.

Two days later, the boy whose intestines had left was discharged from the hospital. The nurses and I clapped for him as he walked out the front door with his parents.

As I watched him leave, I wondered if Togolese parents are like American parents, reminding children of the medical adventures they've had during their childhood.

"Remember that time you threw up on Grandma's shoes at Uncle Tim's wedding? Remember the time you crashed your bike into a parked car and broke your arm? Remember when you had to get stitches in your chin when you were four?"

I wondered if Togolese kids would hear stories as they get older. "Remember that time you were having a seizure and we took you to the Hospital of Hope? Remember when you got gored by a steer in the middle of the rainstorm and your dad picked you up and sprinted to the hospital with you in his arms?"

Or maybe these kids will remember all on their own the times they were sick and came here. The times we gave them medicine, and they felt better. The night they were lying in their hospital bed with a high fever, when they opened their eyes to find a *Bachuray* woman with her hand on their forehead, smiling, praying over them while they were sleeping.

O N MY NEXT on-call shift, I worked with Laura. I was returning from radiology, where I'd just wheeled a patient for a chest X-ray, when I heard a loud commotion and saw Laura and two nurses running toward an ER bed with the crash cart and an Ambu bag.

And then, a second later, all the nurses slowly walked away.

As the crowd dispersed, I saw a three-year-old girl's limp body on the gurney. Laura had her hand on the girl's chest, and was slowly shaking her head as she spoke to the girl's father.

"She was already gone," Laura said to the father in French. "When you brought your little girl to us, she was already gone."

The father began to cry. The little girl had vomited a few times the night before, he said, but it didn't seem to be anything serious. He had told the mother that if the girl was still sick in the morning, they would bring her to the hospital. The little girl had vomited twice that morning, so the father carried her to the hospital.

Sometime between when he left the house and when he arrived at the hospital, his little girl had passed away in his arms.

Her body was still warm when she arrived, but she had no heartbeat and her pupils were blown—her brain had already stopped working from the lack of oxygen.

The chaplains came to pray with the father, and a few minutes later he wrapped the little girl in a bright-blue panya of fabric. I held the door open for him as he carried her body out. The mother was outside, sobbing, holding herself up against the wall. The father strapped the dead little girl to the mother's back and, weeping, they slowly walked toward the main road.

After that, we admitted a five-year-old boy who came in with fevers and a nosebleed. At first we thought maybe he had leukemia, but his white blood cell count was normal. Then he vomited blood. Then he passed bloody stools. We ordered all the tests we could think of, and they all came back normal.

"I hope he doesn't have Ebola," Laura whispered as we looked over his labs, trying to find an explanation for why this boy was bleeding out of every orifice.

When the boy first came in, he was tired but awake, lying on the gurney, asking for his mom.

"She's coming," the father said to him. "She's coming." The boy seemed content with that, and he fell asleep for a while.

In the middle of the night, he started seizing. Then he stopped breathing.

He got medicine to stop the seizures, and his breathing went back to normal, but he never regained consciousness.

"I'm afraid your son is bleeding into his brain," Laura told the father. "And there's nothing more we can do."

He nodded his understanding. And then he spent the night in his son's small bed in pediatrics, sitting up against the headboard, cradling his son's head in his lap.

Two of Laura's sons had malaria. I offered to take call that night so she could go home.

At 1 a.m., I was asleep on the futon in the doctors' lounge when the phone rang. A woman had walked into the hospital with a fever, tachycardia, and low blood pressure.

I went to examine her, then ordered labs. Her malaria test came back positive, so I ordered IV fluids, Tylenol, and Coartem.

When I finished taking care of her, a forty-two-year-old man walked in. He'd had surgery to repair a hernia the week before, and now, for the past twenty-four hours, he'd been unable to urinate.

"Put in a Foley catheter and see how much urine you can get out," I told the nurse. "In the morning, the surgery team can come see him."

Then I was called to the bedside of a twenty-three-year-old woman who had severe abdominal pain. The pain had started three months before. She had lost so much weight, she looked skeletal. The surgeons had done an exploratory laparotomy to discover the cause of her symptoms, but they hadn't found anything during surgery.

"She needs a CT scan, a colonoscopy and upper endoscopy, and some specialized labs," Todd had said the day before. But the Hospital of Hope didn't have any of those resources. All we could do was give her medicine for pain and nausea.

The woman was writhing in her bed, doubled over with pain. Then she vomited onto the floor.

I told her nurse to double the morphine dose, and I added another anti-nausea medicine.

Then I returned to the doctors' lounge and fell asleep.

THE PHONE RANG, waking me out of a deep sleep.

It was a Togolese nurse's aide speaking rapid French.

"Wait, wait, I don't understand," I said.

Then he said in deliberate, thickly accented English, "Come now. He's not breathing."

I thought he meant "she." I thought either the woman with the abdominal pain, or the woman I'd admitted with malaria, was decompensating.

I put on my shoes, grabbed my stethoscope, and ran down the hall. Before I opened the screen door, I heard the sound of chest compressions. The regular, rapid thud of the mattress hitting the metal bed frame.

I came around the corner and saw a crowd of nurses and nurse's aides standing over the bed of the man who had come in unable to urinate.

"What happened?" I asked. Just an hour before, he had been awake and talking, with completely normal vital signs. How did urinary retention turn into cardiac arrest?

"His friend couldn't wake him up, so he started yelling for a nurse," Mallory, one of the American nurses, said. "I ran over to find him in full arrest."

He had no pulse, and he wasn't breathing.

While the aide did chest compressions, Mallory started an IV and gave him a dose of epinephrine.

I stood at the head of the bed and bagged him.

After the epi, he was still pulseless.

We gave him another round.

We continued CPR.

Still no pulse.

Another round of epi.

More CPR.

There were three Togolese nurse's aides who stood side by side at the bed, taking turns doing chest compressions. Every time we stopped CPR to check for a pulse, the next aide would step up and do the next round of chest compressions. Then they'd switch again. Their movements were smooth and their transitions were seamless, like a choreographed dance.

We coded the man for twenty minutes, and never got a pulse back.

I finally conceded that he was gone—though why he had died was still a complete mystery. When I talked to Todd about the case the following morning, his best guess was that the man had undiagnosed kidney failure, and his potassium suddenly spiked, sending him into cardiac arrest.

"There's nothing else you could have done," Todd said. "Even if you had diagnosed his kidney failure, we don't have a dialysis machine, so the outcome would've been the same."

The man's friend had been standing at the foot of the bed the whole time, watching us try to resuscitate his friend.

"Let's call it," I said when I knew that the man had died and he wasn't coming back. "Time of death, 3:42 a.m.

"*Je suis désolé*," I said to his friend as I gently laid my hand on his arm.

His friend nodded as tears welled up in his eyes. As I left to fill out the death certificate, the man knelt at the bedside, laid his head on his friend's silent chest, and cried.

THE DECEASED MAN'S friend notified the family, who came to pay the bill and take the man's body away. After they left the hospital, I excused myself and went to the staff bathroom, which was attached to the outside of the building. The bathroom light was left on and the door was always a little ajar because the hospital compound had no outside lights, so it was pitch-black at night, and we didn't want to risk stepping on poisonous snakes, scorpions, or camel spiders in the dark.

The downside to leaving the bathroom light on and the door open was that the light attracted an inordinate number of mosquitoes.

After I lost that patient unexpectedly, I went to the bathroom to find that, once again, there were too many mosquitoes to count, climbing on the walls and the floor and the toilet and the sink.

Usually when I killed an insect, I did it hesitantly, with a wad of toilet paper in my hand.

But suddenly, overcome by the grief, frustration, and anger of the day, I slipped off my sandal and began bringing the force of my emotions to bear on the mosquitoes, slamming my shoe against the wall and the sink and the toilet and the door over and over and over again, killing every insect I could see.

The annihilation finally stopped because I was crying so hard, I could no longer see.

AFTER MASSACRING MOSQUITOES in the bathroom, I returned to the doctors' lounge. Before I even opened the door, the phone was already ringing.

"Please come!" It was the same Togolese nurse's aide. The same rapid French. The same breathless urgency.

Once again, I grabbed my stethoscope and went running.

This time, it was the young woman with abdominal pain. She had suddenly gone into cardiac arrest.

The nurses were already doing CPR.

I started bagging her and called out the orders.

Epi, bicarb, CPR, check for a pulse, continue CPR.

We coded her for thirty minutes.

I had no idea why she had gone into cardiac arrest. We had no diagnosis for her pain and vomiting and weight loss.

She was married and had two small children.

I didn't want to stop coding her. I didn't want to stop trying. Because it seemed senseless for a woman to die so young—to die without a diagnosis.

I was angry that she was dying so young.

I was angry that she was dying without any explanation of why.

I was angry that a man was going to lose his wife, that two little children were going to lose their mom.

I was angry that this woman was gone and, even though I'd done everything possible, there wasn't anything else I could do to bring her back.

The aides were standing in a line by her bed, rotating as they did round after round of CPR. I watched as they heaved forward over and over and over again, putting their whole weight into each compression. I wondered if they were angry, too. I wondered if the compressions were therapeutic for them, giving them an outlet for the anger. In that case, maybe the next code we had, I should stand in line and do compressions as well.

The woman's pupils were blown. She'd gone so long without a pulse, her brain was dead from the lack of oxygen.

"Let's call it," I said, for the second time in less than two hours. "Time of death, 4:58 a.m."

I RETURNED TO THE doctors' lounge, but I was too upset to sleep, too exhausted to cry.

"God, I'm done," I said as I sat on the edge of the futon, holding my weary head in my hands.

I called Laura. Her husband, Chad, groggily answered the phone and then handed it to her.

"Laura, can you come?" I asked, my voice breaking.

She was suddenly awake. "Of course. Is there an emergency?" she asked.

"No," I said. "But I've lost two patients and I don't know why and the little boy in pediatrics is dying, too, and I can't do this by myself anymore."

"I'll be right there," she said.

I was out of determination, out of energy, out of motivation, out of hope. I had worked hard shifts at the ER in the States, but they were never this hard or this long—and I was always well compensated for my efforts. In Togo, I was working for free, so there wasn't even a financial reward to look forward to. I was completely depleted, completely out of reasons to keep going. I couldn't imagine another minute—let alone another month—of working in Togo.

Twenty minutes later, with her curly red hair still wet from the shower, Laura walked into the doctors' lounge with two travel mugs of steaming black coffee.

As she sat next to me on the futon, she asked, "When's the last time you ate something?"

I definitely hadn't eaten dinner, and I was so exhausted, I couldn't remember if I'd eaten breakfast or lunch the day before. "I have no idea," I said in a weary whisper.

She reached into her purse and took out a plastic sandwich bag with a dozen mini muffins.

"They're banana nut," she said. "I made them myself."

As I reached my hand into the bag to take one, I felt more grateful for this food than I'd ever felt for breakfast in my life.

In between bites of muffins and sips of coffee, I told Laura about the two patients who had died, and everything we'd done to try to save them.

She put her hand on my knee and said, "Sarah, I would've done exactly the same thing. You did everything you could."

And then she said the words with which I would soothe myself over and over in the months after I left Togo, when I relived patients' deaths so vividly in my dreams that I woke up with sweaty palms and a pounding heart.

"Sarah, it's not your fault," Laura said.

It's not your fault.

It's not your fault.

It's not your fault.

As LAURA AND I were talking, the phone rang again, and I jumped—not because I was startled, but because I was terrified that another patient was dying.

"Would you get that?" I asked Laura.

When she hung up she sighed and said, "The little boy in pediatrics has begun agonal breathing," meaning that he was taking his final breaths. "Also, Levi is on his way to the OR to do a C-section for twins who are breech, and needs an extra pair of hands. Do you want pediatrics or OR?"

"I'll go to the OR," I said, thinking that there was at least a chance of a positive outcome with the C-section, and there was no hope for the boy in pediatrics who was dying of massive hemorrhaging we could neither stop nor explain.

Minutes later, I had changed into scrubs and was standing at the deep sink, scrubbing my fingers, hands, and forearms with the *pensée du jour* staring down at me like the eyes of T. J. Eckleburg in *The Great Gatsby*.

I can accept failure,
but I can't accept not trying.

"I don't believe you," I whispered to the quote as I walked into the OR.

Levi, the surgeon, and Grace, the midwife, were already scrubbed in when I arrived. We decided that when he delivered the babies, he would hand the first baby to Grace, and the second baby to me.

Levi made a horizontal incision over the woman's pubic bone, then cut through layers of skin and muscle to get to the uterus, which was large and shimmering. I held a large metal retractor that both pulled the lower edge of the incision wider and helped to protect the bladder from being accidentally nicked by the scalpel.

When he had made an incision in the uterus, he set down the scalpel. He inserted his right hand into the uterus. A second later, he pulled out the first baby. "It's a boy!" he said as he held the baby up for the mom to see. She smiled and nodded. Levi cut the cord and handed the baby to Grace. The baby began to cry immediately, which was a good sign.

I was wrapped up in the moment, watching the mom's expression as she saw her baby for the first time, when I felt a strange sensation on the back of my hand. I looked down to see that the second baby's arm was sticking out of the incision, and his tiny fingernails were scratching the back of my hand.

"Look!" I said to Levi. "He's really eager to get out!"

"Well, let's do it!" he said as he reached his hand into the uterus a second time and emerged with the other twin. "It's another boy, Mama!" Levi said as he cut the cord and handed the second crying baby to me.

I carried him over to the nearby table, the same table where I had seen the dead baby two months before on that first Saturday morning in Togo.

I was grinning as I cleaned the baby, weighed him, assessed his Apgar scores, wrapped him in a blanket, and put a knitted cap on his tiny head. The baby was crying loudly, and he had good muscle tone and normal reflexes—all positive signs that gave him a high score.

It was a relief to witness not disease, but health. Not death, but birth. Not failure, but success. Not a wrinkled hand clutching, "Please don't let me go," but an infant's tiny fingernails clawing at my hand, reaching for the light.

I STOOD IN THE corner of the OR holding the baby boy while Levi finished suturing the C-section incision.

Joyful tears welled up in my eyes as the baby gripped my index finger, and I let them flow. I was too tired to care what the mom or the OR staff thought of me.

"Welcome to the world, little man," I whispered to him. "We're glad you're here, but it's a crazy place and I have so much to tell you."

I wondered what I would tell him about the world if he were old enough to understand.

In PA school, the pediatrics professor taught us never to lie to children. When a clinician is preparing to give a child a shot and the child asks if it will hurt, a lot of clinicians and parents want to say no so the child will cooperate and not fight against the coming pain. It's easier to deal with the emotional reaction after the shot is completed than before, when you're in a hurry to see other patients and you're holding a needle in your hand.

But if you lie to a child about pain, the professor said, you will break their trust and in the future, they won't believe you.

So before giving shots or doing painful procedures, I began telling my patients of all ages, "This is going to hurt." And then I inflicted the pain as quickly as possible, because the anticipation of pain is almost worse than the pain itself.

As I held the baby in my arms, I kept wondering how to explain the world to him—how to explain the world to myself.

To say that life is painless is as dishonest as saying a shot won't hurt. On the other hand, there's something that's stronger than pain that makes life worth it.

Our world is very beautiful, and very broken, filled with places like Togo that are so beautiful, they take your breath away—and so cruel that sometimes, after they take your breath away, they never give it back.

The baby drifted off to sleep. I kissed his forehead and whispered a blessing, a promise that gave me hope for all the souls who lived their days in this difficult place.

"Little man," I said. "You were born into Love, you will die into Love, and you will be held by Love all the days of your life."

Levi and the surgical assistant wheeled the mom to the maternity ward, and Grace and I walked behind them, carrying the babies. When we walked past the nurses' station, nurses and medical assistants and patients' families came over to take a peek at the newborns. We were all in need of a glimmer of hope.

I LAID THE INFANT next to his twin in a bassinet next to the mom's bed, and then I left maternity to round on my patients so I could give sign-out to Tanya, who was on call that day.

I went to pediatrics, where I learned that while I was in the OR assisting Levi with the C-section, the boy with internal hemorrhaging had died. His bed was empty, and his father was already carrying the boy's body home. My heart ached for the father, but I was also relieved that I'd been able to witness the C-section, the arrival of new life, instead of yet another death.

A few cribs down, a four-year-old boy was sitting up in his crib, crying. Three days before, his parents had carried him into the hospital, unconscious and seizing, and we'd admitted him to pediatrics with cerebral malaria. For the first twenty-four hours, he didn't respond to treatment—and then, suddenly, he had begun to improve.

Now he was sitting up in bed, pointing to the floor where his mom had left two bowls. One held cooked white rice and the other a common Togolese sauce made of tomatoes, herbs, salt, and piment—a spicy red pepper. Typically, the Togolese would roll the rice into a ball, dip it in the sauce, and eat it with their fingers.

The boy and his family only spoke Tchakosi, so I used hand signs to communicate with him. I touched my thumb and fingers together and tapped my mouth with the tips.

"Hungry?" I asked.

He nodded eagerly.

He had been unconscious for nearly seventy-two hours, with only IV fluids to sustain him. I couldn't imagine how hungry he must be now.

I asked one of the other moms where the boy's mom was, and she told me the woman had gone to run errands.

"When will she be back?" I asked her.

The woman shrugged and said she didn't know.

I turned to the boy, who was still crying, looking mournfully at the food he couldn't reach.

I lowered the side of his crib and lifted the bowls to where he was. He wouldn't move his hand because it had an IV in it. So I rolled the rice into a small ball, dipped it in the sauce, and fed it to him. He ate it quickly and opened his mouth for more.

So I gave him another bite. Then another. Then another.

Feeding him reminded me of taking communion at the Episcopal church I attended back in the United States, where every Sunday, the priest took a piece of bread, dipped it in a chalice of wine, and placed it in the mouth of each parishioner.

"The body of Christ, broken for you. The blood of Christ, spilled for you," the priest said.

"Thanks be to God," I said each week as I savored the bread and the wine.
Thanks be to God.

The boy opened his mouth, and I gave him another ball of rice dipped in sauce. It was hard to believe that just three days before, he had been on the brink of death. And now here he was, eating out of my hand, giggling as sauce dripped from his chin.

Feeding him was not only an honor; it was a miracle.
Thanks be to God.

It gave me a taste of the joy Jesus must have experienced as he multiplied the five loaves of bread and two fish to feed the five thousand—and the joy Jesus must feel now as each week, sinners and saints come back to the communion table to be nourished again by grace.

The body of Christ, broken for you. The blood of Christ, spilled for you.
Thanks be to God.

I HAVE ALWAYS LOVED the sacrament of Communion, because broken-ness and beauty, opposites and enemies, converge in the center like the two beams that form the crux of Christ's cross.

One of the details of the communion story that I never thought of before Togo was that before Jesus breaks the bread at the Last Supper, turning it into a beautiful and holy sacrament that continues to revive our souls two thousand years later, Jesus blesses it.

He blesses it.

It's as if Jesus says to the bread, "Something violent is about to happen, but you can trust me. I promise to use it for good." As Jesus is praying all night in the Garden of Gethsemane the night before his crucifixion, I imagine the Father saying something similar to Jesus. "Something violent is about to happen, but you can trust me. I promise to use it for good."

In communion, as the bread is broken it mysteriously transcends from sustenance to sacrament. Even more mysteriously, and paradoxically, it undergoes transformation not despite the breaking, but because of it.

Every day, I experienced Togo's brokenness—metaphorically and literally. I lived amid its fractured political system and crippled economy. And every day I touched broken bones and bleeding wounds and cracked teeth.

And somehow in that brokenness, in the "least-happy"-ness and in the pain, Jesus kept showing up in ways I had never experienced him before.

Somehow, in the rooms of the dying, as I held their hands and witnessed their last breaths, there was a Presence I had never felt before. When the Nigerian man paid the bill so the father could take his deceased son home, and the mother gave the grieving father her panya to wrap his dead daughter in, I saw a depth of kindness I had never witnessed before.

When the tiny baby reached his hand out of the womb during the C-section and touched mine, I felt a spark of life I had never felt before.

I was beginning to more deeply understand Leonard Cohen's words: "There's a crack in everything. That's how the light gets in."

And Rumi's line: "The wound is the place where the Light enters you."

The Japanese express this idea in an art form called Kintsugi, where pottery is purposefully broken, and the cracks are repaired with lacquer flecked with silver or gold or platinum. A piece of pottery that has been shattered and then repaired with expensive lacquer is far more valuable than a vessel that has never been broken.

Maybe this is what Paul was trying to express when he wrote,

We have this treasure in jars of clay to show that this all-surpassing power is from God and not from us...
We always carry around in our body the death of Jesus,
so that the life of Jesus may also be revealed in our body. (2 Cor. 4:7, 10)

Something inexplicably beautiful appears in brokenness, not despite the cracks but because of them.

Our bodies and our souls and our hearts break as we go through life. The hope we can hold on to is not that we will remain unbroken, but that when we do inevitably break (and we all do), God will restore us as only a Kintsugi master can: carefully, artfully, beautifully—with extravagant, glimmering grace.

Our Potter Who Art in Heaven.

When Massiko said, "Love looks around," I had taken his words to heart. I tried to see my patients in Togo through the eyes of God, to look on them with compassion and kindness and love.

Now I realized that not only does Love look around and see us, and not only does Love motivate us to look around and see others, but also, when we look around, at even the most broken places and situations that surround us, we see Love.

Love looks around. And when we look around, we see Love.

Love that instills dignity and uniqueness and value in the vessels it repairs. Love that sparkles and shimmers and shines. Love that seeps into even the most broken places and fractured situations. Love that appears not despite— but because of—all the cracks.

I FINISHED MY SHIFT and walked out of the hospital into the bright morning light. A few days before, Hazel had moved me from my room at the guesthouse to a three-bedroom duplex on the hospital compound that I would share with Elle, a nurse, and Bekah, a physician assistant, who were here from the United States to work at the hospital for two weeks. They were both in their thirties, and they were funny and kind. The three of us hit it off immediately.

After living in a small room by myself for two months, I was looking forward to having some company. Plus, the duplex had a kitchen, which meant that instead of eating unhealthy American food in the dining hall, I could get fresh food at the market and cook for myself.

So after my shift, I returned to the duplex for a shower and a nap. When I woke up a few hours later, I walked to the market and bought eggs, tomatoes, okra, onions, bananas, and a fresh-baked loaf of bread.

On my way home, I saw my FIFA Boys, who had gathered at the soccer field.

"Sarah, Sarah!" they called. I waved and walked toward them. Two boys who had been climbing in a nearby tree swung down and ran over to give me high-fives.

They asked if I could play with them and I said no, not today, because I was tired from being up all night, and I needed to get the groceries home. I promised to come back and play with them the following Saturday.

THAT EVENING, I was going to make soup from the okra and tomatoes and onions, but I realized that there were no pots in the kitchen at the duplex, so I walked over to the dining hall to borrow one from the big kitchen.

Several nurses were taking their dinner break, eating together at one of the long tables, and I waved to them. Then I felt a tap on my shoulder. I turned around to see Fred scowling at me.

"Can I talk to you?" he asked.

I nodded and followed him to a couch in the corner of the room, next to the bookshelves and board games.

"You broke the rules," he said.

I had no idea what he was talking about. I had been trying very carefully not to break any rules, because I wanted to be a good teammate and not disrupt the community, and because I didn't want to give legalistic people reasons to judge me.

I showed up to meals on time. I was never late for my clinic or on-call shifts. I attended church services every Sunday night. Even though the hospital hired a Togolese woman to clean my room and do my laundry every week, I kept my room very clean.

I abided by the dress code. Hazel had a large piece of fabric that the team nicknamed the Panya of Shame because if female American guests came to tour the hospital and they weren't appropriately dressed, Hazel would loan them the panya and make them cover up until they left. I hadn't had to wear it, so I assumed I was dressing appropriately.

I thought I was doing pretty well keeping all the rules. So when Fred told me I had broken one, I was baffled. I raised my eyebrows, waiting for him to tell me what I'd done.

"The first day you came, we told you there was a manual in your room," he said. "And in the manual, one of the rules listed is do *not* give the Togolese people any money or gifts."

I nodded. I had read the manual. I knew the rule he was talking about. I hadn't given anyone money or food. I did occasionally bring Omari a cold Coke on busy clinic days, but that hardly seemed like a "gift."

I asked Fred what I'd done to break the rule.

"Do you play soccer with Togolese kids on your days off?" he asked.

I nodded.

"Did you buy those kids a ball?"

"Yes," I said. "I bought them three rubber balls that cost the equivalent of one dollar each. And then when those broke, I bought them a FIFA ball, which cost me six dollars."

"Did you give them the ball?" he asked.

I nodded. I didn't hold on to the ball myself because I didn't want to make them wait several weeks, until my next day off, before they could play soccer. So I had handed it to the oldest boy and asked him to keep it at his house. Then, I said, every time they played soccer, he was to designate a new boy to keep the ball at his house until they played again.

"Make sure everyone gets a turn to keep the FIFA ball," I had told him. He, and all the other boys, agreed to the plan.

I explained this to Fred.

He shook his head. "It was a gift," he insisted. "You gave them a gift after we told you not to and when you give these kids gifts, you make beggars out of 'em."

I didn't press the point. Clearly, this was a dressing-down, not a discussion.

Then the dressing-down turned into a diatribe.

For the next ten minutes, he went off about how easy it was for Togolese people to become beggars. He said that he'd read a book in which a man went to a remote developing country and didn't give the people anything. He just held a weekly Bible study in their language. He didn't help them build anything, he didn't help them find food or medicine, he didn't offer any tangible help to them. He just taught them for one hour a week—because he didn't want them to take advantage of him. He wanted to convert them—not because they had any physical needs met, but because what he was preaching to them was the truth.

The longer Fred talked, the redder his face became.

I wanted to remind him that Jesus healed sick people and fed hungry people. He touched people and let them touch him. If Jesus was into meeting people's tangible needs, not just talking at them or waiting to help them until they acknowledged the truth, why would we do it differently? Who were we to challenge, let alone try to improve upon, Jesus' model of expressing Divine Love?

But I kept my mouth shut. When Fred finished, he said, "Are we clear?"

I nodded and, hurt and embarrassed and confused, I left.

I ate a banana for dinner that night, because I had forgotten to take a pot from the kitchen, and there was no way I was going back there now.

THE FOLLOWING MORNING, Omari brought in more bouille and beignets for breakfast. As we started seeing patients, I noticed my stomach was gurgling a lot. I thought maybe it was because I had skipped dinner the night before.

But the gurgling turned to intense nausea, and then I ran to the bathroom to throw up.

That's weird, I thought. I don't usually have a sensitive stomach. I made a mental note to keep an eye on my symptoms. If I started having diarrhea, I would do a lab test for parasites. And if I started having abdominal pain or a fever, I would start on antibiotics for typhoid fever, a particularly virulent strain of salmonella.

Throughout the morning, I felt worse and worse, until I could think of nothing but lying in a dark room, taking whatever medicine was required for the nausea and throbbing joints and clamminess to disappear.

By noon, I was pretty sure I had malaria.

At noon, I went next door to Bekah's exam room to ask her to write me a prescription for Coartem. If I did have malaria, I wanted to start treatment as soon as possible.

Massiko was translating for her that day. As soon as I walked into the room, before I could say anything, Massiko looked at me and said, "Sarah, you are very sick."

I nodded and handed Bekah my carnet. I asked her to write me a prescription for Coartem.

I went to the pharmacy and filled the prescription. Four tablets twice a day for three days. I had written the prescription so often, I could recite the directions in my sleep.

I told Matt and Omari I was done seeing patients for the day.

I went back to my room, swallowed the first dose of Coartem, changed into shorts and a T-shirt, and climbed into bed.

Five minutes later, I felt my stomach contracting harder and harder, and then my mouth started watering. I ran to the bathroom and threw up.

And that's how I spent the afternoon. Lying on the bathroom floor, raising myself up every few minutes to vomit into the toilet before lying down again.

For the first time since I'd arrived in Togo, I worried that maybe I didn't have the physical stamina to fight virulent pathogens in such an austere climate.

Maybe I would die here.

By that evening, I had been lying on the floor for hours. My joints were throbbing, I couldn't stop throwing up, and my head was pounding. I was ten thousand miles away from the comforts of home.

I threw up again.

And as I lay back down on the cool tiled floor, I was pretty sure I was dying.

And then I blacked out.

ELLE AND BEKAH came back from dinner and found me unconscious on my bedroom floor near the door, my arm outstretched, as if I was reaching for something, though I don't remember what.

They called the guesthouse. Fred was there with a few nurses and Allan, an OB/GYN who was visiting from the United States for a month. Allan and the nurses ran over to the duplex while Fred raced over with a golf cart.

The nurses carried me to the golf cart, and Allan jumped on the back and held my head while Fred sped across the compound.

One of the nurses stayed behind at the duplex and called the nurses' station. "We're bringing Sarah over," she said. "We found her passed out on the floor, and we can't wake her up."

Wade, the jovial nurse from Indiana who was in Togo with his wife, Patty, for six months, was working that night. He met the golf cart at the side door. Together with a few others, he carried me to an empty bed.

Emilie was the doctor working that night.

My heart rate was in the 190s. My blood pressure was dangerously low.

Emilie ordered an IV and blood work and a shot of anti-malaria medicine.

My labs came back a few minutes later. My malaria test was positive.

And that's when I came to, with half a dozen nurses, plus Emilie and Allan, standing over me. They had called Todd at home. As I was waking up, Todd came around the corner, out of breath from running to the hospital.

Todd sighed with relief when he saw that my eyes were open.

"What happened?" I asked Emilie in a hoarse whisper. That was my first question.

Am I going to die? was my second question, but I was too afraid of the answer to ask it out loud.

Emilie admitted me to ISO 3, with IV fluids, anti-malaria medicine, Tylenol, and anti-nausea medicine.

My nurse that night was Kojo, the head Togolese nurse.

He came in with a small paper cup of pills and a cup of water.

As soon as I swallowed the pills, I threw them up.

As he watched me retching over a small plastic basin, he held my hair back and shook his head. "*Du courage*," he said.

"*Du courage*," he said throughout the night, as I threw up over and over again.

Emilie added another anti-nausea medicine to my orders. Finally the vomiting stopped, and I was able to get some sleep.

As I was nodding off, Elle came into my room with gusto, holding a blanket and a pillow.

"What are you doing?" I asked.

"I heard you had the Malares!" she exclaimed. "We don't like the Malares, do we?"

No, I thought as I shook my head. *No, we don't like the Malares—or people who call malaria the Malares.*

She straightened up my bedside table, brushed my hair into a ponytail to get it out of my face, helped me take a sip of water, and then made her bed on the floor next to mine.

"What are you doing?" I asked her.

"Well, you're sick in Togo. And when in Togo…" she said with a happy shrug. She was right—I hadn't noticed it before, but patients never slept alone at the hospital. There was always a friend or relative who slept on a mat next to their bed, helped them walk to the bathroom, and brought them water and food.

You might get deathly ill in Togo—and you might even die—but you would never do it alone.

THAT NIGHT, MY blood pressure dropped to 70/40. I felt achy and clammy.

Kojo came to check on me, and asked me how I was feeling.

"Not awesome," I said in English, because I didn't know how to say *not awesome* in French.

In addition to feeling not-awesome, I was mad that even though I'd taken anti-malaria pills faithfully every day since I got to Togo, sprayed my sheets and my skin with bug spray every night before bed, and seen only two visible mosquito bites on me—at some point, I had been bitten by a female mosquito who injected her parasite-ridden saliva into my bloodstream.

I don't know if it was a dream or delirium, but that night I imagined that I recovered from malaria, returned to the United States, and wrote my story into an award-winning Broadway musical comedy called *Malarious.*

In a surprising-but-genius casting twist, Nathan Lane played my character, the lead character, who led a ward of patients in a choreographed opening number in which the patients were dancing on their beds.

The dream didn't last long enough for me to iron out all the other details.

When I woke up, it was Saturday morning, and Elle was shaking my shoulder. She said she'd gotten permission to move me to the hospital's only private patient room, which had a bathroom attached.

She left to get a wheelchair and returned a few minutes later with the wheelchair and, to my surprise, Omari. He had heard through the grapevine that I was ill and had come to the hospital on his day off to check on me.

I was wearing long pajama pants, which I'd rolled up to my knees because it was so hot in my room.

Omari picked me up and set me in the wheelchair, then, while Elle collected my things, Omari wheeled me to the private room and helped me into bed. He promised to return the following day to check on me, and then he left.

Once he was gone, I suddenly remembered that in Togolese culture it was considered immodest to let a man see your ankles. And Omari had seen not only my ankles but my kneecaps.

How embarrassing, I thought.

And also, *Of all the things I could be thinking about while I'm delirious from malaria, why do Nathan Lane and kneecaps top the list?*

IN MOST OF the hospital wards, there was a TV/VCR unit on the wall that showed either *The Jesus Film*, a dramatization of the life of Jesus, or Bible cartoons dubbed in Tchakosi or French.

I never knew how much of *The Jesus Film* made sense to the people here—I wasn't sure if they understood where Israel was, or that the story happened two thousand years ago—but during my rounds, I had seen several of them smile and clap during the resurrection scene. And when the film ended, they often asked the nurses if they could watch it again.

In the hospital room where I stayed, there was no TV. I had no podcasts downloaded onto my phone. My head ached too much to read a book. So I just lay there in bed, feeling small and depleted. For the first time since I was a little girl, I wished someone would pull a chair up to my bed and tell me a story.

When no one came to entertain me, I said, "Well, God, maybe you can tell me a story."

But God didn't say anything.

Wade, the large, gregarious American who was in Togo for six months with his wife, was my nurse on Saturday afternoon.

He was laughing to himself as he changed my bottle of IV fluids and inspected the tubing.

"I don't think the maintenance guys are very happy with me," he said quietly, shaking his head.

"What?" I asked him, unsure if he was talking to himself under his breath or if he was talking to me.

"I said I don't think maintenance is happy with me," he repeated, louder.

"Why not?" I asked, wondering what he'd done now—he was full of humorous stories that usually involved him breaking something or getting into some kind of trouble.

"'Cuz I broke down the door," he said, pointing down the hallway to the door where the gurney had come out to get me the night before.

"Why did you break down a door?" I asked.

"Well, I saw the nurses coming with you last night, and I saw how pasty you looked and I was really worried about you. I couldn't figure out how to undo the latch in the screen door, so…" He shrugged and his belly started shaking as he chuckled. "I just broke it down."

He finished what he was doing and went to leave, calling over his shoulder as he winked and closed the door, "I broke down the door to get to you, kid."

"Thanks," I said, as loudly as my hoarse voice would allow.

THAT AFTERNOON, I thought about the patients who come to the Hospital of Hope, hearing the story of Jesus for the first time. The theology, dogma, religion, and religious traditions we've created around the Bible (especially in America) can make Christianity seem so complicated and unintelligible, not to mention unattractive.

But at the heart of it is the simple good news, which, after all, is what the word *gospel* means.

"For God so loved the world…"

As I lay in that hospital bed, I thought of how sick I was feeling, and how far away home seemed. I had asked God to tell me a story, and instead he'd sent Wade to tell me about breaking the door.

But maybe that's exactly the story I needed to hear in that moment.

Maybe that's all the story I'll ever need to hear.

For a long time to come, whenever I hear John 3:16, "For God so loved the world…," or whenever I think of what I learned in Africa, or whenever I try to explain to anyone what's at the heart of my faith, I'll think about the gospel—the simple good news—as God the Father, a jovial man with a handlebar mustache, shaking his head and smiling with a chuckle that makes his belly shake.

"I was worried about you," God says to the world, with laughter in his voice and love in his eyes. "So…I broke down the door to get to you, kid."

I broke down the door to get to you.

ON SATURDAY AFTERNOON, I was asleep in my hospital bed when I woke to commotion. Nurses yelling, a monitor beeping loudly, people running past my room.

Wade came in to give me another dose of anti-nausea medicine. I asked him what was happening.

He told me that the baby with burns had contracted meningitis the day before, and had been moved to the room next to mine. Now she was coding.

When he left, I lay there in bed, staring at the ceiling, listening to the commotion in the room next door. The monitor alarming because the baby's oxygen saturation and heart rate were dangerously low. Tanya yelling commands to the nurses.

"Keep doing compressions."

"Another round of epi."

"Check for a pulse."

I lay there helplessly, listening to the code, tears trickling onto my pillow.

I prayed for the baby to feel no pain. I prayed for a miracle. And if the miracle didn't come, I prayed for Jesus to gently hold this mother in her grief.

All through the sound of chest compressions, through the rounds of epi, through the monitor alarms, and then into the quietness afterward, when the code was over and the baby was gone, when the mother's wail settled into quiet weeping as she held her dead baby in her arms and said good-bye for the last time, the tears continued to trickle onto my pillow as I sang in a quiet whisper,

Swing low, sweet chariot
Comin' for to carry me home.
Swing low, sweet chariot
Comin' for to carry me home.

THE BABY DIED that afternoon. I spiked a fever and started throwing up again. My body ached so badly, it hurt to move. It even hurt to blink.

Before I left for Togo, the missions agency required me to purchase an insurance policy that would cover medical expenses if I was injured or ill. The policy also included "repatriation of remains," a euphemism that meant the insurance company would spend up to a hundred thousand dollars to fly my body home if I died.

As I lay in that hospital bed in Togo, I was convinced that I was going to have to exercise that "repatriation of remains" clause.

"Eli, Eli, lama sabachthani?"

My God, my God, why have you forsaken me?

My God, my God, why have you left me to die in this God-forsaken place?

And then I fell into a deep sleep.

Allan told me later that he gathered some nurses together, and they came to my room that night, stood around my bed, and prayed for me. Before Allan left for Togo, one of his patients had given him a vial of "holy oil" she'd brought back with her from a trip to Israel. He brought the vial with him to Togo, and as the nurses prayed for me, Allan anointed my head and my hands and my feet with oil.

I woke the following morning to find that the vomiting had stopped and my pain, while still significant, had improved. Later in the day, Betsy discharged me home.

Fred and Hazel came with the golf cart. They each held one of my elbows to help me into the cart, then Hazel held my shoulders to keep me upright for the short drive to the duplex. As we were driving, Hazel said, "By the way, there's a water shortage, so we're asking people to take very short showers, and the housekeepers will not be doing your laundry this week."

Fred explained that there was a large pump in the Oti River that was supposed to take water out of the river and send it to the water treatment plant. Once the water was treated, it was sent through pipelines to the pumps scattered throughout the village, as well as to the hospital compound. When the water arrived at the compound, it was put through another filtration system and stored in the water tower, which had the capacity to store a three-day supply.

But the pump in the Oti River had broken and the government hadn't been able to find the parts needed to fix it. So the water pumps in the village weren't working at all, and the hospital only had a three-day supply of water. With strict conservation, Fred estimated we could make that supply last for a week.

"And then what happens?" I asked, my voice weak and hoarse.

"Then we're out of options."

He pulled up to the front door of the duplex. Hazel helped me walk down the hall to my bedroom, where I climbed in between cool sheets and quickly fell asleep.

I WAS ADMITTED TO the hospital on Friday night, and discharged from the hospital on Sunday afternoon. I had three weeks before I was scheduled to fly home to the United States. I was on the fence about whether I could last that long, or whether I'd have to change my ticket and fly home early.

For the first few days after I got out of the hospital, it was a struggle to even stand up. I was exhausted, and my joints still ached. I was nauseated, and no food sounded good to me. Hazel brought me chicken soup, but even that made me want to vomit. Every few hours, I forced myself to get out of bed and walk to the kitchen for a sip of water before going back to bed.

When I wasn't sleeping, I lay there, praying to God for healing and strength. And hope.

"How is it possible that your power raised Jesus from the dead, and yet I can barely get out of bed?" I wondered.

I prayed for God to give me a sudden, overwhelming, blinding burst of energy to restore me to health, so I could get back to work—and then, in three weeks, leave Togo as fast as possible.

"God, you can do this," I prayed. "Remember the resurrection? Kinda like that. Only maybe just half the amount of power you used that Sunday morning because I'm not dead. I'm just really tired."

As I was thinking about Jesus rising from the dead, the narrative began to play itself backward in my head, like a movie rewinding. The resurrection, then the crucifixion, then the trial, then the night before the trial, when Jesus was on his knees in Gethsemane, praying, "Not my will but yours" (Luke 22:42).

And I realized that the power that raised Jesus from the dead on Sunday morning was the same power at work in his life on Friday night.

On Sunday, the power gave him strength to rise. On Friday, the power gave him strength to die.

When I was praying for God's power to be at work in my life, I wanted the Sunday-morning power. I wanted to be resurrected and imbued with energy.

But maybe the power at work in my life was the power that gave me strength to surrender.

I had wanted Togo to be a Sunday-morning experience. I wanted to fly back to the United States on the edge of my seat, just waiting to tell people about all my miraculous, amazing experiences in Africa, and how much I'd loved my time there.

But as I lay in bed with malaria, I began to realize that maybe the rest of my time in Togo was going to be a Friday-night experience. Maybe God was asking me to surrender, to fully give myself to Togo, to be emptied of all energy and strength.

Maybe the best I could hope for was to live long enough to fly from Togo to Chicago, where my parents would be waiting to meet me. I was down to ninety-six pounds, so my dad could probably carry me to the car or, at least, catch me on the way down if I collapsed.

THE DAY AFTER I got out of the hospital, half our clinicians flew back to the United States. Allan and Levi returned because their time in Togo was up, and Todd, Beth, Tanya, and Grace all left to attend the wedding of the midwife who had worked at the Hospital of Hope for the past year.

Nelson agreed to stay for an extra two weeks, filling in at the hospital until Todd, Beth, Tanya, and Grace returned.

When I was discharged from the hospital, Tanya had told me to take as much time off as I needed. She said if I wanted, I could just rest for the next three weeks, until it was time for me to fly home. But every morning I looked out the duplex's front window and saw the long line of patients waiting in triage, desperate to be seen.

I couldn't handle the idea of lying in bed while the hospital was so short-staffed and so many patients were waiting to be seen. So one week after I was discharged from the hospital, I went back to work.

On my first shift back, I worked with Omari in the clinic. "You do not look well, Sarah," he said when I walked into the exam room.

I knew he was right. I was pale, I had dark circles under my eyes. I had lost weight because even the sight of food made me want to throw up. But I had dragged myself to the clinic anyway because I wanted to give Togo everything I had left. I was resigned to the power the Father gave Jesus to lay down his life on Friday instead of the power he gave Jesus to rise on Sunday morning.

I was determined to give Togo all I had, even if it literally killed me.

At noon, we saw our last patient of the morning. I went to the sink to wash my hands, and no water came out. *That's strange*, I thought.

I walked over to the dining hall because there was a sink there. But again, no water came out.

Then Fred came in and announced the news we had all been dreading: We were completely out of water.

EVERYTHING WENT DOWNHILL from there.

The temperatures over the next few days soared to 110 degrees. Even though it was the rainy season, it was one of the driest rainy seasons on record, and it hadn't rained for weeks, so humidity hung in the air and it felt like we were breathing through a waterlogged sponge.

Fred sent two of the maintenance workers into town to buy all the bottled water they could find. They went to all the stands in the market, but they weren't able to find much. The men returned with reports that the people in the village were so thirsty, they had begun drinking out of the town's old cisterns—which meant they were drinking stagnant, bacteria-laden, foul-smelling water that sometimes contained the remains of rodents that had fallen into the cisterns and drowned.

Our pharmacy had several gallons of distilled water they were using to mix liquid medications and IV fluids, but that ran out in a day, so Cheryl, a pharmacist from the United States in her mid-fifties who was volunteering in Togo for two years, rode her bike to the town's two bars and bought all the bottles of water they had.

Massiko left for Lomé to buy water there, but it would take him at least two days to drive down and back.

Matt hung a handwritten sign at the nurses' station: IV FLUIDS FOR EMERGENCIES ONLY.

That night, all the staff members who weren't working at the hospital met in the dining hall. For three hours, we prayed for the pump to get fixed. And we prayed for it to rain.

WHEN THE WATER shortage first began, we all abided by the well-known bathroom saying, "If it's yellow, let it mellow. If it's brown, flush it down."

When the water ran out, the saying turned into, "If it's yellow, let it mellow. If it's brown…well…unfortunately, you're gonna have to let that mellow, too."

The hospital and clinic and dining hall and guesthouse rooms and duplexes stank. Patients, who already smelled of body odor because most of the Togolese people didn't use deodorant, smelled even worse. When a wind kicked up, the odor from the Cuisine and the latrines blew across the compound, and the pungent, nearly palpable odor hung over the compound like a cloud.

Despite our best efforts, we Americans began to smell, too. After going several days without a shower, I was desperate to feel clean, so one evening Bekah and I jumped into the pool, only to quickly discover that all sixty hot, sweaty, grimy American missionaries had probably had the same idea and, despite being chlorinated, the pool water smelled worse than we did.

Never in my life had I been in a place where, for days in a row, I turned on the tap or flushed a toilet or turned on the shower—and nothing happened. Never before had I wondered where my next sip of drinking water was going to come from. Never before had I so tightly rationed the amount of water I drank, wondering how dehydrated I could get without passing out or going into renal failure.

A S THE DAYS wore on, I grew more and more worried. What if the pump never started working again?

What if we ran out of the small supply of water bottles we'd been able to buy in town, and what if Massiko couldn't find enough water bottles in Lomé, or what if the old Land Cruiser he was driving broke down on his way back?

I had been fine with the idea of coming to Africa to love and care for marginalized people whose suffering often went unnoticed by the rest of the world, the Invisible People whom Jesus called "the least of these" (Matt. 25:40).

But contracting malaria and then running out of water made this experience so much more intense, and costly, and uncomfortable than I'd ever expected it would be.

I wasn't just loving the least of these here in Togo; I was becoming the least of these.

I wasn't just here for the Togolese people; I was here with them.

I didn't just have sympathy for people who don't have access to clean, readily available drinking water; I had empathy for them. Because I was one of them.

One night I woke up in the early hours, sweaty and thirsty, unable to fall back asleep. As I lay there in the dark, I started thinking about the word *compassion*, which comes from the Latin words *co*, which means "with," and *passion*, from the word *pati*, which means "to suffer." So the word *compassion* literally means "to suffer with."

I had always thought of compassionate people as people with tender hearts. But after my Togo experience, I realized that in order to practice compassion, your heart needs to be tender but the rest of you—including your emotions and your commitment and your will—needs to be tough as nails.

Compassion, in its most extreme forms, is not cute; it is costly. It isn't always sweet; sometimes it is downright scary. Compassion makes you suffer and sweat and smell. It requires you to pour yourself out, sometimes, until there's nothing left.

Togo gave me a new appreciation for Jesus. Instead of having sympathy for the human condition, Emmanuel, God With Us, came down to suffer with and for us. He took the cup of hardship, loss, grief, pain, and death, and he drank it to the dregs.

Maybe, I thought as I lay in the dark that night in Togo, maybe Jesus was calling me to that same level of compassion, calling me to love the world at a great personal cost that I never would've chosen if it was up to me. To take the cup of suffering and drink it all, down to the dregs.

I didn't know yet what radical compassion would look like for me when I got back to the United States, but in Togo, when the sun came up the next morning, for me, having compassion meant picking up my nearly empty water bottle, walking over to the clinic, and seeing patients in a malodorous, muggy exam room while I was hot and thirsty and tired.

It meant sharing with the Togolese people in this hardship, drinking the cup of suffering down to the dregs.

Down to the very last drop.

THREE DAYS AFTER we ran out of water, I was on call with Nelson. We were inundated with patients who were suffering the effects of the water shortage.

Elderly people came in with heatstroke.

People of all ages came in with dysentery and typhoid, which they'd contracted from drinking the dirty cistern water.

Babies came in dehydrated and lethargic because their mothers' breast milk had dried up.

Two pregnant women came to the hospital in premature labor, a result of significant dehydration. One was thirty-four weeks pregnant and the other, twenty-two weeks pregnant with twins. We admitted them to maternity and gave them IV fluids and magnesium to try to stop the contractions.

At the nurses' station, there were two handwashing options. We could use hand sanitizer gel or swish our hands in a bucket of murky three-day-old water, neither of which erased the stains or the stench of feces and urine and blood from our hands.

On top of everything else, Tanya (the hospital's chief of staff) and Todd (the hospital's medical director) and Grace (the hospital's full-time midwife) were still back in the United States, and they weren't scheduled to return to Togo for another week.

IN THE EARLY evening, Nanci, a Togolese nurse who was working in maternity, came running to the nurses' station. "Dr. Nelson! Dr. Nelson!"

Nelson and I went running back to maternity to find that the woman who was twenty-two weeks' pregnant with twins had not responded to the fluids and magnesium. Her labor had progressed and she was now fully dilated, and feeling the urge to push.

Nelson and I quickly sprang into action. As we donned gowns and gloves and set up the sterile delivery tray with forceps, umbilical cord clips, and a suction bulb, Nelson said, in a low voice, "As soon as the babies are born, check their weight. If they weigh less than a thousand grams each, there's no point in beginning resuscitation efforts. We just have to let them go."

I nodded.

Minutes later, Nelson delivered the first baby, a tiny girl who wasn't moving or crying. Nelson cut the cord and handed the baby to me. I laid her on the scale, holding my breath, waiting for the digital numbers to appear, praying for the scale to read a thousand grams or more, praying these babies would stand a chance.

A number blinked on the scale's small LCD screen: 790 grams.

I just looked at Nelson and shook my head.

He nodded slowly, sadly, and prepared to deliver the second baby.

I wrapped the baby girl in a small blue towel and cradled her in my arms. She was as tiny as a small cucumber. She was so premature, her eyelids were still fused together. And she wasn't crying.

But she had a heartbeat and she was breathing. Her breaths were irregular gasps, but still. She was trying to live, fighting for air with all of her God-given Ninja strength.

I knew that in a few minutes, her heart would stop and she would stop breathing and her little soul would pass into eternity.

Nanci left maternity and returned a few minutes later holding a cardboard shoe box. She motioned that I should put the baby in the box so the parents could take the box home and bury the babies in their yard.

But this baby was still alive. There was nothing I could do to save her life, but at least I could spare her from dying alone in a box. So I shook my head at Nanci.

No, not yet.

The second baby was born. It was another girl, who was even tinier than her sister. She wasn't crying or moving, either. Nelson cut the cord, stood up, and laid the baby on the scale. This time, I wasn't holding my breath.

I peered over his shoulder to see the number: 740 grams.

Nelson sighed, wrapped her in a blue towel, and handed her to me. Her heart was beating, too, but she wasn't breathing at all.

Dear Ninjas, keep fighting! I wanted to say. And yet I knew that there was nothing we—or they—could do to force their souls to stay.

Nelson returned to the mom. While he was waiting for her contractions to resume so he could deliver the placenta, he explained to her that she had delivered two baby girls, but they were too tiny to save. He asked if she'd like to hold them, and she shook her head.

So I held them. It was a surreal moment, standing in the middle of the maternity ward on a hot summer night holding a tiny baby girl in each hand, my fingertips resting on their chests, feeling their hearts beating slower. And slower. And slower.

By the time Nelson delivered the placenta, the babies' hearts had completely stopped beating.

I lowered them into the shoe box and positioned them so they were facing each other and their hands were touching each other.

And then I closed the lid.

For months afterward, I had nightmares in which I dreamed I was laying two dead babies in a shoe box. I would startle awake with my heart pounding in my chest and leap out of bed to turn on the light in a desperate attempt to dispel the dream as quickly as possible.

But even after I turned the light on, even after I was fully awake, I could still feel the sensation of two tiny hearts beating slower and slower beneath my fingertips. I could still see their motionless faces. I could still remember how warm their bodies were when I lowered them into the box.

I laid babies in a box.

I laid two dead baby girls in a shoe box.

This was not a bad dream. This actually happened.

And that, I came to realize, is the difference between a memory and a nightmare.

Nightmares disappear when you wake up.

Memories never do.

A FTER THE PREEMIES died, we lost three more patients that night. In the morning, I stumbled outside to see the sun on the horizon. I fell to my knees in the same patch of dirt where I'd found the father weeping after he lost his two-year-old daughter to cerebral malaria. And I cried "Uncle."

I was so depleted, my prayer was only three words long: "I. Am. Done."

I wanted to help the people in Togo, I wanted to honor my commitment and stay, I wanted to be a person of compassion, I wanted to be tough as nails, but I was not physically or emotionally capable of enduring this experience.

I felt like I needed to leave Togo immediately because if I didn't, either I was going to have a complete mental breakdown, or I was literally going to die. I didn't know which, I didn't care which. All I knew was that I needed to leave.

I made up my mind that the shift I had just worked, during which I had laid two babies in a box and unsuccessfully coded three other patients, would be my last shift.

Hospital of Hope? Yeah, right, I thought. *Try, The God-Forsaken Place That Keeps Trying to Kill Me.*

THAT AFTERNOON, I returned to my room in the duplex to find there was still no water, so I couldn't take a shower, and now the Internet wasn't working, so I couldn't change my plane ticket.

I thought maybe kicking around a ball with the FIFA Boys—which had become one of my favorite activities—would help me feel better.

I was lacing up my shoes to walk to town when I heard the patter of a few heavy raindrops on the roof and then, seconds later, there was a deluge.

I took off my shoes and went outside barefoot. It felt good to be cool and wet for the first time in nearly a week. There was no point in walking to town now. The dirt paths would be inches-deep in mud, and there was no way the FIFA Boys and I could play futbol in this downpour.

I looked across the compound and saw two Togolese maintenance workers dragging large, empty plastic barrels from the maintenance shed outside to collect the rainwater. The pack of goats and sheep was sprinting toward the Farm for shelter. Several of the missionary kids were running around the compound, jumping in the puddles that were starting to collect.

And then there was deafening thunder, followed by flashes of lightning, that drove us all back inside.

I changed into dry clothes, toweled off my dripping hair, and tried the Internet again. It was still "unemployed," and would probably be out for hours, until the storm passed.

There was nothing else to do, so I ended up listening to a random podcast I had downloaded a few days before—a lecture about the story of Sisyphus.

In the Greek myth, Sisyphus makes the gods angry, so they condemn him to an eternal punishment. For the rest of eternity, Sisyphus would have to carry a large rock up a hill but, just before he reached the top, the rock would roll down to the bottom, and Sisyphus would have to do it again. Over and over and over again.

The lecturer said that the myth of Sisyphus gave rise to the adjective

Sisyphean, a word describing a task that is futile, hopeless, frustrating, and useless.

I had never heard of the myth before, but I immediately fell in love with the story because *Sisyphean* perfectly described what the Hospital of Hope felt like to me. No matter how hard I worked, no matter how many hours I spent on my feet, no matter how much sleep I sacrificed, no matter how much energy I expended, patients kept dying anyway. And every shift, I had to start all over again.

The lecturer went on to say that anyone who wanted to read a more in-depth analysis of the story could read "The Myth of Sisyphus," an essay by Albert Camus. The lecturer went on to say that Camus's take was interesting because he concluded that Sisyphus was the victor, not the victim, of the story. That he was, in fact, the hero. Camus even went so far as to write, "One must imagine Sisyphus happy."

What the heck? I thought as the podcast concluded.

How could a man condemned to an eternal, useless task possibly be happy? And what could motivate him to keep going?

That evening, in preparation for leaving early to go back to the United States, I cleaned my room and packed my suitcase. The Internet came back on around ten o'clock, as I was getting ready for bed.

Instead of logging onto the airline's website to switch my ticket, I was so curious about why Camus thought Sisyphus was happy, I researched that first instead.

I read the Camus essay, and then I kept reading everything I could find about the myth, trying to figure out why Sisyphus could possibly have been happy. Why Camus, who, in addition to saying that "one must imagine Sisyphus happy," also said that Sisyphus concluded that "All is well."

It was after midnight when I stumbled upon words by Stephen Mitchell, who wrote that Sisyphus was happy for a single reason: because he fell in love with the rock.

> The truth is that Sisyphus is in love with the rock. He cherishes every roughness and every ounce of it. He talks to it, sings to it. It has become the Mysterious Other.

Sisyphus was the happy victor and hero of the story because he had fallen in love with the rock! The first time I read Mitchell's words, that simple truth was so stunning to me, it literally took my breath away. I read the words at least a dozen more times, letting the truth sink into my heart like water into parched ground.

What made Sisyphus happily persist in an impossible situation was the same thing—arguably, the only thing—that could make me stay at the Sisyphean Hospital of Hope.

It was, in a word, Love.

LOVE! IT WAS Love! The answer had been in front of me all along, and I hadn't seen it.

There was Massiko, who told me that love looks around.

And the father of the two-year old who had said, "There is love in your eyes. You looked at my little girl with love."

And Omari, who had said, "I want to see patients like you do. You look at them with love."

I had been looking through eyes of love in a way that made it invisible for me to see love myself, but now I saw it clearly.

It was as though I had arrived in Togo blind. And then God mixed my tears with the dusty red dirt and put mud on my eyes—but the mud was all I could see. And now it had been washed away and like the blind man Jesus healed, I could see for the very first time.

Now these three remain: Faith, hope and love. But the greatest of these is love (1 Cor. 13:13).

I had never thought to question why love was the greatest of the three—but now, in light of the story of Sisyphus, I understood.

If Sisyphus had only had faith, he would've been waiting at the bottom of the hill for God to perform a supernatural act, to suspend the law of gravity so the rock wasn't heavy anymore, or so that it didn't roll downhill.

If Sisyphus had only had hope, he would've been looking forward to a time in the future when he could set the rock down and be done with it. Or he would be hoping that someone would come along to help him; waiting for circumstances to change before taking action.

But it was love that kept Sisyphus present and engaged in the moment. It was love that made him fall for the rock and pick it up. It was love that kept him going. It was love that helped him carry that rock farther and farther up the hill.

I realized that Jesus was the ultimate Sisyphus, who loved the world so much that he came down, put the world on his back, and carried it up Calvary.

When I was in Israel, I had the opportunity to see the Via Dolorosa, the path Jesus walked from his sentencing to his crucifixion, carrying the cross on his back. Until I saw it, I never knew that the Via Dolorosa goes uphill.

It was literally an uphill climb for Jesus to walk from central Jerusalem to the outskirts of town.

Because of love, Jesus walked up the Via Dolorosa, up the steep side of Golgotha, the Place of the Skull. Jesus walked up to his suffering, up to his death, all the while carrying the cross on his back.

I wonder what was going through his mind as he lay down on the beams, stretched out his arms, and felt the nails pounding his body into the wood. I wonder if, like Sisyphus, Jesus sang to us, talked to us, cherished us as he felt his life ebbing out through the wounds the soldiers had made.

Because of love, Jesus laid down his body, and then he laid down his life, to make us whole. To set us free.

By his wounds we are healed (Isa. 53:5).

My friend Porter once told me he loved to take communion because it reminded him that at the cross, everything converges and everything belongs. I love taking communion for the opposite reason. Because to me, the cross is the place where everything converges and *nothing* belongs.

The Prince of Peace meets a violent end. The religious leaders, who claim to know God best, act like God the least. Jesus dies to bring us back to life. The Healer is wounded to make us whole. The Son is forsaken by the Father so we can understand how close God is to each of us. Even the beams of the cross are pointing in exactly opposite directions.

And yet, despite the contradictions and opposites and enemies, despite the fact that nothing makes sense and nothing belongs, I love taking communion because the cross is the place where nothing belongs so that I can belong. So I can bring all the pain and hope, all the light and darkness, all the good and all the evil that coexist in my heart—and in the world around me.

The cross reminds me that I am deeply and desperately loved, and that what was true for Mama the night she was dying is true for every soul that has, does, or ever will exist. Which means it's true for me, too.

I was born into Love, I will die into Love, and I am held in Love all the days of my life.

UNTIL I HEARD the story of Sisyphus that day in Togo, I had been insisting that love wasn't enough. Love wasn't enough because despite love, the little girl with malaria died and we ran out of water and I laid dead preemies in a cardboard box and a little boy screamed *"Why, why, why"* every morning when his bandages were changed.

Now these three remain: Faith, hope and love. But the greatest of these is love.

I now knew why love is the greatest. Because it is higher, longer, wider, deeper, and stronger than anything in the world. It is the thing—the only thing—that is stronger than death itself. Divine Love is the only constant in this world and the next.

What can separate us from the love of God?

Nothing. Absolutely nothing.

What can put an end to God, who is Love?

Nothing. Absolutely nothing.

What can snatch us from the Arms of Love that hold us in birth, death, and the life in between?

Nothing. Absolutely nothing.

We can run out of everything else—emotion and energy and motivation and breath. But we can never run out of Love.

Love makes us stay and dig deeper when we're heresick and in pain. Love motivates us to persevere in difficult situations when we'd rather give up. Love pushes us to keep trying *anyway.*

When we reach the end of ourselves—and when we reach the end of our lives—we find that Love is all we have.

And when we reach that place, we suddenly see what it took me three months in the least happy country in the world to learn:

That in the end, Love is all we have.

And in the end, Love is all we need.

I GOT ONLY A few hours of sleep that night. When my alarm went off at 6 a.m., I woke up feeling completely empty, but this time in a good way. A way that made me feel light and unhindered and free.

With more determination and hope than I'd felt in months, I threw off the covers and walked to the kitchen to make coffee. While I waited for it to brew, I made up my mind that instead of trying to leave Togo early, I was going to stay. Instead of praying that God would get me out of here as soon as possible, I was going to pray that God would help me fall in love with the rock on my back, and give me the strength to advance Togo and the Hospital of Hope farther up the hill.

I poured myself a cup of coffee and headed back to my room to journal before getting ready for my clinic shift. On the way to my room, I caught a glimpse of myself in the hallway mirror. My hair was disheveled, my skin was pale, and there were dark circles under my eyes. I still had bruises on my hands from where my IVs had been, and there were several new mosquito bites on my arms. I had lost so much weight, my shoulder bones looked like they were poking through my skin. In other words, I was a wreck.

And yet somehow, instead of making me feel sad or embarrassed or discouraged, my pathetic appearance just made me laugh.

"Jesus, I'm a *mess*!" I exclaimed.

When I got to my room, instead of spending time in somber prayer or doing earnest writing, I simply set my coffee mug down on the temporary nightstand I'd constructed from an overturned plastic bucket and a stack of books, and I fell on the bed laughing.

Laughing out loud, laughing so hard, my gaunt body shook, laughing at the contrast of the sacred and the ridiculous. Laughing at how little I had to offer God, laughing at how it didn't matter.

Laughing because I was so desperately, so overwhelmingly, so happily, so invincibly loved.

I thought about Paul's words,

O Death, where is your sting?
O Grave, where is your victory? (1 Cor. 15:5)

The resurrection reminds us that dysfunction, pain, sorrow, and death are ultimately overcome by Love's never-ending life.

Before they've even left the grave, Jesus' crucified feet wake, and his heart begins to beat again as *Nevermore* is transformed to *Ever after.* I imagine Jesus dancing his way out of the shroud, his laughter rolling the stone away.

The resurrection stands forever as a promise that Love always comes back to life. Our bodies wear out and die—but our souls never do. Which means that in this world, we are merely shadowboxing with danger.

Death will one day defeat my shadow, but it can never defeat me, the real me, because I exist in a dimension where danger cannot go.

In the end, death is swallowed up into resurrected Life, and Joy has the last laugh. A deep, divine, tears-streaming-down-your-face, invincible laugh.

AFTER I LEARNED about Sisyphus and started praying to fall in love with the rock, my heart and my attitude changed. But nothing about Togo or the Hospital of Hope changed. The days were still hot, the shifts were still long, I still had to deliver bad news to patients on a regular basis, and several patients still died each day.

As I sang with the fundamentalists on Sunday nights, as I saw patient after patient in the clinic, as I tried to sleep on the hard futon in the doctors' lounge during my on-call shifts, I prayed over and over again, "God, help me fall in love with this rock. Because it's really heavy, and it's really hard to love."

I had been praying to fall in love with the rock for a few days when an overcrowded van crashed on its way to our hospital.

Patients in Burkina Faso had pooled their money and hired a van and driver to bring them to the hospital for medical care. There were several government clinics closer to where they lived, but they thought that our hospital was a specialty hospital and would offer them better care. None of them were fluent in French, so when they heard the name of our hospital, L'Hôpital de l'Espérance, they didn't understand that *espérance* meant "hope." They transliterated the word, and thought it meant "experience." They thought we were touting ourselves as the hospital with the most experienced providers, and that's the primary reason why they wanted to come see us.

The drive was fifteen hours long. They drove through the night, hoping to make it to the hospital early in the morning to be in the front of the triage line. They crammed twenty people into a van that should've held twelve. When they were an hour north of the hospital, near a town called Dapong, the driver fell asleep at the wheel and the bus crashed and rolled over multiple times.

Several people, including the driver, died at the scene. Others who were unconscious were rushed to the government hospital in Dapong. Those who were conscious and able to walk hired a new van and continued to the hospital. Around dawn, they walked into the hospital with gashes, broken bones, and sprained joints.

Two men carried in an eighteen-year-old woman who was unable to walk. X-rays showed that she had a fractured vertebra in her thoracic spine and, likely, a partially severed spinal cord. Her diaphragm was partially paralyzed, and it took all the effort she had to move air into and out of her lungs.

A fifty-year-old man who had been in the crash died a few hours after he arrived at the hospital. We didn't have a CT scanner to prove it, but we suspected he had massive intracranial bleeding from head trauma.

We admitted the eighteen-year-old woman and put her on a CPAP machine to help her breathe. The mask helped improve her oxygen saturation, but it made her feel claustrophobic, and she panicked. When I walked by her bed, she grabbed my hand and held on to it with a desperate look in her eyes. She couldn't breathe without the mask, but she couldn't tolerate it on, either.

I asked her nurse, Ibrahim, to give her a few milligrams of Valium in her IV—enough to quell her anxiety without hindering her breathing even more.

She had no bowel or bladder control, so every few hours the nurses had to turn her on her side, wipe her bottom, and change her diaper. That night, as the nurses rolled her onto her side, the movement was enough to sever her spinal cord, leaving her completely unable to breathe.

Her monitor started alarming as her oxygen fell from 90 percent to 75 to 40. I was on call with Emilie, and we went running to her bedside, where the nurses told us what had happened.

"You bag her while I talk to the family," Emilie said.

So I stood at the bedside, squeezing the Ambu bag every few seconds. The girl stared up at my face, her eyes wide and panicked.

What she really needed was to be intubated and put on a ventilator that would breathe for her, but we didn't have those capabilities. I knew that if she couldn't breathe on her own, she would die.

No, it was more grave than that. *Because* she could no longer breathe on her own, she *was going* to die.

Emilie spoke with the patient's older brothers, the men who had carried their sister in. After Emilie had explained the situation to them, she told the brothers that if they wanted, we could teach them how to operate the

Ambu bag to breathe for her until the rest of the family was able to reach the hospital to say good-bye. Or we could just let her go.

They decided to let her go.

The brothers pulled up chairs to the woman's bedside and spoke to her in a language I hadn't heard before. I assumed they were explaining what was about to happen, and telling her good-bye. She remained motionless, staring at their faces.

I asked Ibrahim to bag her so I could hold her hand.

"You were born into Love, you will die into Love, and you will be held in Love every second in between," I whispered to her as I traced a cross on the center of her forehead with my thumb.

We gave her more Valium and then, when she had fallen asleep, we stopped bagging her. It was the most merciful way we had to help her die without the horrific feeling that she was suffocating to death.

Her oxygen plummeted. Her heart rate sped up, became erratic, and then beat slower and slower and slower until it became a flat line, and the monitor blinked ASYSTOLE.

I reached up and turned off the screen, then Emilie and Ibrahim and I walked away to give the brothers a few moments of privacy with their sister before we prepared her body for them to transport home.

Mercifully, it seemed that she had died without panicking or suffering. After we gave her the Valium, she simply went to sleep—and never woke up.

I FINISHED MY SHIFT and returned to the duplex. I turned on the kitchen faucet and discovered, to my relief, that we had water. I showered for the first time in a week, lingering under the cool running water that washed the sweat, tears, and blood of the last shift out of my hair and off my skin.

I changed into clean pajamas and then, overcome with exhaustion, sank onto the bathroom floor crying, holding my face in my hands.

Help me love this rock, help me love this rock, help me love this rock, I prayed over and over again. I needed supernatural grace to keep me going because, especially after the last round of patient deaths, I felt defeated and ready to give up.

I thought again of Jesus, the ultimate Sisyphus, who for three years of ministry carried the heavy rock of the world up a steep, never-ending incline. I wondered if, when Jesus was alone, he sat down with his head in his hands and, with tears streaming down his face, asked his father the same questions I was asking now: Why does it matter that I'm physically present here? Why does it matter that I've sacrificed comfort in order to be tired and sweaty and hungry and thirsty and in pain? Why does it matter that I'm here if I can't heal every person who's sick, or resurrect every person who has died? God, why did you send me here if, even after all the sacrifices I've made to be here, injustice and hunger and death and pain are going to continue?

I wondered what, if anything, was the point of Jesus being physically present in our world. What was the significance of Emmanuel—of *God* being *With Us*?

If we look at everything Jesus left undone when he departed from the earth, then his presence hardly mattered at all. People were still sick, they still died, they were still oppressed, and they still suffered.

So why did it matter that Emmanuel was here?

As I thought about it, the question became its own answer. Emmanuel's value did not lie in what he did or didn't accomplish while he walked the earth. What mattered was that he was here.

He was *here.*

Jesus' presence mattered because it was a tangible reminder that we are not invisible to our Father. We are never lost to him, we are never forgotten by him, we are never abandoned by him. When Jesus was talking to Nicodemus, he said he was here because "God so loves the world."

So why did it matter that the other missionaries and I were here in Togo?

As I showered, put on pajamas, and climbed into bed, the question became its own answer.

Though we tried our hardest and did lots of good for the Togolese people, our ultimate value did not only lie in what we could or could not accomplish.

What mattered most is that we were *here.*

With our physical presence we reminded the Togolese people that they were not forgotten or lost or abandoned. They were not invisible to their loving, compassionate Parent.

I had wondered many times if Togo was a God-forsaken place. And now I knew the answer. No place is God-forsaken if people, who experience and express the love of God, go there.

Jesus came to earth to show us that God is here, that God is now, that there is no place where Divine Love cannot or will not go. As followers of Jesus, we have the opportunity to say the same thing with our lives.

For me, this was the point of going to Togo, and of seeing the Invisible Girls on the train in Portland. This is why it's important that all followers of Jesus go into the corners of the world where others cannot, will not, dare not go—from jail cells, homeless shelters, crime-ridden neighborhoods, and underperforming schools to Ivy League universities, Fortune 500 companies, Fifth Avenue marketing firms, and everywhere in between.

None of us is capable of single-handedly changing the world. But if we each reach out to the people around us, we can bring healing to the cracks within our reach. We can remind people with our physical presence and with acts of tangible kindness that Love is here, Love is now, and there is no place on earth that Love cannot or will not or dare not go.

That night, I fell asleep with tears spilling onto my pillow, partly from exhaustion and partly from relief.

I knew that in two days, when it was time for my next shift, I would return to the hospital and start again. Not because I could fix every problem or diagnose every illness or alleviate all the suffering there. But because just by being there, I made a statement.

God still loves me.

God still loves you.

And despite all the dangers and toils and snares...

God still so loves the world.

I WORKED MY LAST clinic shift on Thursday. The following day, I planned to drive down to Lomé with Todd and Brett, who were picking up a church group that was going to spend two weeks volunteering at the hospital.

After the clinic closed, I sat in the exam room with Omari. We exchanged email addresses and hugs, and then we exchanged gifts. I gave him a six-pack of Coke, and he gave me a panya of fabric he'd bought at the market.

I handed in my keys to registration, and then I walked into town to buy some apples and bottles of water at the market for the next day's long car ride. On my way to town, I walked past the soccer field where a handful of my FIFA Boys were practicing penalty kicks. I told them I was leaving the following day, and that I would remember them and pray for them. They once again thanked me profusely for the soccer balls.

In the distance, I saw several more FIFA Boys who were herding goats on a thin dirt path that wove through cornfields, where the stalks were now several feet tall. I waved to them, and they jumped up and down as they waved back.

The sun was setting, and the expansive sky was awash in vibrant orange, purple, and pink as I walked the dusty red road that led from the village to the hospital one last time.

As I walked, I remembered all the unexpected ways in which I had encountered Jesus in Togo, and it reminded me of the Gospel of Luke's account of the two disciples walking down the Emmaus Road. They are talking about the Messiah's crucifixion, and their faces are "downcast" (Luke 24:17), when the resurrected Jesus suddenly appears and begins walking and talking with them—though they don't recognize him at first. The three men have a deep conversation in which Jesus recites prophecies and answers their questions. But the men don't recognize Jesus until they invite him home for dinner—and he blesses and breaks the bread.

What helps them see Jesus is not his resurrected body or his brilliant mind or his sage wisdom. They recognize him in the blessing and the breaking of the bread.

The epiphany is in the breaking.

By some mercy, and some mystery, brokenness shows us the way to healing. Wounds become windows into the promise of resurrection, and we recognize Jesus in a way we never could have seen him before.

The wounds Jesus sustains in the crucifixion, the rending that the bread undergoes to become a sacrament, and the brokenness I encountered in my patients' bodies at the Hospital of Hope are all living forms of Kintsugi pottery, with redemption shining through brokenness and priceless mercy seeping through the cracks.

When I returned to my room, I packed my large blue duffel bag with the clothes and toiletries that had gotten me through the past three months. The only souvenir I had from my time in Togo was the rope I had found in the basket in my room on my first day in Mango. I had learned that the rope was intended to tie groceries and goods to the back of a moto taxi on the way back from the market. Since I walked everywhere I went, I hadn't used the rope. Instead, I had kept it as a reminder that the same rope that can be used as a noose can also serve as a lifeline in times of despair. That Divine Love rescues us when we feel like giving up.

I gently laid the rope on top of my clothes.

"Thanks be to God," I whispered as I zipped the suitcase closed.

EARLY THE NEXT morning, I climbed into the same Land Rover that had brought me to Mango three months before, only this time, instead of Massiko driving, Todd was behind the wheel. Brett sat in the front passenger seat, and I sat in the backseat behind him.

We drove across the hospital compound and turned left out of the main entrance. More than five hundred people had shown up at triage that morning, and the line stretched for half a mile.

As we made our way out of town, I caught my last glimpses of the soccer field where I had played with the FIFA Boys, the market, which would be buzzing with activity in a few hours, and the mosques that broadcast the loud, mournful prayers five times a day.

When we got to the paved road, I felt as if three months of heat, sleep deprivation, grief, malaria, and heresickness caught up with me, and I fell fast asleep, using my large duffel bag as a pillow.

I woke up when we were at the outskirts of Lomé. When we reached the dump, we turned onto a narrow dirt road that led to a small motel near the beach. Todd, Brett, and I got keys to our rooms. The guys invited me to have dinner with them, but I was so tired, I turned down their offer, preferring to sleep instead.

My motel room was similar to the room at the guesthouse where I'd spent my first night in Lomé—tiled floors, cracked paint, a hard mattress with coarse sheets, and a broken TV.

I took a quick shower, climbed into bed, and spent my last night in Togo dreaming of home.

A T FOUR O'CLOCK the following morning, I was wide awake, unable to go back to sleep. The motel's restaurant didn't start serving breakfast until 6 a.m., so I had two hours to kill.

I spent some time journaling and praying, and then I went online and did some reading about conditions in the developing world. I had a lot of anecdotes about people who were suffering in Togo, but I was also hungry for concrete data to know what people in the developing world were facing, and whether things were getting better or worse for them.

In my online research, I came across a column that Nicholas Kristof had recently written for the *New York Times*, highlighting all the progress that's been made in the past two decades. I learned that rates of infant mortality, starvation, and extreme poverty were not gradually declining; they were dropping dramatically. The World Bank predicted that if international efforts stayed on track, extreme global poverty, defined as living on $1.25 a day or less, could be eradicated by 2030.

After all the pain and death I had witnessed, here was a glimmer of hope. Our global community could end extreme poverty, improve the quality of life for people in the developing world, and save the lives of vulnerable children, if we continued to invest in solutions and refused to give up.

It was easy to look at all the problems in Togo, not to mention other countries in Africa and the rest of the world, and feel overwhelmed by all the problems and needs.

But as I continued to read, a pathway forward began to emerge. First, you start with hope that not only *can* the world get better, it *is* getting better. And then you invest your life and your talents and your resources into the people and the problems within your reach. You catch people *comin' thro' the rye* who are within your grasp to save.

It's possible to bring healing to our beautiful but broken world—but it will only happen if we each do our part. Because the world never has been, and never will be, changed by one person doing it all. The world is much more likely to be transformed by a billion people doing one thing than by one person trying to do a billion things.

As we each contribute all the beauty, love, kindness, and resources we can, soon the cracks in our broken world will become windows into redemption as we pour the precious lacquer of Divine Love into the cracks within our reach.

AT 6 A.M., I dressed, bought a coffee from the motel's restaurant, and walked a few yards from the restaurant to the beach. I held the paper cup of steaming coffee in my cold hands as I sat in the sand, waiting for the sun to rise.

I watched the sky's familiar transition from lavender to periwinkle to light blue. And I saw the sun appear on the horizon as a sliver, then a crescent, then a half circle, then a shimmering orb that hung in the distant sky, casting a warm orange glow on the world below.

I was mesmerized by the sight, soaking in my last sunrise in Togo, when Todd tapped me on the shoulder. "Sarah, it's time to go," he said.

I retrieved my luggage from my room and checked out at the front desk. Todd drove me to the airport. I was scheduled to fly from Lomé to Brussels, and then Brussels to Chicago, where my parents would pick me up. On the drive, Todd thanked me for all my help, and asked when I was coming back. I laughed. "I have to recover from this trip before I even think of another one!" I said.

When we got to the airport, Todd helped me retrieve my heavy bag from the back of the Land Rover. He gave me a hug, and then drove away. I had no idea, as I stood on the sidewalk in front of the airport waving at him as he drove away, that it was the last time I would see him alive.

Todd fell ill four months after I left Togo. He was admitted to the Hospital of Hope. After two weeks of antibiotics and anti-malaria medicine, he was getting worse instead of better, and the staff still had yet to figure out what was causing his fevers and multi-organ failure.

He was airlifted to a hospital in Germany, and passed away a few hours after arriving there, leaving Beth and their four sons behind. His autopsy revealed that he had died of Lassa fever.

A few months after Todd passed away, Cheryl, the American pharmacist who biked to bars to buy bottled water during the water shortage, passed away at her home in the hospital compound of an unknown illness.

Just like Jesus, Todd's and Cheryl's love cost them their lives.

Their deaths are sobering reminders of what it takes to love the world.

And their deaths leave the rest of us to grapple with significant questions:

Will we choose to be people of Love?

And if so, what does it mean for us to fall in love with the world, put it on our back, and carry it higher?

I IMAGINED IT AT least a hundred times.

When I was sick with malaria, when I was exhausted after a twenty-eight-hour shift, when the hospital ran out of water, when I lost a patient I'd tried so hard to save, I closed my eyes and imagined coming home. I dreamed of stepping on the plane in Togo, falling asleep with headphones and a blanket, and waking up on US soil, hugging my family for the first time in months.

Despite how unlikely it seemed at times, the day had finally arrived. After Todd dropped me off, I checked in and handed the airline agent the large blue wheeled duffel bag that the man had been determined to "help" me with when I arrived three months before.

The agent was a lanky Togolese young man. "When are you returning to Togo?" he asked.

"I don't know," I said with a weary smile.

"Please come back," he said, his voice sounding more like desperation than hospitality.

Then I went through security, where the guard who checked my passport and ticket asked the same question. "When are you returning to Togo?"

"I don't know," I said again.

"Please come back," he said, handing my documents back to me.

It took seven hours to fly to Brussels. I had a three-hour layover, so I sipped an Americano at an airport café while I journaled about my last days in Togo.

I was mid-sip when all of a sudden I saw his face—the face of one of the patients I'd lost in Togo. The man who failed BiPAP and CPAP and looked at me with terror in his eyes saying, "Madam—I—can't—breathe."

I saw the monitor above his head alarming because his heart rate was so high and his oxygen saturation was so low.

I saw his chest heaving, every muscle in his body straining to suck oxygen in and then blow it out.

I felt the desperation in his grip.

"Madam—I—can't—breathe," he said, maddeningly polite despite being in severe respiratory distress.

"We're coming," I had said. "We're coming," because at the time it was all I knew how to say in French, and it was all he needed to know.

I remembered the emotional journey from *we'll do everything* to *there's nothing else we can do*, from *we might lose him* to *we're going to lose him* to *we've lost him*.

He was gone, and there was nothing we could to do bring him back.

As I sat there at the airport café, unable to shake the horrific scene from my mind, tears streamed down my cheeks at a furious pace, and I buried my face in my napkin to keep my grief from giving me away.

When the tears didn't stop, I packed up my laptop, went into a nearby restroom, locked myself in a stall, and let the tears flow. Soon I heard the gate agent announce that my flight to Chicago was boarding. So I washed my face, boarded the flight, wrapped myself in a blanket, put headphones on, and closed my eyes, tears still seeping out of the cracks.

I had tried. I had tried so hard to catch him—and many like him—*comin' thro' the rye*, but they had slipped through my fingers and fallen to their deaths.

I wondered if I was experiencing culture shock as I transitioned from the developing world to the Western world, or if it was the beginning of PTSD. (In hindsight, it was both.)

The lead flight attendant made the usual safety announcements, then said, "If there's anything we can do to help you, please ring your flight attendant call button."

I wanted to ring the button. I wanted someone to comfort me, to help me, to hold my hand and assure me that despite everything I'd experienced in the past three months, somehow everything was going to be okay.

Instead, as the plane took off, I fell asleep repeating the words Laura had spoken to me a few weeks before.

Sarah, it's not your fault.

It's not your fault.
It's not your fault.
It's
not
your
fault.

I WOKE UP SOMEWHERE over the mid-Atlantic to realize that I'd been so sound asleep, I had missed the first beverage service as well as the meal service. It didn't matter—I wasn't hungry anyway.

Even though I had hope for the future, and I was looking forward to how God would use me and the story of Togo to help heal the world, I felt like the experience had used up my malaria-depleted body, leaving me weary and empty.

I turned on music, wrapped the blanket tighter around me, and closed my eyes, hoping to go back to sleep. The song that happened to come up first on my iTunes playlist was "It Is Well," a hymn written by Horatio Spafford.

I had heard the story behind the hymn many times. Spafford's wife and four daughters were traveling from America to Europe in 1873 when their ship sank in the middle of the ocean, and the four daughters drowned. Spafford's wife was the only family member to survive the incident. When she reached Europe, she sent Spafford a two-word telegram: "Saved Alone."

As he boarded a steamer to travel to meet his wife, Spafford asked the captain to let him know when they were crossing the place where his daughters had died, and so the captain did.

As Spafford peered into the deep waters of the Atlantic where his precious girls had drowned, he penned the words,

When peace like a river attendeth my way
When sorrows like sea billows roll
Whatever my lot, Thou hast taught me to say,
"It is well, It is well with my soul!"

As my plane traversed the Atlantic Ocean, crossing over the waters where Spafford had penned those well-known, heart-wrenching words, I wondered what it meant, and what it took, to say the words "It Is Well" in the face of unimaginable grief and tragedy.

I had witnessed the deaths of hundreds of Togolese people over the past three months. I had watched an HIV-positive man die as his infected brain herniated. I had listened to a man desperately pleading with me, "Madam— I—can't—breathe." I had laid two dead premature baby sisters in a shoe box. I had handed lifeless children back to their parents with the words, *Je suis désolé*. I had held fourteen-year-old Felix's hands and prayed for him as he was dying. I had made the sign of the cross on the foreheads of Mama and the eighteen-year-old woman injured in the van accident, whispering, *You were born into Love, you will die into Love, and you will be held in Love every second in between*. I had performed CPR on dozens of Togolese chests, willing their silent hearts to beat again. I had administered morphine and Valium, the sacraments of the dying, to more patients than I could count.

Could I say with Horatio Spafford, *It is well with my soul*?

Or with Sisyphus, *All is well*?

Or with Julian of Norwich, *All shall be well, and all shall be well and all manner of thing shall be well*?

*W*ELL. A SIMPLE, at times seemingly impossible, beautiful word.

In medicine, being well is an even higher ideal than being healthy. Because health is the absence of disease from the body. But wellness is a sense of balance and peace in your entire being. You can be healthy but still suffer from anxiety, narcissism, hypochondria, and other conditions and not be well. Alternatively, you can have a terminal diagnosis and yet be well because you experience peace and harmony and a sense of okay-ness despite the disease your body is facing.

Well is also a monosyllabic metaphor for how God fills us when we're weak and weary.

In a TV show I saw once, a couple is talking about being emotionally available for each other. One person says, "I want to be the well into which you can pour your emotional water," and the other person laughs and says, "You don't pour water into a well!"

No, I realized on the plane as I remembered that scene—you don't pour water into a well; you pour water into a cistern. And as I had witnessed in Togo, and as the prophet Jeremiah writes about in the Bible, water in cisterns gets stagnant and contaminated. Water in cisterns can make you dangerously ill.

But wells are different. Wells fill up from the inside out, from the bottom up, receiving from a deep, life-giving spring. When Jesus talks to the woman at the well in John 4, he says he is the fountain of living water. When we drink from this water, Jesus says, it will quench and satisfy our souls. Also, when we choose to stay *heresick*, being patient in difficult times while our roots grow deeper, I think it's this same life-giving spring that we tap into.

It is Well.

Even though it would take a long time for my emotions and my body to heal from the experience of Togo, it was possible to be well in the process.

It is Well.

Even though many people around the world continue to suffer and die, it is possible to be well because we know that no matter what happens to our bodies, no matter how badly death defeats our shadows, our souls exist in a dimension danger cannot go.

It is Well.

No matter the pain we witness and experience in this world, we can trust it is well because we are born into Love, we die into Love, and we are held in Love every second of the life we live in between.

It is Well.

When we are weak or empty or weary, we can have hope because it's not up to us to fill ourselves up from the outside—to frantically grab at transient supplies of energy or pleasure or motivation. We simply need to be surrendered and still and wait for the Spring of Living Water to renew us. In the words of Isaiah, it's the people who *wait* who renew their strength and rise up with wings like eagles, who soar not by flapping their wings harder but by letting the gust of the Spirit catch them and carry them to new heights.

It is Well, It is Well with my soul.

*L*ADIES AND GENTLEMEN, *we'd like to be the first to welcome you to Chi-cago, where the local time is 1 p.m.*, the flight attendant said when we touched down at O'Hare. I had been sleeping for the past few hours, and I startled awake.

I deplaned with the other passengers and made my way to the long immigration line.

When it was my turn, I stepped up to the glass window, and an agent flipped through my passport. I had been to eight other countries that year. I had stood before lots of border patrol officers, and I had been asked a lot of questions. I was expecting the usual barrage of questions from an officer who was trying to read my microexpressions to see if I was lying.

Instead, he asked me a single question: "What were you doing in Africa?"

"I worked at a hospital there," I answered wearily. In those words, in those six words, a lifetime of stories and indelible memories. A world of grief. And a new understanding of Love.

"Good work," the agent said as he stamped my passport and slid it under the glass partition toward me. "Welcome home."

I nodded silently, because I was crying too hard to speak.

I DRIED MY TEARS of relief and exhaustion as I walked to baggage claim to retrieve the large wheeled duffel bag that held three months of belongings.

The walls in baggage claim were awash in pink—pink ribbons, pink posters, pink banners—and it took me a minute to remember that it was October, Breast Cancer Awareness Month. As a breast cancer survivor, sometimes I celebrated Breast Cancer Awareness Month with gratitude, and other times I loathed the ubiquitous reminder of the disease that had nearly cost me my life.

As I waited for the conveyor belt to start moving, I thought about how, for several years now, whenever I told the story of the Invisible Girls, I had said that because my breast cancer diagnosis disqualified me from serving as a full-time missionary in Africa, God had brought Africa to me. God had given me a consolation prize of working with Somali refugees on my soil because, for a long time, my cancer diagnosis had made it impossible for me to travel to theirs.

Standing here now, minutes away from my feet touching American soil for the first time in three months, I suddenly had the humbling realization that I had been making unfair and untrue value judgments for a really long time.

I had assumed that loving people while standing on the soil of West Africa was more valuable than loving people while standing on a sidewalk in the United States.

That traveling for hours on a plane to get to people who were suffering was more significant than driving ten minutes in my car to the local rescue mission, or the Somali girls' apartment—or even walking to the neighbor's house next door.

Somehow, I believed that I earned more cosmic points for loving people while jet-lagged than for loving people while well rested.

That eating strange food was more significant than eating leftovers from my favorite take-out place.

That serving people who speak a different language from me was somehow more important than serving fellow English speakers.

It took a hard three months in Africa to open my eyes to the fact that the Somali girls were never a consolation prize. That cancer didn't deprive me of God's Plan A for my life. That I was where I was meant to be, and if I never used my passport again, the life waiting for me in the States was just as significant as the life I thought I'd have as a missionary overseas.

As I pulled my heavy bag off the carousel, I thought, *Maybe in God's eyes, the soil under our feet doesn't matter nearly as much as the compassion in our hearts. Maybe the love we show to others is infinitely more significant than the ground on which we stand.*

I carried my bag to the sliding doors that separated baggage claim from the International Arrivals lobby, where my parents—and the next chapter of my life—were waiting for me on the other side.

The doors began to slide apart.

I took a deep breath and stepped across the threshold with these words echoing in my soul:

IT IS WELL.

ALL IS WELL.

I AM WELL.

AUTHOR'S NOTE

I hope this book has encouraged and inspired you to participate in healing our beautiful, broken world. If you would like to contribute to organizations that are making a positive and tangible difference in the developing world, here are a few suggestions!

(Of course there are other organizations to choose from. I recommend using a resource like www.charitynavigator.org that can help steer you to nonprofits that will use your contribution well.)

If you'd like to support the Hospital of Hope, you can give here: www .hospitalofhopemango.org.

If you're interested in sponsoring a child in the developing world, combating the HIV/AIDS epidemic, providing pre- and postnatal care to women, or supporting effective disaster relief efforts, visit http://www.compassion.com /sarahthebarge.

To buy jewelry, accessories, home goods, apparel, and gifts made by women in the developing world, check out www.globalgoodspartners.org.

To offer loans to entrepreneurs in the developing world who are innovating in the areas of education, agriculture, retail, textiles (and more!), go to www.kiva.org.

To support the goal of bringing "clean and safe drinking water to every person in the world," check out www.charitywater.org.

To help families out of hunger and poverty by providing them with livestock, donate at www.heifer.org.

To provide college scholarships and leadership training to young adults in Africa, head to www.thesenumbers.org.

QUESTIONS TO CONSIDER

1. Have you ever said, "I'm going to change the world someday?" If so, what did you mean when you said those words?
2. Have you ever been involved in a ministry, missions trip, humanitarian effort, or other endeavor to make a positive difference in people's lives? If so, what did you learn from the experience?
3. One of the book's humorous moments is when Sarah tries to speak French to Hugo and Jori at the guesthouse. Have you had an embarrassing cross-cultural experience? If so, what insight did it give you about immigrants and refugees who come to your country?
4. When Sarah arrives in Togo, she faces fear, anxiety, frustration, and doubt in her first few hours. Have you experienced that in your life? What kept you going in that experience, or caused you to turn around and go back?
5. One of the most memorable lines of the book is Massiko's statement that "love looks around." How did that line hit you when you first read it? How would the world look different if you saw it through the eyes of God?
6. What does it look like to live out the idea that "love looks around" in your own life?
7. As Sarah described her first few days at the Hospital of Hope, what details stood out to you?
8. Several times in the book, Sarah talks about the gospel, which means "good news." If you're a person of faith, can you articulate what the gospel means to you? What makes the "good news" good?
9. Sarah uses her skills in medicine and writing to try to make a positive difference in the world. What skills and interests do you have? How can you use them to make the world a better place?

10. Tragically, many patients die at the Hospital of Hope. Has someone close to you died? What was your experience of that loss?

11. If you're a person of faith, what difference does God make when you contemplate the mortality of yourself and others?

12. Despite the suffering, Sarah encounters bright spots—like the natural beauty of Togo, her friendship with Omari, and the joy of the FIFA Boys. Thinking back to hard chapters of your own life, what have the bright spots been?

13. Sarah encounters what the Celtic Christians called the Thin Space as she sits with Mama, who is dying of metastatic cervical cancer. Have you had this experience? What were the circumstances? How did the experience impact you?

14. Sarah describes some challenges in trying to integrate into the American team in Togo. Have you tried to work as part of a team in the past? What were the challenges? What were the rewards?

15. When the team loses the twenty-seven-week-old baby, the one "born under the bed," Sarah remembers the words the Father spoke to Jesus: "My soul wanted you." What, in your understanding, is the reason why you—and others—exist in this world?

16. After losing the five-month-old baby to tetanus, the question "Why does God allow suffering in the world?" comes up at staff devotions. If someone asked you that question, what would you say?

17. Sarah says the question she's more interested in is not why God allows suffering in the world, but why we do. What's your response to that question?

18. At the deathbed of several patients, Sarah whispers the words, "You were born into Love, you will die into Love, and you are held in Love every second of the life you live in between." Do you believe you're held in Love? Why (or why not)?

19. Sarah is told that she looks at patients with love. What does it mean in your life to look at those around you with love?

20. Have you ever had the feeling that, even though you loved people—or felt that God loved you—that "love is not enough"? Why did it, or didn't it, feel enough?

21. While Sarah is recovering from malaria, Wade tells her, "I broke down the door to get to you." In what ways have God and other people broken down the door to get to you? How have you broken down doors to get to others?

22. After her malaria diagnosis and the subsequent water crisis, Sarah prays a very simple, short prayer: "God, I'm done." At what points in your life have you prayed a prayer like that?

23. Sisyphus is "happy" after falling in love with the rock, and concludes that "all is well." What task in your life currently seem Sisyphean? How can you fall in love with that rock?

24. Flying over the Atlantic Ocean, Sarah contemplates Horatio Spafford and the hymn "It Is Well," which he wrote after his daughters drowned. Have you experienced—or witnessed—a tragedy in your own life? What was your response?

25. Sarah writes about the difference between health and wellness, and points out that despite things going wrong in our bodies (or in our lives), it's possible to be well. What changes can you make in your life to promote wellness in your heart, mind, body, and soul?

26. *Well* describes Sarah's journey from trying to change people to offering to heal them. In your day-to-day life, what can you do to bring healing to the world around you?

27. Kintsugi pottery demonstrates that beauty can be seen in brokenness. As you look at your life and at the world around you, what broken places and cracks do you see? What beauty shows up there?

28. Toward the end of the book, Sarah contemplates the difference between a cistern and a well. When you spend energy to love the people around you, how can you recharge in a healthy, sustainable way?

29. Name three things you learned about West Africa from reading *Well* that you didn't know before.

30. Serving at the Hospital of Hope cost Todd and Cheryl their lives—and nearly cost Sarah her life as well. What cost have you paid to follow Jesus' leading in your life?

ACKNOWLEDGMENTS

To Adrienne, Greg, Jim, and Andrea, for bringing this book to life.

To Sue and Tom, for your profound generosity.

To Jody and Alan, for your physical and emotional hospitality.

To Jeanne and Rick, for inspiring me to see the Invisible People in our world.

To Angie and Keith, for your never-ending encouragement. .

To Mary Beth and Rick, for introducing me to an epic adventure.

To Allan and the Sawyer family, for living your lives (and your love) out loud.

To Jack, for walking this road with me.

To Doug, for always being up for an adventure.

To Karina, for your constant love and prayers.

To Stephanie, for reminding me to hope.

To Douglas, for cheering me on.

To Karen, for believing in me.

To Kristin, for your tenacity.

To Reba, for your courage.

To Kat, for your wisdom.

To Carren, for being an incredible human being and spiritual leader.

To Nate and Porter, for your wisdom and shenanigans.

To Jordan, John, Amber, Betsy, and Karrie, for being faithful friends.

To Phil, Tasha, and First Presbyterian, for offering me community.

To my family, for...well, everything. I am honored to be your daughter, granddaughter, sister, aunt, sister-in-law, niece, cousin, and friend.

To Divine Love. Because you're alive, I live.